PERFORMING
IN
MUSICALS

PERFORMING IN MUSICALS

ELAINE ADAMS NOVAK

SCHIRMER BOOKS
A Division of Macmillan, Inc.
NEW YORK

Schirmer Books
A Division of Macmillan, Inc.
866 Third Avenue, New York, N.Y. 10022

Collier Macmillan Canada, Inc.

Library of Congress Catalog Card Number: 87–20669

Printed in the United States of America

printing number
1   2   3   4   5   6   7   8   9   10

Library of Congress Cataloging-in-Publication Data

Novak, Elaine Adams.
   Performing in musicals.

   Bibliography: p.
   Includes index.
   1. Musical revue, Comedy, etc—Production and
direction.   2. Music—Performance   3. Title.
MT955.N7 1988   782.81'07   87–20669
ISBN 0-02-871731-7

CONTENTS

LIST OF
ILLUSTRATIONS

photographs; and to the copyright owners for permission to reprint songs and dialogue excerpts from the following:

From *42nd Street*, produced by David Merrick and directed by Gower Champion, Copyright © by Michael Stewart and Mark Bramble. Used by permission of Michael Stewart and Mark Bramble.

From *Applause*, Copyright © 1971 by Betty Comden and Adolph Green. Reprinted by permission of Random House, Inc.

From *West Side Story*, Copyright © 1956, 1958 by Arthur Laurents, Leonard Bernstein, Stephen Sondheim, and Jerome Robbins. Text reprinted by permission of Random House, Inc. Lyrics Copyright © 1957 by Leonard Bernstein and Stephen Sondheim. ALL RIGHTS RESERVED. Lyrics used by permission of G. Schirmer, Inc.

From *Dames at Sea*, Copyright © 1966, 1967, 1969 by George Haimsohn, Robin Miller, and Jim Wise (book, music, and lyrics). Reprinted by permission of International Creative Management, Inc.

Amateurs wishing to arrange for the production of *Dames at Sea* must make application to SAMUEL FRENCH, INC., at 45 West 25th Street, New York, NY, 10010, giving the following particulars:
1. The name of the town and theatre or hall in which it is proposed to give the production.
2. The maximum seating capacity of the theatre or hall.
3. Scale of ticket prices.
4. The number of performances it is intended to give, and the dates thereof.
5. Indicate whether you will use an orchestration or simply a piano.

Upon receipt of these particulars SAMUEL FRENCH, INC., will quote the terms upon which permission for performances will be granted. Anyone presenting the play shall not commit or authorize any act or omission by which the copyright of the play or the right to copyright same may be impaired. No changes shall be made in the play for the purpose of your production unless authorized in writing. The publication of this play does not imply that it is necessarily available for performance by amateurs or professionals. Amateurs and professionals considering a production are strongly advised in their own interests to apply to Samuel French, Inc., for consent before starting rehearsals, advertising, or booking a theatre or hall.

From *My Fair Lady*, Copyright © 1956 by Alan Jay Lerner and Frederick Loewe. All rights to perform excerpts and songs are reserved to the copyright owners thereof. Excerpts are reprinted by courtesy of the estate of Alan Jay Lerner.

From *Camelot*, Copyright © 1960, 1961 by Alan Jay Lerner and Frederick Loewe. Text reprinted by permission of Random House, Inc. "Camelot," words by Alan Jay Lerner, music by Frederick Loewe. Chappell & Co., Inc., owner of publication and allied rights throughout the world. International Copyright Secured. ALL RIGHTS RESERVED. Used by permission.

From *Kiss Me, Kate*, Book-Copyright © 1948 by Bella Spewack; Book Revisions-Copyright © 1953 by Samuel and Bella Spewack. "Wunderbar," words and music by Cole Porter. Copyright © 1948 by Cole Porter. Copyright renewed, assigned to John F. Wharton, Trustee of the Cole Porter Musical and Literary Trusts. Chappell & Co., Inc., publisher and owner of publication and allied rights throughout the world. International Copyright Secured. ALL RIGHTS RESERVED. Used by permission.

From *Funny Girl*, Book Copyright © 1964 by Isobel Lennart, Jule Styne, and Bob Merrill. Reprinted by permission of Random House, Inc.

From *Brigadoon*, Copyright © 1947 by Alan Jay Lerner and Frederick Loewe. All rights to perform excerpts and songs are reserved to the copyright owners thereof. Excerpts are reprinted by courtesy of the estate of Alan Jay Lerner. "The Heather on the Hill," words by Alan Jay Lerner, music by Frederick Loewe. Copyright © 1947 (Renewed 1975) Alan Jay Lerner and Frederick Loewe. World rights assigned to and controlled by

1

THE MUSICAL

PEGGY SAWYER [new to Broadway]:   I'm sorry, Mr. Marsh. Show business isn't for me. I'm going back to Allentown.

JULIAN [a producer-director]:   What was that word you just said? *Allentown?* I'm offering you the chance to star in the biggest musical Broadway's seen in twenty years and you say *Allentown?* Now listen, Sawyer, and listen good. Even if you don't give a damn for me, think of all those kids you'll be throwing out of work if you don't do this! Think of the songs that will wither and die if you don't get up there and sing them! Think of the scenery that will never be seen, the costumes never worn, the orchestrations never heard!... Think of musical comedy, the most glorious words in the English language! Sawyer, think of Broadway, dammit!

—from *42nd Street*

In the above excerpt from *42nd Street,* which is a satire on Broadway productions of the 1930s, Julian is trying to persuade Peggy to stay in New York to star in a musical, a type of show that since World War II has flourished in this country and elsewhere. But what is this entertainment called the musical comedy, the Broadway musical, the American musical, or just the musical? In past years, the label *musical comedy* was often used, as in Julian's speech above, but because some shows like *Show Boat* and *West Side Story* have serious themes, the usual term today is simply *musical.*

The musical is a show that is closely related to others that combine music, singing, acting, dancing, and theatrical production. When we consider the entire American musical theatre, we can see that there are three main divisions—the musical, opera, and revue—with various subcategories, such as:

• Musicals: musical comedies, musical dramas, operatic musicals, rock musicals.

• Operas: grand operas, light operas, comic operas, operettas, popular operas.

• Revues: vaudeville, burlesque, variety shows, nightclub/cabaret entertainments.

1

Figure 1-1.   Wanda Richert, as Peggy Sawyer, and the company of *42nd Street*.
(Photo: © 1984 Martha Swope.)

Although both the musical and the opera tell a story using music, singing, acting, dancing, and theatrical production, usually it is easy to differentiate between them because in operas all or most of the lines are sung, while in musicals there are spoken passages. In operas the singing and music are emphasized, but in musicals the book, acting, dancing, and production may receive as much attention as the singing and music. Also, operas are generally produced by opera companies in opera houses with opera singers whereas American musicals open in Broadway theatres with Broadway performers. Examples of famous operas are *La Traviata* and *Madame Butterfly;* examples of popular musicals are *A Chorus Line* and *Annie.*

But what do you call a Broadway musical such as *Porgy and Bess* or *Sweeney Todd*, in which most of the lines are sung? For these the compromise label of *operatic musical* or *popular opera* may be used.

The *revue*—which may have songs, dances, music, comedy acts, blackout sketches, specialty numbers, and theatrical production—is different from the musical and the opera in that the revue does not have a story line or plot to tie the entire show together, although there may be a theme to provide some unity. For instance, *Sugar Babies* was presented as a "memory of burlesque," which was the theme for this revue; and in *Ain't Misbehavin'* all of the music was written or recorded by Fats Waller, which gave this revue a unifying theme.

While this book is concerned primarily with performing in musicals, much of what is advocated here can also be applied to revues and operas. Now let's examine the musical in more detail.

CHARACTERISTICS OF THE MUSICAL

Musicals come in all shapes and sizes. Consider the following:

- They can be large, spectacular productions or little, inexpensive ones. Typically, when we think of the musical, we think of an elaborate show such as *42nd Street* or *La Cage aux Folles;* but musicals do come in smaller sizes, such as two popular off-Broadway productions, *The Fantasticks* and *You're a Good Man, Charlie Brown.*
- The source for a musical may be a play (*Hello, Dolly!* from *The Matchmaker*), a novel (*Oliver!* from *Oliver Twist*), stories (*Fiddler on the Roof*), poems (*Cats*), a film (*Promises, Promises* from *The Apartment*), the life of a person (*Funny Girl*), history (*1776*), a comic strip (*Li'l Abner*), the work of an artist (*Sunday in the Park with George*), or an original concept (*Company*).
- The musical can be a comedy (*My Fair Lady*), a farce (*Kiss Me, Kate*), a satire (*Of Thee I Sing*), a romantic comedy (*She Loves Me*), a fantasy (*Brigadoon*), a drama (*Evita*), a melodrama (*Sweeney Todd*), a tragedy (*West Side Story*), or any other type that a play can be.

But there are characteristics that apply to most musicals, such as the following:

- Usually, many artists collaborate to produce the show: bookwriter, composer, lyricist, producer, stage director, actors, singers, dancers, comedians, specialists (such as magicians or circus performers), choreographer, dance director, musical director, conductor, orchestrator, arrangers, rehearsal pianists, orchestra, designers of scenery, lighting, costumes, and sound, various assistants, and crews.
- The musical has many stage conventions that audiences must accept: for example, characters talk then break into song; an orchestra and conductor may be visible throughout the show; dancers may appear for no apparent reason except to add their talents to a production number.
- The musical is presentational theatre, not representational. The shows are presented directly to the audience: the performers sing and speak to the spectators much of the time, scenery often merely suggests a location, and there is little attempt at illusion. (In representational theatre, such as a realistic production of a play like *Long Day's Journey into Night* by Eugene O'Neill, there is a greater effort to make audiences believe that they are watching life onstage.) While musicals may not present much illusion onstage, audiences can empathize with a musical as much as a realistic play if they accept the stage conventions.

Figure 1-2. Poster for *The Black Crook*, the show that many consider to be the first American musical.

(Courtesy of the Billy Rose Theatre Collection, the New York Public Library at Lincoln Center, Astor, Lenox, and Tilden Foundations.)

Figure 1-3. The chorus of the *Ziegfeld Follies of 1924*.

(Courtesy of the Billy Rose Theatre Collection, the New York Public Library at Lincoln Center, Astor, Lenox, and Tilden Foundations.)

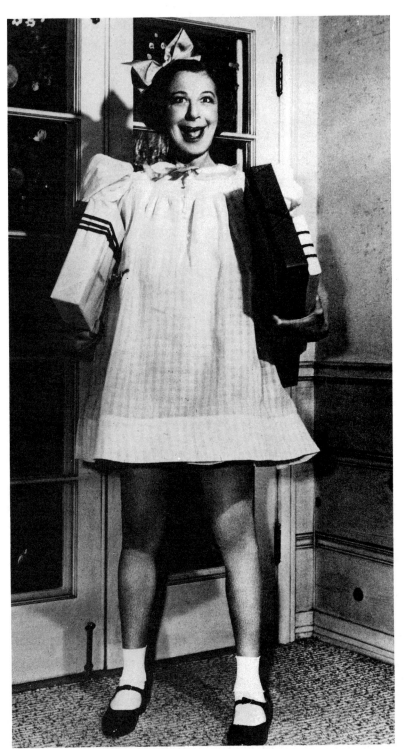

Figure 1-4. One of Ziegfeld's biggest stars, Fanny Brice, playing the character of Baby Snooks.

(Courtesy of the Billy Rose Theatre Collection, the New York Public Library at Lincoln Center, Astor, Lenox, and Tilden Foundations.)

the American musical is the 1943 production of *Oklahoma!* by Rodgers and Hammerstein. With music, song, dance, and book more closely integrated than in previous productions, this show set the pattern for many musicals to follow: a strong book with songs and dances that advance the plot or reveal character; many scenes divided into two acts; a large cast of singers, dancers, and actors; solos, duets, and production numbers carefully routined for maximum effect; a full orchestra; and spectacular scenery, lighting, and costumes. A common plot was boy meets girl, boy loses girl, and boy gets girl at the end of the show.

Other big hits of the 1940s were *Carousel* by Rodgers and Hammerstein; *Annie Get Your Gun* by Irving Berlin and Herbert and Dorothy Fields; *Brigadoon* by Alan Jay Lerner and Frederick Loewe; *Kiss Me, Kate* by Cole Porter and Samuel and Bella Spewack; and, the second winner of a Pulitzer prize, *South Pacific* by Rodgers, Hammerstein, and Joshua Logan.

The next decade brought *Guys and Dolls* by Frank Loesser, Jo Swerling, and Abe Burrows; *The King and I* by Rodgers and Hammerstein; and *My Fair Lady* by Lerner and Loewe. In 1957, *West Side Story* by Arthur Laurents, Leonard Bernstein, and Stephen Sondheim, based on Jerome Robbins's concept, brought to prominence the *dance musical*, a type that featured spectacular dancing as a means to further the plot or delineate character. In 1959, *Gypsy,* by Sondheim, Laurents, and Jule Styne, became another big hit because of a strong book, great songs and dances, and Ethel Merman at her best. In that same year, Rodgers and Hammerstein, with Howard Lindsay and Russel Crouse, wrote *The Sound of Music.*

The 1960s saw many fine musicals, including Lerner and Loewe's *Camelot; How to Succeed in Business Without Really Trying* (another Pulitzer prizewinner) by Frank Loesser, Abe Burrows, Jack Weinstock, and Willie Gilbert; *Hello, Dolly!* by Jerry Herman and Michael Stewart; *Funny Girl* by Jule Styne, Bob Merrill, and Isobel Lennart; *Fiddler on the Roof* by Jerry Bock, Sheldon Harnick, and Joseph Stein; *Man of La Mancha* by Mitch Leigh, Joe Darion, and Dale Wasserman; *Mame* by Jerry Herman, Jerome Lawrence, and Robert E. Lee; *Cabaret* by John Kander, Fred Ebb, and Joe Masteroff; and *1776* by Sherman Edwards and Peter Stone.

In 1968, the popularity of *Hair,* by Galt MacDermot, Gerome Ragni, and James Rado, brought attention to a new form, the *rock musical.* While the plot was minimal, the show made sharp political comments about issues such as the Vietnam War. Simple scenery and properties were carried on and removed as needed, actors changed costumes—and roles—in full view of the audience, and the sound was amplified. The rock music, the informal and spontaneous manner, and the first use of total nudity by most of the cast of a Broadway musical made *Hair* appear different. Other important rock musicals that followed during the 1970s were *Jesus Christ Superstar* by Andrew Lloyd Webber and Tim Rice, *Grease* by Jim Jacobs and Warren Casey, and *The Wiz* by Charlie Smalls and William F. Brown.

Starting in the 1970s, the collaboration of Stephen Sondheim and producer-director Harold Prince brought us innovative productions like *Company* (with George Furth); *Follies* (with James Goldman); *A Little Night*

Music (with Hugh Wheeler); *Pacific Overtures* (with John Weidman); and an operatic musical, *Sweeney Todd* (with Wheeler). James Lapine and Sondheim collaborated in 1984 on *Sunday in the Park with George*, yet another winner of the Pulitzer prize, and in 1987 on *Into the Woods*. The emphasis in these musicals is on the concept—the idea or theme for the show—and not on a "boy gets girl" plot or melodic, singable tunes. Episodes serve to illustrate the concept. The songs, which often reveal the

Figure 1-5. Mandy Patinkin and Bernadette Peters in *Sunday in the Park with George.* (Photo: © 1986 Martha Swope.)

characters' deep feelings or comment on the action, were not written to be popular successes outside of the show, although some like "Send in the Clowns" have been big hits. Rather, they were tailored for specific characters to sing in particular situations needed by the plot. The result was sophisticated, intricate, witty shows, some akin to opera, that pointed the musical in a new direction. Of course, some composers admired and admitted the Sondheim influence; however, others preferred the more traditional form of musical with simple plots and singable melodies.

Other important shows of the 1970s and 1980s were *Applause* by Charles Strouse, Lee Adams, Betty Comden, and Adolph Green; *Pippin* by Stephen Schwartz and Roger O. Hirson; *Chicago* by John Kander, Fred Ebb, and Bob Fosse; *A Chorus Line* (another Pulitzer prizewinner) by Michael Bennett, Marvin Hamlisch, Edward Kleban, James Kirkwood, and Nicholas Dante; *Annie* by Strouse and Martin Charnin; an operatic musical, *Evita* by Andrew Lloyd Webber and Tim Rice; *42nd Street* by Harry Warren, Al Dubin, Michael Stewart, and Mark Bramble; *Barnum* by Cy Coleman, Stewart, and Bramble; *Dreamgirls* by Henry Krieger and Tom Eyen; *Nine* by Maury Yeston and Arthur Kopit; *Cats,* based on poems by T. S. Eliot, with music by Lloyd Webber; *My One and Only*, with book by Peter Stone and Timothy Mayer and music and lyrics from previous shows by the Gershwins; *La Cage aux Folles* by Harvey Fierstein and Jerry Herman; a revival of a 1937 London hit, *Me and My Girl* by L. Arthur Rose, Douglas Furber, and Noel Gay; *Les Misérables*, an operatic dramatization of Victor Hugo's novel by Alain Boublil and Claude-Michel Schönberg, with lyrics by Herbert Kretzmer, adapted and directed by Trevor Nunn and John Caird; and *Starlight Express* by Lloyd Webber and Richard Stilgoe.

During the 1970s, the workshop method of writing musicals evolved. This gives writers and composers the chance to develop their show working with performers and rewrite. It also allows potential backers to see singers, actors, and dancers doing the material. If the money for production is raised, then the show can be put into rehearsal. For example, in a process that took well over a year, *A Chorus Line* went from workshops to an off-Broadway production to a Broadway hit in 1975. It went on to become the longest-running show on Broadway.

Some writers, composers, directors, and producers like workshops because they give them time to develop the material in a situation that costs much less than a Broadway production. With large musicals requiring millions of dollars to produce, it seems sensible to create and experiment in workshops first. However, there are those who do not enjoy working in a group and prefer adhering to traditional ways.

One unfortunate result of Broadway's high production costs has been high ticket prices. Now, some theatregoers can no longer afford to attend Broadway shows, and many who pay large sums for tickets expect to see costly, elaborate productions. As the financial stakes get higher, producers become hesitant about attempting expensive musicals and are quick to close marginal shows that are not certain of success.

As of the 1980s, Broadway appears in danger of losing to London its title of world leader of musical theatre. England's comparatively low production costs and ticket prices make it a desirable location to try out a show; then, if it is a London success, it may be brought to New York. British composers, writers, and directors such as Andrew Lloyd Webber, Tim Rice, and Trevor Nunn have come to the forefront by creating spectacular hits like *Evita, Cats, Les Misérables,* and *Starlight Express,* all of which were produced in London before Broadway. Whether this trend continues depends on several factors, including the creativity of American writers and composers and finding a solution to the problem of high production costs and ticket prices.

The performers who work in musicals must be talented singers or dancers or actors or comedians, and for some roles they must be all of these. Some of the top stars of Broadway musicals have been George M. Cohan, Al Jolson, Fanny Brice, Ed Wynn, W. C. Fields, Bert Williams, Eddie Cantor, Bert Lahr, the Marx brothers, Victor Moore, Bobby Clark, Gertrude Lawrence, Noel Coward, Beatrice Lillie, Ethel Merman, Mary Martin, Danny Kaye, Ethel Waters, Alfred Drake, Nancy Walker, Carol Channing, Robert Preston, Angela Lansbury, Barbra Streisand, Zero Mostel, Julie Andrews, Gwen Verdon, Chita Rivera, Jerry Ohrbach, Liza Minnelli, Joel Grey, Jim Dale, Ben Vereen, Tommy Tune, Bernadette Peters, Mandy Patinkin, and Patti LuPone.

DEVELOPMENT OF MUSICAL PRODUCTION

Now let's briefly consider how the technical elements of the musical developed to what they are today.

The tradition of elaborate scenery for musicals goes back to the seventeenth century in Italy when designers used imaginative *wings, drops,* and *borders*—all beautifully painted in perspective—for the opera. Both then and now, the main purpose of scene designing was to add excitement and spectacle to the production. Today designers are also concerned with providing a visual environment for each scene that will help the audience understand the plot, characters, theme, style, and mood.

In order to go quickly from one scene to another, wing-drop-border sets have proved to be immensely practical for proscenium stages with *fly lofts,* which all Broadway theatres have. When a scene is finished, the drop can be lifted to the flies by means of a rope and pulley system and another drop can be lowered. Wings can be flown, turned, or pulled offstage to disclose others for the next scene.

To accommodate set changes, musical writers have often alternated scenes needing the full stage with scenes that can be done in a shallow downstage area. While the downstage scene is being played in front of the first set of wings and a drop, curtain, or traveler (this is called playing in "one"), a full-stage set can be erected in back. For this reason, you will find that large chorus numbers requiring the entire stage often alternate with dialogue, solos, or duets that only need a shallow space.

Since the nineteenth century other devices have been used to facilitate scene changes: revolving stages, wagons, treadmills, jackknife stages, escalators, and elevators, some of which today may be operated by com-

c. Minstrel shows
d. Vaudeville
e. Operettas
f. *Ziegfeld Follies*

5. Research the careers of the following famous writing teams:
a. George and Ira Gershwin
b. Richard Rodgers and Oscar Hammerstein II
c. Alan Jay Lerner and Frederick Loewe
d. Andrew Lloyd Webber and Tim Rice

6. Stephen Sondheim is considered to be one of the chief innovators of the contemporary theatre. Research his career.

2

ELEMENTS OF A MUSICAL

BUZZ [a writer]: The play is actor-proof!

MARGO [an actress]: Actor-proof! If you knew the bits, the schtick, I have to dredge out of the vaudeville trunk to give the illusion that something amusing is going on. . . .

BUZZ: You empty-headed, conceited bass fiddle! You're just a body and a voice! Don't ever forget—I'm the brain!

—from *Applause*

To understand the musical, let's look at what the bookwriter creates—the book—and then the other elements of lyrics, score, and dances. In the next chapter, the production elements will be considered.

BOOK

In creating a musical, the first element to be written is usually the book. This contains the plot, characters, thoughts, dialogue, placement of songs and dances, and some stage directions, all of which are described below. After the lyrics of the songs are written by the lyricist, they are added to the book; and the book and lyrics are typed and reproduced to make the scripts for the show.

For operas, and sometimes for musicals, the text is termed the *libretto*—which means "little book" in Italian—and the writer may be called the *librettist*.

Plot

The plot or story line is the plan for the musical; that is, an outline of what happens in the show. In formulating the plot, the bookwriter structures the events to tell the story, delineate character, and express the theme and other thoughts. He or she may also indicate where songs and dances may occur for maximum effectiveness.

At the beginning of a typical plot, the writer will attempt to arouse the audience's interest, set the mood and style, give any exposition that the audience needs to understand the story, introduce the major characters, and get the action started by presenting to a major character a problem that disturbs the equilibrium. In the middle, which is the longest part of the plot, there is usually a conflict between two or more leading characters and the building of suspense with complications and surprises that lead to a climax at the end of Act I. Normally, the writer tries to leave the spectators "hanging" at the end of the first act to be sure that they return for the second.

In Act II, which is almost always shorter than the first act, there is another build with more suspense and surprises until the major climax is reached. This is followed by a short, satisfying ending or resolution in which the complications are settled.

To illustrate a musical plot, let's look at Lerner and Loewe's *My Fair Lady*. In the first scene, which takes place outside of a London opera house, the writer gives exposition about the leading characters: Higgins is a well-to-do professor who studies phonetics, Colonel Pickering is also interested in languages, and Eliza is a poor flower girl who speaks with a cockney dialect. During this scene, Higgins boasts that after six months of work he could pass Eliza off as a duchess at a ball.

In the second scene, set in a tenement section of London, the audience meets Eliza's father, Doolittle, and learns more about her background. Next, in Higgins's study, the action rises when Eliza enters to ask for speech lessons and Pickering proposes a bet that Higgins cannot make people believe she is a duchess in six months. As the lessons begin, Higgins is thoughtless and insensitive to Eliza's needs, and this attitude causes a conflict that enlivens the scenes in which he is trying to teach her Standard British speech and good manners. Will Higgins be able to deceive aristocrats into thinking that a flower girl is a duchess? The suspense builds, but at the end of Act I, the audience is left in doubt as Eliza is waltzing at the ball with a speech expert, Karpathy, who may detect her humble origins.

In the first scene of Act II in Higgins's study, the audience learns that Eliza was successful, and the tension is abated—only to build again as the conflict between Eliza and Higgins erupts into a bitter fight. (Part of this scene may be found in chapter ten.) At a confrontation between the two the next day at the home of Higgins's mother, Eliza informs him that she will marry a young man, Freddy, and that she will not see Higgins again. Later that day, Higgins makes the discovery that he has grown accustomed to Eliza, and in the last scene, he reveals how unhappy he is at losing her. The major climax is reached when Eliza returns, and in the very short ending that follows the conflict is resolved as they are reconciled.

A musical plot typically includes a subplot that provides a contrast to the main one. In *My Fair Lady* the subplot centers on Eliza's father, Doolittle, a dustman, who because of Higgins receives a bequest of four thousand pounds a year. He is thereby thrust into middle-class respectability and even marries his mistress.

While this sort of pattern of a simple, linear plot with subplot is found

Figure 2-1. Rex Harrison as Henry Higgins and Julie Andrews as Eliza Doolittle in the Broadway production of *My Fair Lady*.

(Courtesy of the Billy Rose Theatre Collection, the New York Public Library at Lincoln Center, Astor, Lenox, and Tilden Foundations.)

in many musicals, some shows are quite different. If you look at the plot of *A Chorus Line* or *Company*, two "concept musicals," you will discover that they do not fall into the common mold. Consider *A Chorus Line:* At an audition for a Broadway musical, various dancers tell about their lives in speech, song, and dance. Near the end, dancers are selected for the show, and this announcement is followed by a big finale. This type of construction may be called "episodic" or a "string of beads." To understand the latter term, think of a necklace. It has a thin string to hold the beads together, just as a musical of this type has a thin plot line to hold the episodes together.

Characters

The characters are the people in the musical who do the actions of the plot, speak the dialogue, and perform the songs and dances. To create "well-rounded" characters, the writer must know each character intimately: age, appearance, size, posture, movements, voice, dialect or accent, personality, intellect, education, occupation, socioeconomic status, nationality, ethnic origins, religion, moral beliefs, politics, likes and dislikes, desires, motivations, and relationships. Also, the writer must decide whether a character changes during the course of the musical or stays the same. Consider how much Eliza grows during *My Fair Lady:* she develops from a cockney flower girl into a refined lady. Higgins also changes as he comes to realize how much he needs Eliza. Doolittle changes too, but the other characters stay about the same from the beginning to the end of the plot.

Often the writer will have one or more *protagonists* (leading characters) who want to achieve a goal. A protagonist is usually appealing and likeable—a person that the audience can care about and empathize with. Opposition to the protagonist may come from one or more antagonists or society in general. After all, without an antagonist, the protagonist could easily achieve the goal, and there would be no conflict, no suspense, and no musical. Examples of protagonist-antagonist conflicts are King Arthur and Mordred in *Camelot,* Dolly and Horace Vandergelder in *Hello, Dolly!,* and Curly and Jud in *Oklahoma!.*

In addition to the protagonists and antagonists of the main plot, there may be other characters in a subplot, friends and relatives of these people in whom they can confide, comedians who are in the musical to get laughs, and, of course, singers, dancers, and extras. Plotting the interaction of these characters to maintain the audience's interest is the goal of the writer.

Thoughts

The thoughts of the book include the show's theme (the main underlying idea) or message. This may be implied or given directly to the audience in dialogue, actions, songs, dances, or even in signs. For example, the theme of *West Side Story* concerns the tragedy of prejudice. The song entitled "A Boy Like That," Lieutenant Schrank's speeches ("... a room with half-breeds in it. ..."), the rumble between the Jets and the Sharks, and the senseless killing of Riff, Bernardo, and Tony—all exemplify the theme.

Tying in with the theme may be other important ideas; for instance, in *West Side Story,* Tony and Maria look for a better life together as they dance to "There's a place for us,/Somewhere a place for us." In a few musicals, such as *The Threepenny Opera* by Kurt Weill and Bertolt Brecht, signs may be displayed onstage to tell the audience the main ideas of the scenes.

Dialogue

The words that comprise the spoken dialogue of the book are carefully chosen by the writer to reveal the characters, plot, and thoughts. Each word must be appropriate for the character, the situation, and the style of the show. Because a musical must have time for songs, dances, and music, the spoken dialogue is often cut to a minimum; consequently, words cannot be wasted. Every speech must be understandable, concise, and clear.

When a speech provides a lead-in to a song, the spoken passage must progress logically and easily into the adjoining lyrics. Even though different people may write the dialogue and the lyrics, their efforts must blend so that the words of both sound as though they come from the same character.

Placement of Songs and Dances

Since a musical number will usually provide the climax of a scene, its correct placement is crucial to the success of the show. The bookwriter may indicate where songs and dances may be, but these are likely to be changed during the composing and songwriting period and during rehearsals and previews. The bookwriter, lyricist, and composer, often in consultation with the stage director, choreographer, and musical director, consider where to place solos, duets, ensembles, choruses, and orchestral passages for maximum effectiveness.

Stage Directions

In stage directions (which in a script are usually indented and/or put in parentheses to distinguish them from the dialogue and lyrics), the bookwriter tells how he or she sees and hears the show. To guide the work of those involved with interpreting the script, the author may give some directions to performers and directors on characterizations, line interpretations, dialects or accents, makeup, movements, and stage business and to designers on scenery, properties, costumes, lighting, and sound.

LYRICS

Most songs for musicals are written by two people, a composer and a lyricist. As to which comes first, the music or the lyrics, that depends on the preference of the team.

The technique in writing a song is similar to writing a plot. Words cannot be wasted in the lyrics—every word should carry meaning, be simple to sing, easy to understand, and right for the character. A song should have a beginning that tells the listeners what the song is about and gets them interested in the subject, a middle that expands on the idea, and an ending that provides a satisfactory conclusion.

South Pacific, Emile's two children and Nellie, who do not know whether or not Emile has been killed in the war, are singing "Dites Moi" as Emile enters behind them. When the three stop singing, Emile finishes the song. The children rush to embrace their father, and they all sit down to eat. Then, as Emile and Nellie look at each other and clasp hands, the music swells, highlighting the moment that the lovers are reunited.

The music for scene changes (or sometimes costume changes) may involve a *bridge* or *segue,* a *crossover,* or a *throwaway* song or dance. These may be short or long depending on the difficulty involved in changing the set. A bridge or segue may be new music, or it may be music from the scene just ended blending into music to set the mood for the next scene. A crossover involves performers moving across the stage in "one," usually in front of a downstage drop, while the scene change goes on upstage. For example, in *Camelot* near the end of the first act, the audience sees a corridor in the castle and knights parading with banners to the Grand Hall. At the end of the parade, the corridor drop rises revealing the spectacular Grand Hall set. A throwaway song or dance has the same purpose, which is to hold the audience's attention while a scene change takes place. An example is the chorus number "I Sing of Love" from *Kiss Me, Kate* that is done in front of a downstage curtain while a full-stage set is erected behind the curtain. In recent years, however, advances in scenic practices have speeded up scene changes so that such devices are no longer needed as much.

Music specifically for dances is often arranged by a dance arranger from music in the score. To do this, the arranger works closely with the choreographer, the composer, and the musical director.

DANCES

Dance is a succession of harmonious and rhythmical movements or poses. In every movement there are three factors to be considered: *time, intensity,* and *space.* The time factor includes the tempo (or rate of speed) and duration (or length of time) of the movement. Intensity, or force, pertains to the amount of energy used. Space refers to the direction of the movement (forward, back, diagonal, and so forth), the size or range (from large to small), and the level (high to low) in which it occurs.

Dance numbers in musicals come in all sizes from solos and duets to large production numbers. And all types of dancing are called for in musicals: jazz, tap, ballet, *pointe,* modern, acrobatic, social, folk, period, ethnic, ballroom, soft shoe, eccentric, exotic, break, and a mixture of these that is sometimes called "show dance" or "stage dance."

Dance is a universal art whose origins are unknown, but we do know that dance was a part of the ancient Greek theatrical productions in the fifth century BC and has often been a part of musical shows ever since. An interest in social or folk dancing occurred in the Middle Ages and grew in the Renaissance. Today, popular social dances of the past, such as the pavane, the galliard, and the minuet, may also be termed "period" dances. Ethnic dances are a part of the traditions of a particular ethnic group, such as the Irish jig or the Scottish Highland fling. In the twentieth century, social or ballroom dancing has included the waltz, two-step, fox trot, rhumba, tango, jitterbug, twist, frug, disco, and many others.

The ballet grew out of Italian and French social dancing of the sixteenth century and developed into a performance art. It is comprised of traditional movements, positions, turns, and leaps that demand great skill, agility, and many years of training. One form of ballet is dancing *en pointe* (French for "on point"), which requires special toeshoes. From the beginning of opera, ballet was either a part of the show or a special performance at intermission, and it has continued to be an important part of modern musicals, such as *Oklahoma!*, *Carousel*, and *On Your Toes*.

Figure 2-2.   Dancers in the original Broadway production of *Oklahoma!*.
(Courtesy of the Billy Rose Theatre Collection, the New York Public Library at Lincoln Center, Astor, Lenox, and Tilden Foundations.)

Tap dancing developed in the last century from folk dances such as the clog, the Irish jig, and African dances. Using metal taps on the heels and toes of shoes to accentuate complex foot movements, tap dancers are still in demand for musicals like *My One and Only* and *42nd Street.* Similar to tap but done to slower music in shoes without taps is another old favorite, the soft shoe dance.

In the twentieth century, an American revolt against the conventional, formal movements of ballet resulted in modern dance, which has more emphasis on natural, emotional, personal expression. Led by dancers like Isadora Duncan, Martha Graham, and Hanya Holm, this type has also contributed to dancing for musicals. Showing the influence of modern, tap, ethnic, and ballet is jazz dance. Calling for relaxed legs and a flexible spine and hips, it was first used to interpret the rhythms of jazz music but is now done to other forms of popular music.

The word *eccentric* applies to a humorous form of jazz dancing that may involve weird contortions of the body and an individual style, such as Ray Bolger's in *Where's Charley?* and in the movie of *The Wizard of Oz.* As the loose-jointed straw scarecrow in the latter, his funny kicks and rubbery legs won many laughs. *Exotic* refers to sensual, sexy dancing, such as the strip tease numbers in *Sugar Babies* and *Grind.* Acrobatic is a very old form of dance in many countries, but "break" dancing, a blend of acrobatic dance and mime that originated on urban streets, is a recent addition to the list. A combination of some of the above, which may be termed show or stage dance, is often used today in musicals. It is the exciting, dynamic type of dance that Michael Bennett did for *A Chorus Line* and Bob Fosse choreographed for *Dancin'.*

In early musicals, dances were added with little reason other than to display pretty girls in beautiful costumes in order to add entertainment and spectacle to the show. Today dance not only adds variety, it is often an important part of the plot and theme, as in *A Chorus Line.*

Dance can be narrative, as it is in *The King and I* when the dance entitled "The Small House of Uncle Thomas" tells the story of *Uncle Tom's Cabin,* or it can be nonnarrative, as in *Funny Girl's* "Downtown Rag." The latter is also a good example of another function of dance: a number that is used to showcase the dancing talents of its performers.

Dance can reveal character as in *Cabaret's* "Don't Tell Mama," a song-and-dance number that helps to establish the character of Sally and the other entertainers at the Kit Kat Klub. In *Brigadoon,* Harry Beaton's sword dance reveals his stern, sharp nature.

Dance can be a substitute for realistic action. In *Man of La Mancha,* dance is used as Aldonza fights with the muleteers who beat and ravage her. In *West Side Story,* instead of a naturalistic fight, the Jets and Sharks show their antagonism through dance.

Dance can add comedy to a show as in the dance number that opens Act II of *South Pacific* in which Nellie and some nurses, sailors, and marines perform rather ineptly but humorously a dance for the "Thanksgiving Follies."

Dance can enhance and enlarge almost any song number. Consider two numbers from *Funny Girl,* "Cornet Man" and "Rat-Tat-Tat-Tat." If the performers only sang them, they would not be half as interesting. The dancing, which recreates the style of show dancing in the early twentieth century, contributes to the fun of these numbers.

Dance can help to establish the proper mood for a scene, such as the wedding dance in *Fiddler on the Roof*, which shows the great happiness of the celebrants. This contrasts sharply with the fright that occurs when the constable and his men enter to begin their destruction.

Finally, dance can also help to get across to an audience a change in characters, the passage of time, and shifting of places. In *Gypsy*, one dance number shows Gypsy Rose Lee's progress in stripping from her first awkward routine in Wichita to later shows in Detroit, Philadelphia, and, at last, the big time—Minsky's in New York.

EXERCISES

1. Read and analyze the book of a famous musical.
   a. What happens in the beginning?
   b. What happens in the middle?
   c. What happens in the ending?
   d. Is there a subplot?
   e. Does this musical have a protagonist-antagonist conflict?
   f. What is the theme?

2. What kinds of songs are in this musical?
   a. Are there ballads?
   b. Rhythm songs or jump tunes?
   c. Narrative songs?
   d. Comedy songs?
   e. Patter songs?
   f. Dramatic songs?
   g. Special material?
   h. A reprise?

3. Look at the score for this musical to determine the following:
   a. Is there an overture?
   b. Entr'acte music?
   c. Is music used for underscoring dialogue and action?
   d. Is music used to cover scene changes? Are there bridges or segues? A crossover scene? A throwaway song or dance?

4. Is there dancing in the musical?
   a. What types of dances are used? (Jazz? Tap? Ballet? Other kinds?)
   b. Is there a dance that contributes meaning to the plot?
   c. Is there a dance that is narrative? Nonnarrative?
   d. Is there a dance that reveals character?
   e. Is there a dance that substitutes for realistic action?
   f. Is there a dance that is funny?
   g. Is there a dance that contributes to the mood of a scene?
   h. Is there a dance that helps to communicate to an audience the change in a character, the passing of time, or a shift in locale?

3

PRODUCTION OF A MUSICAL

PIANO PLAYER: Hi, Mr. Benedict! How's the new musical in Philly?

HOWARD [a producer]:   Lousy book, lousy score. Naturally everyone is blaming the costumes.

—from *Applause*

A musical consists of just words and music on paper until a producer takes an option on the show and starts the process of turning the book, lyrics, and score into a production. If it is a new professional show, the book-writer, lyricist, and composer will probably attend auditions, rehearsals, and previews to offer their advice and make changes in the script and music. In addition to the authors, performers, and orchestra, the following are the people most involved in creating a professional production: the producer, stage director, musical director/conductor, orchestrator, arrangers, choreographer, designers of scenery, lighting, costumes, and sound, and the stage manager. The work of these persons will be described in this chapter.

If you are cast in a new, original amateur show, you will find more or less the same staff as listed for professional productions. However, if the musical has already been done professionally and your group is renting the orchestrations, scores, scripts, and dialogue and vocal parts, there should be no need for an orchestrator and arrangers. Also, the typical amateur theatre usually lacks a general or company manager, a casting director, and some of the other assistants listed below.

Most popular musicals can be produced by amateur organizations after payment of royalty and rental fees to the company holding the amateur production rights. To select a musical for amateur production, you should consult the catalogs of the following companies, which handle the most musicals in the United States:

Tams-Witmark Music Library, Inc.
560 Lexington Avenue
New York, NY 10022

Music Theatre International
810 Seventh Avenue
New York, NY 10019

Rodgers and Hammerstein
598 Madison Avenue
New York, NY 10022

Samuel French, Inc.
45 West 25th Street
New York, NY 10010

When you are cast in a musical, either amateur or professional, you will need to know who is responsible for what, and that is the reason for providing in this chapter a brief description of each of the important positions. While they are described separately below, it sometimes happens that one person may hold two jobs, such as stage director and choreographer or as the designer of both scenery and lighting.

Now let's look at those involved in mounting and running the professional production.

PRODUCER

The producer selects a show and takes an option on it. To do this, he or she must pay money to the bookwriter, lyricist, and composer to have the exclusive right to produce the show during a specified time period. Then comes the task of raising the money for its production. Producing a large musical today means that millions of dollars must be acquired before going into rehearsal, and it is the producer's job to persuade others that investing in this production will be profitable. Because so much money is needed, there are usually several people or organizations involved as producers and many more as financial backers.

The producer organizes the business side of the production. This person: is responsible for seeing that a budget is prepared and that all stay within it; hires everyone who works on the show, which requires dealing with various unions; rents rooms for auditions and rehearsals and a theatre for performances; sees that salaries, bills, and taxes are paid; keeps all financial records; arranges for publicity; forms additional companies; pays the backers if the show is a success; and closes the musical when it becomes unprofitable to keep it open. While the producer is the top business person on the show and, as such, oversees everyone's work, he or she may or may not be involved in the artistic aspects of the musical.

The producer may have various assistants, such as a general manager, company manager, press representative, casting director, lawyers, accountants, and secretaries.

STAGE DIRECTOR

The stage director (usually called simply *the director*) is the creative head of the show, the chief interpreter and coordinator of the production. The director must thoroughly analyze and understand the musical: the plot, characters, theme and thoughts, dialogue, songs, dances, music, and style. He or she must be able to arrive at a concept for the production—an idea as to how this musical should look and sound in its final form—that brings an added dimension to the show. Then the director must be able to communicate this to the others involved in creating the production. Working within the financial guidelines set by the producer, the director plans the production with the bookwriter, lyricist, composer, choreographer, musical director, and the various designers. Then the director must supervise their work so that the result is a unified production.

At auditions, the director usually casts the show with the advice and consent of the producer, bookwriter, lyricist, composer, musical director (on singers), and choreographer (on dancers).

After casting, the first meeting of the entire company is normally a discussion of the show, at which the dialogue is read and the music is played. Then, the director schedules separate rehearsals so that he or she can work on the acting, the musical director can rehearse the singing, and the choreographer, the dancing. As soon as possible, though, the acting, singing, and dancing must be put together by the director, whose aim is to unify the production. The director customarily stages everything except the dances, although he or she may seek the help of the choreographer in planning the movement and gestures in some singing numbers. In chapter seven, under "Rehearsing," you will find a description of the types of rehearsals conducted by the stage director: reading, blocking, developing, polishing, technical, and dress.

The director's assistants are the stage managers and often an assistant director and a rehearsal secretary. When the director leaves a show after opening night, the stage manager is charged with keeping the production as it was when the director was last present. However, the director must see the show at least once every eight weeks and, if he or she (or the producer) thinks it necessary, rehearse the performers.

MUSICAL DIRECTOR/CONDUCTOR

The musical director advises the staff and performers on all musical matters. This person assists in casting the singers and securing an orchestra, consults with the composer, lyricist, orchestrator, arrangers, stage director, and choreographer on interpretations and tempos of the music, and supervises all singing and orchestra rehearsals.

Usually the musical director is also the orchestra's conductor and as such is responsible for rehearsing the orchestra and conducting at performances. The latter involves cueing performers and musicians, setting tempos of musical numbers, and controlling the loudness and softness of the orchestra and singers, adhering as closely as possible to the interpretations that were decided upon during rehearsals.

Members of the musical director/conductor's staff may include an assistant, choral and vocal directors, an orchestra manager, and rehearsal pianists.

ORCHESTRATOR AND ARRANGERS

Working closely with the composer and the musical director/conductor are the orchestrator and the vocal and dance arrangers. The orchestrator, after selecting the best keys for the music, arranges the orchestra music and prepares a part for each instrument. The vocal arranger, in addition to arranging music for the singers, may also rehearse choral groups, ensembles, and soloists while the dance arranger works with the choreographer to arrange the dance music. Both the vocal and dance arrangers may also be rehearsal pianists.

CHOREOGRAPHER

Before creating the dances, the choreographer must analyze the musical and consult with the stage director, composer, bookwriter, lyricist, musical director, and the designers to determine where dances are to be placed in the show, the music, scenery, and costumes to be used, the dramatic function of the dances, the space available, and the people in the number. Lighting the dances is a major concern that requires close collaboration between the choreographer and the lighting designer.

The choreographer conducts dance auditions and advises the director on the casting of dancers. Working with the dance arranger, he or she devises the dances, taking into consideration the concept of the stage director, what happens in the plot before and after the dance, and the capabilities of the dancers. The choreographer or an assistant teaches the routines to everyone who dances in the show by demonstrating for the dancers what is wanted and correcting their efforts. The choreographer may also help with movement in singing numbers, if asked to do so by the stage director.

Assistants may include an assistant choreographer, a dance director, and a rehearsal pianist. After the show opens and the choreographer leaves, the dance captain (a member of the chorus who is selected for this extra duty by the choreographer) may call brush-up rehearsals for the dancers as needed. Like the director, the choreographer must see a performance every eight weeks and rehearse the dancers if necessary.

DESIGNERS OF SCENERY, LIGHTING, COSTUMES, SOUND

After a careful analysis of the musical, the designers must consult together and with the stage director, producer, choreographer, and musical director to be sure that all have a common understanding of the artistic aspects of the musical. Among matters for discussion are the theme and style of the musical, the director's concept, the number and types of sets and costumes needed, the time and place of each scene, the changes of mood, the colors to be used, and the amount of money that may be spent. As mentioned earlier, the stage director must oversee and approve the work of the designers, so that the result will be a unified production. Each designer may have one or more assistants.

The designer of scenery is responsible for providing an appropriate environment for each scene that aids the audience in understanding the time period, location, and the socioeconomic circumstances of the characters. Major concerns are to design sets that evoke the proper mood for each scene, furnish different levels, steps, and platforms for variety in staging, and contribute to the style and spectacle of the show.

After doing any needed research, the set designer makes rough sketches, floor plans, and perspective sketches or models, all of which must be discussed with and approved by the stage director. The set designer then makes working drawings for the people who will do the construction and painting and sees that this work is done according to these specifications. This designer is also responsible for "dressing" the sets with suitable furniture, decorations, and other properties.

After the scenery is constructed and painted at a scenic studio, it is delivered to the theatre where the designer supervises the placement and shifting of the sets and props. After opening night, when the set designer leaves the show, the stage manager, master carpenter, property master, and their crews keep the scenery and properties in working order.

The designer of lighting also helps the audience to understand the play by making visible what the spectators need to see. He or she can help them know the time of day and weather conditions, add variety to the stage picture, and provide special effects (such as a sunset or slide projections). Other concerns are changing the lighting to suit the moods, coordinating the lighting with the music, using lighting that enhances the colors of the scenery and costumes, and directing the audience's attention to a soloist, a group, or whoever or whatever is supposed to be emphasized in a scene.

The lighting designer sees to the acquisition of the equipment needed, makes a light plot and an instrument schedule, and supervises the placement and focusing of the lighting instruments, the use of color filters, the preparation of cue sheets, and the operation of the control board. After the show opens this designer also departs, leaving a master electrician in charge of the lighting crew.

The designer of costumes can help the audience to understand the play by designing or purchasing ready-made garments that are appropriate for each character. Often clothes can establish the sex, age, personality, occupation, or economic status of a character. Costumes can also help to indicate the time, place, and mood of scenes and add greatly to the excitement, beauty, style, and spectacle of a production. This designer must be certain that the costumes can be worn through the entrances of the set and used with the furniture, steps, ramps, and platforms that are onstage; that the colors of the costumes are compatible with the scenery and lighting; and that the garments are comfortable for the performers to work in, strong enough to withstand great stress and perspiration, and easy to get on and off for fast changes.

Designing costumes may require research and the preparation of numerous sketches to show to the director, producer, choreographer, and others. The final color sketches with instructions and swatches of material are then given to the costume house that will make the clothes. This designer is also responsible for preparing a chart that shows what every character will wear in each scene and for supervising the acquisition of accessories, such as jewelry, parasols, and fans.

After the garments are made at the costume house, the costume designer oversees the various fittings and a "dress parade," at which performers wear their costumes for the director and others to approve so that problems can be corrected before dress rehearsals. When the musical opens and the designer leaves, the costumes are in the care of the wardrobe supervisor and the dressers.

Like the other designers, the designer of sound (also called the sound engineer) is concerned with helping the audience to understand and appreciate the play. When a musical is performed in a large theatre or one with poor acoustics, this designer must make audible what the audience needs to hear. This designer handles the amplification of performers' voices and musical instruments, the mixing of sounds, and the placement, control, and safety of microphones and speakers. He or she is also responsible for creating or obtaining recorded sound effects (such as traffic noises or an explosion), recording music, preparing cue sheets, and operating the control console, which is usually located somewhere in the house (i.e., the audience area) so that the audio technician can tell immediately how the sound is being perceived by the audience.

When the sound designer leaves after the opening, audio technicians operate, maintain, and safeguard the equipment. They also make sure that the sound from the stage is fed to the various locations in the theatre where cue information is needed; these include the dressing rooms, greenroom, and light control booth.

STAGE MANAGER

The stage manager is the stage director's assistant at cast interviews, auditions, and rehearsals. He or she keeps an up-to-date list of addresses and telephone numbers of the company, helps to plan the rehearsal schedule and makes sure that everyone concerned is aware of it, and posts or makes announcements about such matters as fittings and photo sessions. The stage manager, who sees that the regulations of the Actors' Equity Association are observed, is the disciplinarian, enforcing necessary rules of conduct. He or she must also be certain that local fire, police, and city regulations are observed. On a Broadway musical, the responsibilities of this job are so numerous that there are at least two assistant stage managers.

For rehearsals, the stage manager marks the floor of rehearsal rooms to correspond to the floor plans of sets, provides makeshift furniture and properties, prompts, and keeps the promptbook up-to-date. When changes are made in the show, the stage manager must notify those involved. Eventually, he or she records in the promptbook all blocking and business; cues for lights, sound, curtains, music, and movements of the sets and properties; floor plans of sets; lighting, costume, and property plots; and all other information needed to produce the show.

During technical rehearsals, the stage manager and assistants are concerned with supervising the work of the various crews, organizing quick set and property changes, and finalizing technical cues. At dress rehearsals and performances, the stage manager is responsible for running the show by seeing that performers are properly made up and costumed, prompting, giving cues for the technical elements, and getting all to do their work correctly at the right time. Backstage, the stage manager is the boss.

Before a performance, the stage manager calls "Half hour, please," "Fifteen minutes, please," "Five minutes, please," and "Places, please." If a performer is not present at "half hour," the stage manager must telephone the absentee and start hastily to prepare the understudy or standby to go on. The stage manager makes sure that the orchestra goes into the pit to warm up and that the conductor enters just before starting time. During intermissions, the stage manager calls "Five minutes, please," and "Places, please." The stage manager is also responsible for keeping an accurate time record of the acts and intermissions.

After the musical opens and the director departs, the stage manager gives notes on performances, calls rehearsals as needed to keep the show as the director left it, and rehearses understudies, standbys, and replacements. The stage manager is also responsible for getting scenery, props, lighting and sound equipment, and costumes repaired, cleaned, or replaced as needed so that all production elements stay as they were at the opening of the show.

EXERCISES

1. Interview a person who has held one of the following positions on an amateur or professional musical production to find out what it takes to be successful in this job.
   a. Producer
   b. Stage director
   c. Musical director/conductor
   d. Orchestrator or arranger
   e. Choreographer
   f. Designer of scenery, lighting, costumes, or sound
   g. Stage manager
2. Research the careers of the following:
   a. Producers: Harold Prince, Joseph Papp, David Merrick
   b. Director-choreographers: Jerome Robbins, Michael Bennett, Bob Fosse, Tommy Tune
   c. Bookwriter-directors: George Abbott, Joshua Logan, Anthony Newley
   d. Directors: Rouben Mamoulian, Tom O'Horgan, Trevor Nunn
   e. Choreographers: George Balanchine, Agnes de Mille, Twyla Tharp
   f. Musical directors: Jay Blackton, Harold Hastings, Lehman Engel (Note the books written by Engel under Suggested Reading.)

4

MOVEMENT EXERCISES

JOAN [an experienced performer]:   You still wanna be a Broadway star?

RUBY [new to Broadway]:   Oh, yes!

JOAN: (*With grim seriousness*) Well, Ruby, there's only one way.

RUBY: How?

JOAN: Practice, kid, practice... 5, 6, 7, 8. (RUBY *begins to tap*)

—from *Dames at Sea*

The following movement exercises are designed to get you ready to perform. You will find in this chapter exercises for relaxation, body alignment, flexibility, balance, coordination, sense memory, emotional memory, imagination, rhythm, and observation. To practice them, you should wear exercise clothes and either sneakers, ballet slippers, flat shoes, or no shoes.

You should do all of the exercises in this chapter and the next at least once; and when you see the word *repeat*, use your own judgment as to how many times you should do the exercise. Some may only have the time or inclination to do it twice while others may find ten repetitions to their liking. Your goal should be to develop control of your body and voice so that they can respond effectively to the demands of a variety of characters.

You should exercise every day. After you become familiar with all of the exercises in this chapter and the next, devise your own routine for a daily workout of thirty to forty minutes and a shorter warm-up to do prior to an audition or performance.

For a daily workout, consider relaxation exercises 1, 3, 4, 7, and 8; body alignment exercise 1; flexibility exercises 7, 8, and 9; balance and coordination exercises 3, 4, 5, and 7; in chapter five, breathing exercises 6 and 7; phonation exercises 1, 3, 6, and 7; resonation exercises 1, 2, and 4; articulation and pronunciation exercises 1, 2, 3, 10, and 11; variety exercise 6; and projection exercises 3 and 6.

For a shorter warm-up, try relaxation exercises 3 and 4; body alignment exercise 1; flexibility exercises 8 and 9; balance and coordination

Figure 4-2.   Relaxation exercise 4.
(Photo: Kimberly Harbour.)

Figure 4-3.   Relaxation exercise 7.

(Photo: Kimberly Harbour.)

Figure 4-4.   Relaxation exercise 7.
(Photo: Kimberly Harbour.)

Figure 4-5. Relaxation exercise 7.
(Photo: Kimberly Harbour.)

8. With feet apart at shoulder width, bend over from the hips and swing your arms freely from right to left. (See figure 4-6.) Swaying rhythmically, gradually come up to an erect position. Now swinging your arms at shoulder height, allow the momentum to turn your body right and left as far as you can go without changing the position of your feet. (See figure 4-7.) Gradually decrease the speed of the swings as you bend over and return to the starting position.

Figure 4-6.   Relaxation exercise 8.
(Photo: Kimberly Harbour.)

Figure 4-7. Relaxation exercise 8.
(Photo: Kimberly Harbour.)

9. Standing in a good posture with feet apart, jump slightly up and down. Be sure to land on the balls of the feet first, then the heels as you bend your knees. Try to feel as relaxed and loose as possible. Vary this exercise by bouncing around the room.

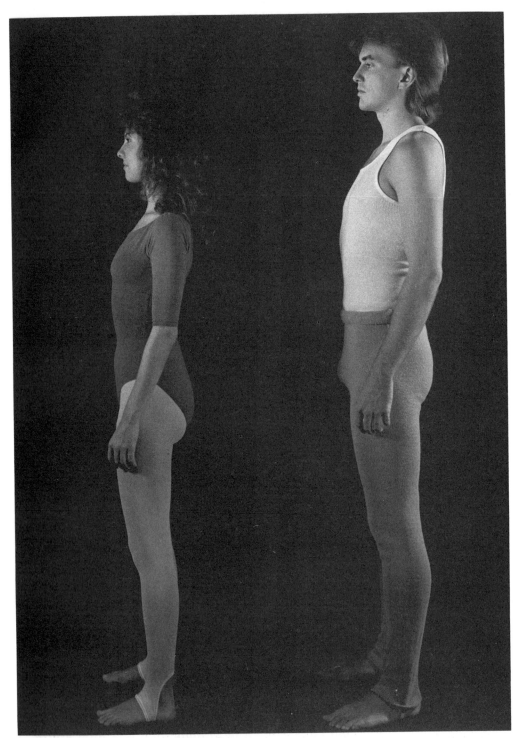

Figure 4-9. Side view of standing alignment.
(Photo: Kimberly Harbour.)

FLEXIBILITY

To be a versatile performer who can play a wide range of parts, you must work on the flexibility of your body and voice. In the "Variety" section in chapter five, you will find exercises for developing a flexible voice. Below are some exercises for a flexible body.

Exercises

To develop flexibility, practice the following:

1. Standing in a good posture, examine the flexibility of various parts of the body. Start with the hands: move each finger in a circle, then forward and backward and to the sides; move your hands in circles from the wrists, then forward and backward and to the sides. Next explore the movement that is possible with your arms: starting with them out to your sides, bring them in to hug yourself, then out and in and out again; then move them up until your hands touch overhead, then down to your sides and up and down again; make large circles and small circles with your arms, then make circles from the elbows. Next examine the flexibility of your legs and feet, your torso, and your head. When you come to the face, move your eyebrows, then your eyes, nose, lips, tongue, and jaw.

2. Lying on your back on the floor, clasp one knee to your chest and hold for four counts, then extend the leg and pull the leg as close to your chest as possible and hold for four counts. Then do the exercise with the other leg. Repeat.

3. Lying on your side on the floor, slowly raise the top leg as high as you can and then lower it. Repeat. Then do the exercise on the other side.

4. Lying on your front on the floor, slowly raise one leg as far as you can and then lower it. Repeat. Then do the exercise with the other leg.

5. Lying on your front on the floor, reach back with your hands and clasp your feet. Try to raise your head, upper torso, and knees off the floor. (See figure 4-10.) Hold for a count of four, then slowly return to the starting position. Repeat.

6. Sitting on the floor with your legs straight before you, bend over, clasp your feet, and bring your head as close to your knees as possible. Repeat.

7. Standing with feet apart and arms stretched overhead, slowly bend directly to one side, then up, then to the other side. Repeat.

8. Standing with feet apart and with arms stretched overhead, lunge forward as far as you can on one leg. Gently stretch for a count of four, and then return to the starting position. Lunge forward with the other leg, stretch, and return. Repeat.

9. Standing with feet apart and arms stretched overhead, bend back as far as you can, hold for a count of four, then return to the original position. Bend forward until your hands touch or come as close to the floor as is possible, hold, then return to the original position. Repeat.

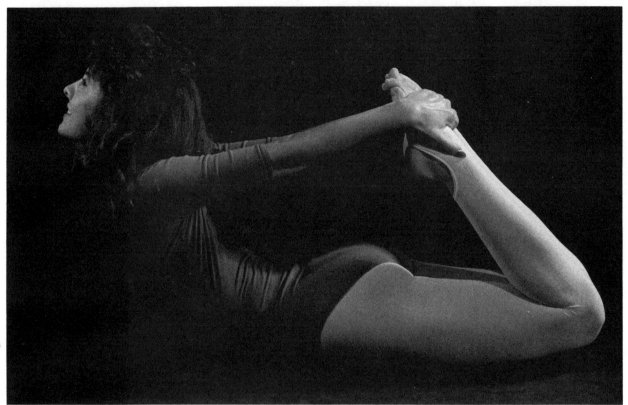

Figure 4-10.   Flexibility exercise 5.
(Photo: Kimberly Harbour.)

BALANCE AND COORDINATION

Balance is a steadiness that results when all parts of your body are properly adjusted to each other. *Coordination* is the harmonious functioning of the various parts of your body for the most effective results. Dancers, actors, and singers all need to work on these skills.

Exercises

Try the following to improve your balance and coordination:

1. Facing a partner, do the "mirror" exercise. One of you is the leader; the other is the follower. Whatever movement the leader makes, the follower should attempt to do it as though the follower is the leader's image in a mirror. After several minutes, change roles.

2. Vary the first "mirror" exercise by adding sounds that the follower must copy as well as movements. No words are permitted—just vocal sounds, such as grunts, groans, screams, and humming.

3. Standing on one foot, swing the other leg forward and backward, kicking as high as you can. Reverse.

Figure 4-11. Balance and coordination exercise 4.
(Photo: Kimberly Harbour.)

4. Standing erect on your left foot, raise your left arm; raise your right foot in back, clasp this foot with your right hand, and bend forward from the waist. Reverse. (See figure 4-11.)

5. Standing with arms overhead and heels together, go up on your toes, then bend your knees to descend to a squatting position. Then, rise to an erect position, staying on your toes. Repeat.

6. Standing in a good posture with feet apart, pat your head with your right hand and rub your abdomen in a circle with your left hand. Reverse.

7. Walk three steps and leap once; then walk two steps and leap twice. Repeat this pattern.

8. Draw a twenty-foot line with chalk on the floor. Imagining that you are a tightrope walker working at a great height in a circus tent, walk across this line holding an imaginary umbrella for balance.

SENSE MEMORY, EMOTIONAL MEMORY, IMAGINATION

One of the first steps in learning to be an actor is to learn about yourself. What makes you what you are today? How have your environment and heredity shaped you? Do you know yourself well enough to understand why you do and say the things you do? For example, do you know why you respond differently to various persons? Think: do you talk the same way to your parents, brothers and sisters, spouse, teachers, and close friends? If not, why not?

In order to analyze and understand dramatic characters and their attitudes toward each other, you must first be able to analyze and understand yourself. One way is to work with your own memories, both sensory and emotional, recalling and examining them to determine why you reacted as you did in that situation. And when a character you are playing has an experience similar to one that you have had, you can and you should make use of your memory to give your acting a realistic honesty. (See the sections on "Personalization" and "Emotional Scenes" in chapter seven.)

If, however, you have never had an experience like your character's, try using your imagination. Ask yourself what would you do if you were this type of person in this situation. (See the section on "Imagination" in chapter seven.)

Exercises

Do the following actions, basing them on your own sensory or emotional memories, if possible. If you have never had an experience that is close to the described exercise, then use your imagination. You can do the following as pantomimes, or speak if you feel motivated to do so.

1. Watch and listen to a band marching down a street.
2. Look at a beautiful sunset.
3. Pick your favorite flower. Examine it carefully: touch it, smell it, and pin it on your clothes.
4. Lie in the sand on a beach, enjoying the sunshine; build a sand castle; run into the ocean and have fun in the waves.
5. You are sleeping when someone throws a bucket of cold water on you.
6. You are sleeping in a tent when slowly you become aware that a rattlesnake is nearby.
7. You are reading at a library in the wintertime when the heat is turned off and the room becomes progressively colder.
8. You are reading at a library in the summertime when the air conditioning is turned off and the room becomes progressively hotter.
9. While reading in the library, you notice a bad odor that permeates the room.
10. Visit a pet store to look at the cages of puppies and birds.

11. You are waiting for a bus on a hot summer day when it starts to rain.

12. You are waiting for a bus on a cold winter day when it starts to snow.

13. Drink some hot chocolate that burns your tongue.

14. Listen to a church bell ringing in the distance.

15. Smell and compare two bottles of perfume that you are considering buying.

16. Examine the blades of two kitchen knives.

17. Taste and compare two soft drinks.

18. Examine closely two fabrics that you are thinking about buying: one is velvet and the other is corduroy.

19. Burn your hand while cooking.

20. Eat your favorite dinner.

21. Listen as a fire alarm sounds in your building.

22. Watch a horror film.

23. Answer the telephone and listen as a relative bawls you out for something you did not do.

24. Answer the telephone and listen as someone informs you that you have won a thousand dollars in a contest.

25. Get dressed; you are happily preparing to meet the one you love.

26. Get dressed; you are furiously planning to leave your home forever.

27. Walking in a circle around the room, walk as you did on an occasion when you were disappointed and disgusted with yourself. Base this on your memory of an experience that you had.

28. Walk as you did one time when you were happy. Again, base this on a true experience.

29. Walk as you did once when you were afraid that someone was following you.

30. Recreate times when you were embarrassed, surprised, worried, sad, in love, and angry. These actions should be based on your memory of experiences that happened to you at some time in your life. Mentally reconstruct what happened and how you acted, then practice recreating what you did.

RHYTHM

The word *rhythm* refers to the beat felt in music, speech, and movement—the recurrent alternation of strong and weak elements and the rate or tempo, which may vary from slow to fast. Your heart beats in certain rhythms. You also walk and talk in rhythms, and these rhythms can change frequently according to your thoughts, moods, and energy. Each character you play will have different rhythms, and studying these is an important part of finding a characterization.

5

VOCAL EXERCISES

HIGGINS: (*Placing marbles in her mouth*) Four . . . five . . . six marbles. There we are. (HE *holds up a slip of paper*) Now, I want you to read this and enunciate each word just as if the marbles were not in your mouth. "With blackest moss, the flower pots were thickly crusted, one and all." Each word clear as a bell. (HE *gives her the paper*)

ELIZA: (*Unintelligibly*) "With blackest moss, the flower pots" . . . . I swallowed one!

HIGGINS: (*Reassuringly*) Oh, don't worry. I have plenty more. Open your mouth.

—from *My Fair Lady*

In this chapter you will find exercises for your speaking and singing voice. They comprise breathing, phonation, resonation, articulation, pronunciation, variety, projection, phrasing, and pausing. Your goal should be a voice that you can use without straining or tiring and a voice that is right for the character. It should be easily heard and understood and have enough variety to capture and hold the audience's attention.

In addition to studying dance, as mentioned in chapter four, musical performers should learn how to sing because most roles demand some singing ability.

BREATHING

All of your life you have been breathing without giving it much thought. It is, of course, essential that you take oxygen into your body during inhalation and breathe out carbon dioxide and other waste products in order to live; our breathing goes on automatically to provide these necessities. Now you are asked to think about your breathing, so that you can develop a quick, silent inhalation and a controlled exhalation.

First of all, let's consider the location and action of the diaphragm. This is a thin, dome-shaped layer of muscle and tendon that separates the thorax (chest cavity) from the abdomen. It is attached to the sternum (breastbone) in front, the lower ribs, and the spine in back; it moves up and down as you breathe. (See figure 5-1.)

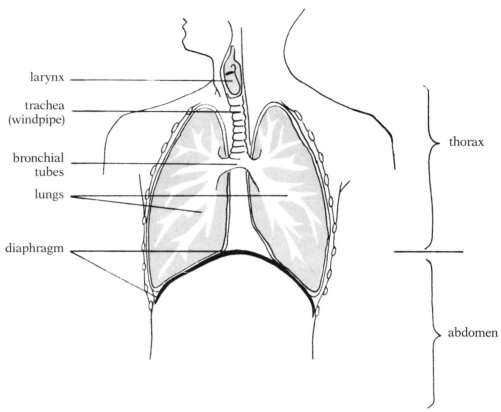

Figure 5-1.   Some parts of the body that are involved in speaking and singing.
(Drawing by Kimberly Harbour.)

On inhalation, when the diaphragm descends and the ribs and rib muscles move out and up, there is more room in the thoracic cavity than previously. The air pressure in the lungs is lowered, and atmospheric pressure forces air to enter the body. When this happens, the air enters through the nose or mouth, goes down the throat to the trachea (windpipe), then to the bronchial tubes and finally the lungs. The lowering of the diaphragm also causes pressure on visceral organs that results in a slight outward movement of the abdomen.

In exhalation, just the reverse occurs: The abdomen moves in, the diaphragm returns to a dome shape, the ribs and rib muscles move in and down, and the air is squeezed out of the lungs. The air then travels to the bronchial tubes, up the trachea, through the throat, and out through the nose or mouth. Note that when you want to control your exhalations, this can be done by contracting the abdominal muscles, which causes them to move inward and affect the rising diaphragm. This is called *diaphragmatic-abdominal* breath control.

Exercises

The following exercises will help you to become more conscious of what happens in your body as you inhale and exhale. During all of these exercises, be sure to relax your neck and throat completely.

1. Lying on your back in a relaxed state, concentrate on feeling the movement of the air into and out of your body as you inhale and exhale.

2. Still lying on your back, put one hand on the lower ribs (at your side) and the other on your abdomen (at the waistline). Do your hands go out as you inhale? Do your hands come in as you exhale?

3. Still lying on your back, inhale quickly and silently, then blow the air out through rounded lips. Do you feel a contraction of the abdominal muscles as you exhale? When you are out of air, inhale. Do you feel the expansion of the midsection on inhalation? On the next exhalation, count out loud until you run out of air. (You speak or sing only on the exhalation, never on the inhalation.)

4. Still lying on your back, inhale quickly and silently, then sing "ah" on the exhalation until you are out of air. Vary this exercise by next singing "oh," then "oo," "ay," and "ee." Avoid breathiness. Keep the tone steady; when it becomes difficult to control the steadiness of the tone, stop singing and inhale.

5. Stand in an erect but relaxed posture with feet about twelve inches apart, and place one hand on the lower ribs at your side and the other at the waistline in front. Open your mouth and pant as though you were gasping for air. Do not let the shoulders rise and fall. The only movement should be in the abdominal muscles and lower ribs which push out on inhalation and come in on exhalation.

6. Keeping your hands in the same positions as for exercise 5, say "hah!" several times loudly with force, inhaling before each word. Then say loudly and vigorously, inhaling before each syllable, "hah! hoh! hoo! hay! hee!" Repeat.

7. Repeat exercises 3 and 4 in a standing position. When inhaling, do not make any sounds, and do not raise the shoulders. Try to keep the neck and throat muscles relaxed, and do not waste air as you speak or sing.

8. Check up on how much air is escaping from your mouth as you speak by holding a lighted candle or match about four inches away from your lips as you count in a soft tone. Is too much air escaping when you say "three," "four," "five," "six," and some of the other numbers? When you run out of air, stop; and start from the beginning again in a loud voice, trying to say the numbers without flickering the flame too much.

PHONATION

Phonation is the process of producing a vocal tone. This happens in the larynx (voice box), which is located at the top of the trachea. On exhalation, if you wish to speak or sing, the air coming up the trachea vibrates the vocal folds of the larynx, thus creating sound waves.

Pitch is determined by the frequency of the sound waves: a low frequency is heard as a low pitch and a high frequency as a high pitch. Factors that influence the pitch of your voice are the length, weight, elasticity, and tension of the vocal folds and the breath pressure striking the larynx from below. Normally, a man's voice is lower in pitch than a woman's because his vocal folds are longer and heavier. When the vocal folds become tense, the pitch rises, which is one reason for encouraging you to relax the throat and neck muscles. How loudly or softly you speak or sing is determined by the pressure of the air coming up the trachea. When you increase the breath pressure on the vocal folds, you produce a louder tone.

For good phonation, you need to have an open, relaxed throat and a relaxed jaw, to avoid breathiness, and to learn to speak at your best pitch level. To find the optimum pitch for your speaking voice, sing up the scale from the lowest pitch that you can sing easily. Usually a person's optimum pitch is about three to five tones above your lowest, but this may not always be true. It will take some experimentation by singing various tones in the lower part of your register until you find the pitch at which your voice seems to function best. Then try speaking at that pitch to see if it is comfortable for you.

Exercises

Practice the following exercises for good phonation:

1. Sitting or standing in a good posture, stretch your arms and yawn. Then, drop your head forward to your chest and slowly rotate your head to one side, to the back, to the other side, and let it drop in front again. Keep your eyes closed and try to feel relaxed in the throat, neck, and face. Rotate the head again. Then with another big yawn, raise your head to an erect position.

2. Turn your head to the left as far as possible and tense the neck muscles as you stretch; then relax completely. Do the same to the right, backward, and forward.

3. Yawn to give your throat an open, relaxed feeling, then sing "ah" on a comfortable pitch until you are out of air. Avoid breathiness and straining. Vary this exercise by singing "oh," "oo," "ay," and "ee."

4. Yawn, then sing "ah, oh, oo, ay, ee" on one breath, holding each syllable for two counts.

5. With a relaxed jaw, yawn, then sing "mah" eight times on a comfortable pitch at a medium rate of speed. Vary this exercise by singing eight times each "bah," "dah," "fah," "gah," "hah," "jah," "kah," "lah," "nah," "pah," "quah," "rah," "sah," "tah," "vah," "wah," "yah," "zah."

6. Yawn, then sing up the scale "do, re, mi, fa, sol, la, ti, do" on one breath; breathe, then sing down the scale. Vary this exercise by singing "yah" on each of the notes. Then use "yoh," "yoo," "yay," and "yee."

7. Instead of singing, yawn then speak "do, re, mi, fa, sol, la, ti, do" on one breath going up the scale; breathe, then speak these syllables going down the scale.

8. Yawn, then sing up the scale "do, re, mi, fa, sol, la, ti, do" starting with a very soft tone and ending with a loud one. As you get louder, do not allow the throat and neck muscles to become tense. Next, sing down the scale starting with a loud tone and ending with a soft one.

9. Vary exercise 8 by singing up the scale using the above syllables, this time starting with a loud tone and ending with a soft one. Then, sing down the scale going from a soft tone to a loud one.

10. Count from one to ten on one pitch. Start softly and end with a loud tone. As you get louder, resist the tendency to go up in pitch. Next, count backwards from ten to one on one pitch going from a loud to a soft tone.

RESONATION

Resonation is the process of amplifying and enriching the sound waves that are created by the vibrating vocal folds. Resonation, which occurs primarily in the throat, mouth, and nose and, to a lesser extent, in the chest, adds strength to the tone and gives your voice its unique quality. (See figure 5-2.)

For good resonance, you need a relaxed jaw, an open throat, and effective use of the resonators. As an actor, you need sufficient flexibility in your voice to vary the quality for different roles, sometimes even using what are termed faults of resonance: nasality, denasality, stridency, throatiness, and breathiness.

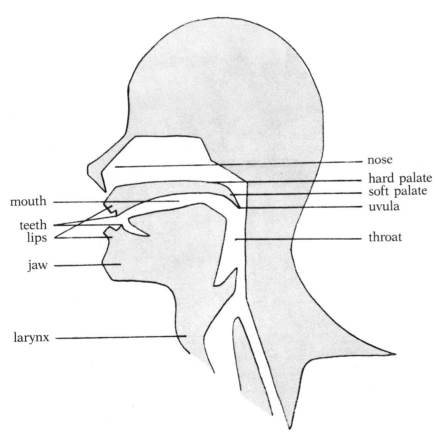

Figure 5-2. Some parts of the head and neck that are involved in speaking and singing. (Drawing by Kimberly Harbour.)

Exercises

Work on these exercises to develop a good basic resonance:

1. Starting with your hands and knees on the floor, bend forward and place the top of your head on the floor. (See figure 5-3.) Yawn, then sing, holding each syllable for a count of two, "mee," "may," "mah," "moh," "moo." Does the tone seem to be hitting against your front teeth? If so, you are getting a "front placement" of your voice. Many singing teachers encourage front placement as a means of getting good nasal and oral resonance and keeping the tone from sounding too throaty. Sit back on your heels and sing the same syllables, trying for a front placement. Repeat in both positions.

2. Standing in an erect but relaxed posture, yawn to relax and open your throat, then sing "mee" on each note while going up the scale for one octave. Feel the front placement of the tone as the tone seems to be hitting against the front teeth. Now sing "mah" on each note as you come down the scale. Try to feel the same front placement on "mah" as you had on "mee." Vary this exercise using "may" and "moh," "nee" and "nah," "nay" and "noh."

3. Yawn, then glide up and down an octave singing one "mee" for all notes. Vary this exercise using "mah," "may," "moh," "nee," "nah," "nay," and "noh."

Figure 5-3.   Resonation exercise 1.
(Photo: Kimberly Harbour.)

4. Yawn, then sing "ee" for four counts and then "ah" for four counts. Get the same feeling of front placement on "ah" as you have on "ee." Repeat. Vary this exercise using "ee" and "oh," "ee" and "oo," and "ee" and "aw."

5. Three consonant sounds, [m], [n], and [ŋ] (as in *m*e, *n*eed, and ri*ng*), are resonated primarily in the nose. Normally the uvula (the end of the soft palate) is against or almost against the back wall of the throat, but when the three nasal consonants are spoken, the uvula comes away from the wall permitting nasal resonance on these consonant sounds. As for vowel sounds, it is debatable how much nasal resonance should be used. You should train your ear so that you recognize what sounds acceptable and what seems to be excessive nasal resonance. To feel and hear the difference in resonance between a nasal consonant and a vowel, yawn then sing "ing" for four counts and then "ah" for four counts. Repeat. Then vary this exercise with "en" and "oh" and then with "em" and "aw."

6. The following faults of resonance should normally be avoided, although ocassionally they may be utilized for a characterization.
   a. Nasality involves too much nasal resonance on all sounds. This may be caused by an inactive uvula or by holding the jaws together tightly so that the sounds cannot come out of the mouth and must go through the nose. Say the following sentence with nasality: "My heavens, I can't get him to do anything!" Now say the sentence opening the jaw adequately with a good balance of mouth, nose, and throat resonance.
   b. Denasality involves too little nasal resonance. Shut off the nasal cavity completely, as though your nose is stopped up with a bad cold, and say this sentence with denasality: "I have a terrible cold, and I'm going home to go to bed." Now say the sentence with a proper balance of mouth, nose, and throat resonance.
   c. Stridency involves a loud, harsh, tense tone, which tends to be high in pitch. Say this sentence with a strident quality, then relax the muscles of the throat and neck before saying it again: "I can't understand why you are doing this to me!"
   d. Throatiness involves a gravelly tone that sounds as though it originates in the throat and does not have enough front placement. The pitch may be too low, and there may be too much tension in the throat. (Do not confuse this term with hoarseness that comes as a result of a medical problem such as a cold.) Say this sentence with a throaty quality, then relax and use front placement when you repeat it: "If you want to see me again, just call."
   e. Breathiness means that too much air is escaping when you speak. Some sexy movie stars like Marilyn Monroe made a fortune out of a breathy vocal quality, but for good projection from the stage a more careful control of the air supply and better resonance are desirable. Try this sentence with breathiness: "Be quiet—you don't know who's listening to us." Now, say it again and do not permit an excessive amount of air to escape.

7. As an exercise in using a full, resonant voice with a good balance of throat, mouth, and nose resonance, work on the following lines from Act I, Scene 1 of *Camelot*, which show the first meeting of Arthur and Guenevere. (More of this scene may be found in chapter ten.)

> (SHE *turns dejectedly towards the foot of the tree. A branch cracks, and* ARTHUR *drops to the floor.* GUENEVERE, *startled out of her wits, runs*)
>
> ARTHUR: A thousand pardons, Milady. Wait! Don't run. (SHE *stops in the corner of the stage and looks at him coweringly*) Please! I won't harm you.
>
> GUENEVERE: You lie! You'll leap at me and throw me to the ground.
>
> ARTHUR: (*Amazed, protesting*) I won't do any such thing. (HE *takes a step toward her.* SHE *takes a step backwards.* HE *stops*)
>
> GUENEVERE: Then you'll twist my arm and tie me to a tree.
>
> ARTHUR: But I won't.
>
> GUENEVERE: Then you'll sling me over your shoulder and carry me off.
>
> ARTHUR: No, no, no! I swear it! By the Sword Excalibur! I swear I won't touch you.
>
> GUENEVERE: (*Hurt*) Why not?

ARTICULATION AND PRONUNCIATION

Articulation involves the distinctness of your speech. It depends upon how well you move the articulators: the lips, tongue, teeth, jaws, hard and soft palate, and for one sound (the *h*), the vocal folds. (See figure 5-2.) On the stage you must always speak distinctly enough so that the audience can understand you, but other concerns with articulation should be governed by the type of character you are playing. For example, one character, perhaps a scholarly professor, might speak in an overly precise way while an illiterate oaf might mumble his words. Onstage, however, both must be understood by the audience in the back of the balcony. Another consideration is how your character's articulation may change throughout a play, as he or she becomes better educated, tired, ill, drunk, drugged, aged, or emotionally disturbed.

While articulation is concerned with producing sounds distinctly, *pronunciation* involves knowing the correct sounds and the right syllables to emphasize for the dialect that you want to use. If in trying to use the Standard American dialect, I say "G*it* me to the *mo*-tel," instead of "G*et* me to the mo-*tel,*" I have made two errors of pronunciation: the vowel sound in *get* and the accent in *motel.* As with articulation, your pronunciation of words onstage must be as the character would pronounce them.

In the Standard American dialect, there are fourteen vowel sounds that can be placed in three groups depending upon whether the front, middle, or back of the mouth is the most involved in their pronunciation. In producing a vowel sound the mouth is open and the articulators do not move. Note the underlined vowel sounds in the following words (the phonetic symbol from the International Phonetic Alphabet for the underlined sound is in brackets):

Front	*Middle*	*Back*
beet [i]	Burt [ɝ]	boot [u]
bit [ɪ]	bother [ɚ]	bush [ʊ]
bait [e]	above [ə]	bone [o]
bet [ɛ]	butt [ʌ]	bawl [ɔ]
bat [æ]		bar [ɑ]

A diphthong is a blend of two vowel sounds in one syllable. In forming the following six diphthongs, the articulators move from the position for the first vowel to the position for the second:

by [aɪ]	bay [eɪ]
boy [ɔɪ]	beau [oʊ]
bough [aʊ]	beauty [ju]

While vowels and diphthongs are open, uninterrupted sounds, consonant sounds are more obstructed. All vowels and diphthongs are voiced: in other words, the vocal folds are vibrating as they are produced. Some consonants are voiced, but some are voiceless.

The plosive consonants, which are made by stopping the air flow briefly by the articulators and then releasing it with a slight "explosion," are the following:

Voiceless	*Voiced*
pet [p]	bet [b]
too [t]	do [d]
kind [k]	go [g]

The following fricative consonants are made by forcing air through two articulators:

Voiceless	*Voiced*
fun [f]	vote [v]
thin [θ]	than [ð]
see [s]	zoo [z]
shall [ʃ]	measure [ʒ]
hat [h]	

The following nasal consonants are all voiced and are made by diverting the air to the nose by lowering the uvula away from the wall of the throat:

met [m]
net [n]
king [ŋ]

The following glides are produced as the articulators move from the position for the glide to the following vowel or from a vowel to the glide consonant. All glides are voiced:

last   [l]   yes   [j]

ran   [r]   we   [w]

The following are blends of a plosive and a fricative consonant:

Voiceless   *Voiced*

church   [tʃ]   judge   [dʒ]

The above are the sounds of the Standard American dialect, but a character you are playing may not speak with this dialect and may use other sounds. For example, a character who has a Bostonian dialect may use, in saying *ask*, a vowel sound that is about halfway between [æ] and [ɑ] that is indicated in phonetics by [a].

A dialect is a variation of a language characteristic of a geographical region or social class, examples of which are the American southern and the London cockney dialects. There are many American dialects, but Standard American is the most common. The British Isles also have a variety of dialects, many of which appear in plays. Note how Eliza Doolittle and her father in *My Fair Lady* speak in the London cockney dialect. Then, during the show, Eliza is taught to speak Standard British (called in England "RP" or "Received Pronunciation").

The term *accent* may be used not only to indicate proper syllabic stress in words but also a way of speaking that involves a carryover of pronunciation, rhythm, and melodic characteristics from a person's original language to a second language. For example, in *The Most Happy Fella*, Tony, an Italian grape farmer in California, has an Italian accent when he speaks English, which is indicated in the script by the use of "omma" for "I am" and various other changes in the spelling of English words. In *Cabaret*, when the German characters speak English, they should have a German accent. In *South Pacific*, Emile should use a slight French accent.

It is not within the scope of this book to undertake a study of dialects and accents as there are many and each requires a great deal of work. A good way to learn one is to listen to an individual who normally speaks in that manner. In some cities a speech or acting coach who specializes in dialects and accents may be available to help you. A third method is to read a book that explains them and listen to the accompanying tapes. (There are several of these listed under Suggested Reading.) Just reading about them without listening to tapes is a poor fourth choice.

In studying dialects and accents, though, remember that not everyone speaks in the same manner, so consequently there is no one "right" way to do a French accent or a Scottish dialect. Variables such as education, socioeconomic level, personality, occupation, environment, and other factors affect the character's speech, so each dialect or accent that you undertake should be acquired with your specific character in mind. Remember, too, that it must never be done so authentically that an audience cannot understand you.

Exercises

The following exercises are for articulation and pronunciation. While doing them, remember to keep your neck and throat relaxed at all times.

1. To exercise the articulators, stick out your tongue and move it rapidly from side to side; try to touch your nose and your chin with your tongue; move the lower jaw in a circle; open the mouth as wide as possible; alternately pucker, protruding the lips, and smile broadly; blow through closed lips, vibrating them.

2. Say the following sounds rapidly eight times each: "bee," "dee," "fee," "gee," "hee," "kee," "lee," "mee," "nee," "pee," "quee," "ree," "see," "tee," "vee," "wee," "yee," "zee." Take two of the syllables and repeat them quickly four times each; for example, "bee-dee," and "fee-gee."

3. Vary exercise 2 by using the same beginning consonants with other vowel sounds: "oh," "oo," and "ay."

4. The following words have difficult sound combinations. Practice them until you can articulate them distinctly.

abominably	indubitably	oaths
adapts	lengths	sects
anesthetists	malingerer	statistics
depths	masts	tasks
eighths	months	thwart
guests	mouths	twelfths
horror	murderer	widths

5. The next five exercises involve common words that are sometimes mispronounced. If you are doubtful about your pronunciations of these words, look them up in a dictionary. The first group concerns words that may be mispronounced because people substitute other sounds for the accepted ones of the Standard American dialect; for example, some people say "git" instead of the preferred "get." Keep in mind, though, that if you are playing a character from certain areas of the United States, you might want to use "git" instead of "get," if that is characteristic of the dialect of that region.

any	hypnotize	push
can't	iron	slovenly
chasm	just	suave
color	oil	woman
fire	orgy	worship
get	pantomime	zoology

6. The following are words that are sometimes mispronounced because people omit sounds that should be heard; for example, some people say "bout" when they mean "about."

about	entertain	possible
afraid	gentlemen	suspenders
almost	government	twenty
candidate	kept	violet
didn't	library	wonderful

7. The following are words that are sometimes mispronounced because people add sounds that should not be used; for example, some do not realize that the *b* in *subtle* is silent and, therefore, pronounce the word incorrectly.

across	heir	psalm
athlete	mischievous	salmon
christen	once	subtle
corps	please	sword
grievous	preventive	victuals

8. The following are words that are sometimes mispronounced because people accent the wrong syllable; for example, some pronounce *comparable* with the accent on the second syllable instead of the first, which is preferred.

admirable	device	irreparable
ascertain	genuine	motel
comparable	incomparable	omnipotent
debate	incongruous	police
demonstrative	infamous	receipt
Detroit	insurance	superfluous

9. The following words may be mispronounced because people transpose sounds; for example, in the word *perspiration*, it is incorrect to say the first syllable as *pre* instead of *per*.

aggravate	perform	predicament
introduce	perspiration	relevant
larynx	pharynx	stubborn

10. It is said that in the fourth century BC in Greece, Demosthenes trained to be an orator by shouting over the sounds of the ocean with his mouth full of pebbles. In *My Fair Lady* Higgins has Eliza speak with marbles in her mouth (see the excerpt at the beginning of this chapter). Instead of pebbles or marbles, which could be dangerous, try biting a pencil placed lengthwise between the front teeth. With your teeth held apart by the pencil, work hard to articulate the tongue twisters in exercise 11 or the excerpts in exercises 12 or 13. After this attempt, remove the pencil and repeat the selections to see if your articulation has improved. If not, try the pencil again.

11. Practice the following well-known tongue twisters until you can say them rapidly with good articulation:
    a. She shall sell sea shells on the seashore.
    b. Around the rough and rugged rock the ragged rascal ran.
    c. Peter Piper picked a peck of pickled peppers.
    d. Better buy rubber baby-buggy bumpers.
    e. Sixty-six sick chicks sat on six, slim, slick, slender saplings.
    f. A big black bug bit a big black bear and made the big black bear bleed.
    g. The sixth sheik's sixth sheep's sick.
    h. Linger longer, Lemuel Lister, lilting limitless lullabies.

12. A patter song by Gilbert and Sullivan is another excellent exercise for articulation. Work on the following trio from *Ruddigore* until you can say it distinctly at a fast pace. In this comic opera, it is sung by Robin, Despard, and Margaret in Act II.

ROBIN: My eyes are fully open to my awful situation—
       I shall go at once to Roderic and make him an oration.
       I shall tell him I've recovered my forgotten moral senses,
       And I don't care twopence-halfpenny for any consequences.
       Now I do not want to perish by the sword or by the dagger,
       But a martyr may indulge a little pardonable swagger,
       And a word or two of compliment my vanity would flatter,
       But I've got to die to-morrow, so it really doesn't matter!

DESPARD: So it really doesn't matter—

MARGARET: So it really doesn't matter—

ALL: So it really doesn't matter, matter, matter, matter, matter!

MARGARET: If I were not a little mad and generally silly
          I should give you my advice upon the subject, willy-nilly;
          I should show you in a moment how to grapple with the question,
          And you'd really be astonished at the force of my suggestion.
          On the subject I shall write you a most valuable letter,
          Full of excellent suggestions when I feel a little better,
          But at present I'm afraid I am as mad as any hatter,
          So I'll keep 'em to myself, for my opinion doesn't matter!

DESPARD: Her opinion doesn't matter—

ROBIN: Her opinion doesn't matter—

ALL: Her opinion doesn't matter, matter, matter, matter, matter!

DESPARD: If I had been so lucky as to have a steady brother
         Who could talk to me as we are talking now to one another—
         Who could give me good advice when he discovered I was erring
         (Which is just the very favour which on you I am conferring),
         My story would have made a rather interesting idyll,
         And I might have lived and died a very decent indiwiddle,
         This particularly rapid, unintelligible patter
         Isn't generally heard, and if it is it doesn't matter!

ROBIN: If it is it doesn't matter—

MARGARET: If it ain't it doesn't matter—

ALL: If it is it doesn't matter, matter, matter, matter, matter!

13. Another patter song is sung by Sir Joseph Porter, First Lord of the Admiralty, in Act I of *H.M.S. Pinafore* by Gilbert and Sullivan. Practice speaking the following at a fast rate with a distinct articulation:

    When I was a lad I served a term
    As office boy to an Attorney's firm.
    I cleaned the windows and I swept the floor,
    And I polished up the handle of the big front door.
      I polished up that handle so carefullee
      That now I am the Ruler of the Queen's Navee!

RUTH: A wife of seventeen! You will find me a wife of a thousand!

FREDERIC: No, but I shall find you a wife of forty-seven, and that is quite enough.

2. For you to deliver every line of your part at the same rate of speed can be very monotonous for your audience. Read the following at a constant pace; then read it a second time with proper variation of rate, pitch, loudness, and quality. The excerpt is from Act II, Scene 9 of a ballad opera entitled *The Beggar's Opera* by John Gay. The time is 1728; the place is Newgate Prison, where Macheath, a notorious womanizer, is incarcerated. He looks upon Lucy, the daughter of his custodian, as someone who can help him to escape.

MACHEATH: The very first opportunity, my dear—have but patience—you shall be my wife in whatever manner you please.

LUCY: Insinuating monster! And so you think I know nothing of the affair of Miss Polly Peachum—I could tear thy eyes out!

MACHEATH: Sure, Lucy, you can't be such a fool as to be jealous of Polly!

LUCY: Are you not married to her, you brute, you?

MACHEATH: Married! Very good! The wench gives it out only to vex thee, and to ruin me in thy good opinion. 'Tis true I go to the house; I chat with the girl, I kiss her, I say a thousand things to her, as all gentlemen do, that mean nothing, to divert myself; and now the silly jade hath set it about that I am married to her, to let me know what she would be at.

3. Usually, the rate, pitch, and loudness rise and fall together according to the emotional and intellectual content of the lines. For example, many actors will build to a climax in a speech by increasing the pace and rising in pitch and loudness; but some may find it effective to do the opposite. Others may go up in pitch and loudness but decrease the rate, or go down in pitch but use a loud tone. Practice various ways of interpreting the end of King Arthur's soliloquy that concludes Act I of *Camelot*. Arthur is debating what he should do about the growing love between his wife Guenevere and Lancelot.

ARTHUR: Proposition: I'm a king, not a man. And a civilized king. Could it possibly be civilized to destroy what I love? Could it possibly be civilized to love myself above all? What of their pain and their torment? Did they ask for this calamity? Can passion be selected? (*His voice rising*) Is there any doubt of their devotion . . . to me, or to our Table? (HE *raises high the sword, Excalibur, in his hand*) By God, Excalibur, I shall be a King! This is the time of King Arthur, and we reach for the stars! This is the time of King Arthur, and violence is not strength and compassion is not weakness. We are civilized! Resolved: We shall live through this together, Excalibur: They, you and I! And God have mercy on us all. (*The decision made*, HE *becomes almost relaxed, almost at peace*) They're waiting for us at the table. (HE *starts to walk off*) Let's not delay the celebration.

4. To see how stress contributes to the meaning of words, list some words that change meaning according to which syllable is stressed. (*Insult* and

subject are two: as nouns they are accented on the first syllable; as verbs they are stressed on the second.)

5. To consider how stress contributes to the meaning of a sentence, take the first sentence of the excerpt from *Camelot* in exercise 3 above: "Proposition: I'm a king, not a man." Actors will vary in their interpretations—and there is no one "correct" way to read any line—but many actors would stress the following underlined words and syllables: "*Propo*sition: *I'm* a *king*, *not* a *man*." Keep in mind that there are various degrees of stress, and not every syllable will receive the same amount; for example, *prop*, *I'm*, and *not* will probably not receive as much emphasis as *si*, *king*, and *man*, although they will get more than the other words and syllables in the sentence. You should notice that our speech consists of stressed and unstressed syllables in various combinations. While every syllable that you say onstage must be heard by the audience, every syllable should not receive equal stress. The meaning and emotional content of the lines will determine which syllables and words should be emphasized. Continue through the rest of the lines of Arthur's speech underlining the syllables and words that you believe should be stressed.

6. As an exercise in varying rate, pitch, loudness, and quality, speak the following patter song that is sung by the Lord Chancellor in Act II of Gilbert and Sullivan's *Iolanthe*. Pay particular attention to the sensory images in these lines. Get a picture in your mind's eye before speaking.

> When you're lying awake with a dismal headache, and repose is taboo'd by anxiety,
> I conceive you may use any language you choose to indulge in, without impropriety;
> For your brain is on fire—the bedclothes conspire of usual slumber to plunder you:
> First your counterpane goes, and uncovers your toes, and your sheet slips demurely from under you;
> Then the blanketing tickles—you feel like mixed pickles—so terribly sharp is the pricking,
> And you're hot and you're cross, and you tumble and toss till there's nothing twixt you and the ticking.
> Then the bedclothes all creep to the ground in a heap, and you pick 'em all up in a tangle;
> Next your pillow resigns and politely declines to remain at its usual angle!
> Well, you get some repose in the form of a doze, with hot eyeballs and head ever aching,
> But your slumbering teems with such horrible dreams that you'd very much better be waking;
> For you dream you are crossing the Channel, and tossing about in a steamer from Harwich—
> Which is something between a large bathing machine and a very small second-class carriage—
> And you're giving a treat (penny ice and cold meat) to a party of friends and relations—

They're a ravenous horde—and they all came on board at Sloane
Square and South Kensington Stations.

And bound on that journey you find your attorney (who started
that morning from Devon);

He's a bit undersized, and you don't feel surprised when he tells
you he's only eleven.

Well, you're driving like mad with this singular lad (by the by, the
ship's now a four-wheeler),

And you're playing round games, and he calls you bad names when
you tell him that "ties pay the dealer";

But this you can't stand, so you throw up your hand, and you find
you're as cold as an icicle,

In your shirt and your socks (the black silk with gold clocks),
crossing Salisbury Plain on a bicycle:

And he and the crew are on bicycles too—which they've somehow
or other invested in—

And he's telling the tars all the particu*lars* of a company he's
interested in—

It's a scheme of devices, to get at low prices all goods from cough
mixtures to cables

(Which tickled the sailors), by treating retailers as though they
were all vege*tables*—

You get a good spadesman to plant a small tradesman (first take
off his boots with a boot-tree),

And his legs will take root, and his fingers will shoot, and they'll
blossom and bud like a fruit-tree—

From the greengrocer tree you get grapes and green pea, cauli-
flower, pineapple, and cranberries,

While the pastrycook plant cherry brandy will grant, apple puffs,
and three-corners, and Banburys—

The shares are a penny, and ever so many are taken by Rothschild
and Baring,

And just as a few are allotted to you, you awake with a shudder
despairing—

You're a regular wreck, with a crick in your neck; and no wonder
you snore for your head's on the floor, and you've needles and
pins from your soles to your shins; and your flesh is a-creep, for
your left leg's asleep, and you've cramp in your toes, and a fly on
your nose, and some fluff in your lung, and a feverish tongue,
and a thirst that's intense, and a general sense that you haven't
been sleeping in clover;

But the darkness has passed, and it's daylight at last, and the night
has been long—ditto, ditto, my song—and thank goodness they're
both of them over!

7. The subtext of the following excerpt from Act I, Scene 3 of *Kiss Me,
Kate* will affect Fred's interpretation of his lines. The situation is that
the flowers and card that Fred sent to his girlfriend, Lois Lane, have
been mistakenly delivered to his ex-wife, Lilli. She is about to read the
card, and he is frantically trying to retrieve it.

FRED: (*Taking both her hands—aghast*) You're not going to read that now!...
Look, I'll tell you what I wrote: "To Lilli, the only woman I've ever loved,
the only artist I've ever worshipped!" Now give me the card and you can
read it after the show!

LILLI: Oh, Fred, did you really mean that? (*Rises, throws arms around* FRED)

FRED: (*Plenty nervous, tries to get card*) With all my heart!

PROJECTION

Projection is the process of aiming or directing your voice to the rear of the
theatre on the assumption that if those in the back can understand you,
those sitting in front should also be able to. Good projection is the ability
to communicate to everyone in your audience, but it is not the same as
speaking loudly, because in acting you often have to project a soft tone or
even a whisper.

To project your voice well, you need breath control, resonance, distinct articulation, and relaxed throat, jaw, and neck muscles. If you cannot
be heard when you speak to an audience, the cause may be:

- *Poor breath control.* Do you drop the ends of sentences? Sometimes
actors get into the habit of taking a breath and talking loudly at the
beginning of a sentence, but as they run out of air they become softer
and softer. You must control your exhalation (or find a place that you
can pause briefly to inhale) because all words must be audible. (See the
following section on "Phrasing and Pausing.")

- *A breathy or throaty quality.*

- *Poor articulation.*

- *Not opening your mouth wide enough.* If your jaw muscles are tense,
you may not be opening the jaw far enough to let the sound out.

- *Speaking at a pitch that is too low for you.* This practice can give your
voice a muffled, inaudible quality.

- *Not expending enough energy.* It takes effort, vitality, and stamina to
perform in musicals. If you do not have this energy, you must build up
your health and endurance before trying to perform.

- *Not estimating correctly the acoustics, the size of the theatre, or the
amount of noise in the audience.* If you always rehearse in a small
room, you may forget that you need to project more in a large theatre,
especially if it has poor acoustics or noisy spectators.

Exercises

To improve your projection, try the following exercises:

1. With eyes closed and feeling as relaxed as possible, let the head fall
to your chest. Slowly raise the head to an upright position, letting the
lower jaw drop so that the mouth is open at least one inch. Vary this
by humming and then singing "mah" as the head is raised.

2. Massage the muscles of the jaw and neck until they feel relaxed. With
your hands gently move the lower jaw from side to side.

3. Yawn, then say, "Here I am!" as though speaking to someone close to you, then to someone ten feet away, twenty feet away, thirty feet, and fifty feet. While there will be a tendency to go up in pitch as you get louder, try to hold the pitch down so that your voice does not become unpleasantly high. Stay relaxed.

4. Ask a friend to go to the rear of a theatre or someplace (a hallway or outside) where he or she can be about forty feet away, and then in a whisper read one of the exercises in this book. If the person cannot understand you, sharpen your articulation.

5. In Act II, Scene 6 of *Camelot*, Lancelot enters Guenevere's bedroom quietly. They speak the following lines softly because they do not want to be overheard; yet every word must be projected to all of the audience. Station someone at the rear of a theatre to tell you if you can be understood in this scene.

LANCELOT: (*Hushed; tremulously, fearfully*) Jenny . . .? (GUENEVERE *rises quickly and looks at him in astonishment.* HE *goes to her*) Jenny, I was in the yard . . . I couldn't sleep . . . I saw the light in your window . . . I knew you were alone . . . I tried to stay away . . . I tried, but I . . . Jenny, I . . . (HE *takes her in his arms and* THEY *embrace passionately. Suddenly* SHE *withdraws in fear*)

GUENEVERE: Did anyone see you?

LANCELOT: No one. The castle is dark. I was careful. Jenny, don't be afraid.

GUENEVERE: But I am afraid.

LANCELOT: I swear we're alone. No one saw me enter. Jenny, there's nothing to fear.

6. Speak the following chorus number from Act I of *Iolanthe* by Gilbert and Sullivan with good projection, breath control, resonance, articulation, and variation. It is sung in this comic opera by a chorus of peers.

> Loudly let the trumpet bray!
>   Tantantara!
> Proudly bang the sounding brasses!
>   Tzing! Boom!
> As upon its lordly way
>   This unique procession passes,
>   Tantantara! Tzing! Boom!
> Bow, bow, ye lower middle classes!
> Bow, bow, ye tradesmen, bow, ye masses!
> Blow the trumpets, bang the brasses!
>   Tantantara! Tzing! Boom!
> We are peers of highest station,
> Paragons of legislation,
> Pillars of the British nation!
>   Tantantara! Tzing! Boom!

PHRASING AND PAUSING

Phrasing is grouping words into thought-units or phrases. Each phrase has one idea, which may consist of just one or two words or as many as you can say on one breath. When you pause, though, you have ended a phrase.

Pausing may not only be used to indicate the end of a thought it may also be done when a character is thinking, having difficulty expressing ideas, reacting to what has been said, performing an action, or waiting until the right moment to spring a punch line.

Both actors and singers must many times consciously figure out where to pause in order to get across the meaning and emotions of the lines or lyrics. Punctuation marks may be of help in this. You will often pause at periods, question marks, exclamation points, semicolons, colons, dashes, and sometimes at commas. But not always. In some cases, it may sound more realistic to pass a mark of punctuation and then, perhaps, pause where there is no mark.

While pausing, you can use that time to inhale because you should never break into the middle of a thought just because you need air. You must work on your breath control so that, if you need to, you can say or sing a long phrase on one breath. Usually, however, if you find that you are running out of air before the end of a phrase, you can locate a logical place to take a quick breath so that you will have an adequate air supply to make all words audible.

Pauses come in all lengths from very brief to lengthy and dramatic. Some playwrights, notably Harold Pinter, are famous for indicating many pauses in their scripts; other authors, however, leave it to the actors to decide where to pause. If you listen to yourself and others talking in real life, you will find we often pause while we formulate our ideas or search for the words to express them. Seldom, while thinking, do we say a long sentence without pausing somewhere. In acting, if you concentrate on listening to the other performers and thinking the thoughts of your character, this should result in a natural interpretation of the lines that will give an audience the appearance that you are saying these words for the first time.

Exercise

Look at the scene from *Funny Girl* in chapter ten and note the pauses and hesitations indicated in that excerpt.

6

ACTING
TECHNIQUES

FANNY BRICE: It's coming too easy—that's what's got me scared! Where's all the suffering you're supposed to do before you click? The hard knocks—the setbacks that you're supposed to learn from?

EDDIE: What about all those years on the road, when you were just a kid. Didn't you have enough hard knocks then?

FANNY: Aaaah—it got me out of school! And I still say this is too quick. I haven't suffered enough yet!

—from Funny Girl

No one can teach you how to act—you must teach yourself through your experiences onstage, through watching the great performers in the theatre, on television, and in films, through your reading, and through exercises. Certainly the guidance of good directors and instructors can be of great help to you, but actually, your success depends on your willingness to work, your dedication, and your devotion to acting. Studying and exercising your acting skills should never stop—these should continue as long as you are performing.

What does it take to be a good actor? Intelligence, a flexible body and voice, energy, stamina, sensitivity, imagination, creativity, and performing skills that have been developed by your training and your experiences in the theatre—these are some of the vital ingredients.

This chapter is concerned with providing a few of the essential elements of your acting training. It will take up stage techniques, comedy techniques, concentration, and improvisations.

STAGE TECHNIQUES

In this section are some of the fundamentals of acting: the names of different types of stages, stage areas, and body positions, how to move onstage, and how to handle special movement problems.

Types of Stages and Stage Areas

When directors block a show, they tell actors where to move on the stage, and in doing so they use terms that you should know. On a *proscenium stage*, which has an architectural arch that separates the audience from the acting area, *upstage* is the area closest to the back wall while *downstage* is the area nearest to the audience. (See figure 6-1.) If you stand in the middle of a medium-sized proscenium stage, facing the audience, you are in *center stage* (C). *Up center* (UC) is in back of you, and *down center* (DC) is in front of you. Left stage is to the actor's left, and right stage is to the actor's right; therefore, to your left, you have *up left* (UL), *left* (L), and *down left* (DL). To your right, there is *up right* (UR), *right* (R), and *down right* (DR). The nine areas are situated as follows:

(BACK WALL OF STAGE)

Up Right (UR)	Up Center (UC)	Up Left (UL)
Right (R)	Center (C)	Left (L)
Down Right (DR)	Down Center (DC)	Down Left (DL)

(AUDIENCE)

If you are working on a large proscenium stage, your director may refer to fifteen areas, as follows:

(BACK WALL OF STAGE)

Up Right (UR)	Up Right Center (URC)	Up Center (UC)	Up Left Center (ULC)	Up Left (UL)
Right (R)	Right Center (RC)	Center (C)	Left Center (LC)	Left (L)
Down Right (DR)	Down Right Center (DRC)	Down Center (DC)	Down Left Center (DLC)	Down Left (DL)

(AUDIENCE)

When you are recording your director's instructions in your script, you can use the abbreviations listed above. If you wish to write "cross to down left" in your script, it is faster to write "X DL." Other symbols you may want to use are a downward arrow ↓ for "sit" and an upward arrow ↑ for "rise."

While the proscenium stage is the most common type in the United States, there are other kinds of stages on which you may perform. The *arena* stage (also known as *theatre-in-the-round*, *circus staging*, *circle staging*, or *central staging*) has the audience on all sides of the playing area, which may be a rectangle, a circle, or an oval. (See figure 6-2.) No matter where you stand onstage, you will always have your back to some members of the audience; consequently, directors may use a good deal of movement in arena staging. In blocking, they may number the aisles and direct actors in terms of the location of furniture, properties, or other

Figure 6-1.   Example of a proscenium stage.
(Courtesy of Museum of the City of New York.)

actors; for example, "enter from aisle three and cross to Jim at the desk." Others may liken the stage to a clock and divide it into twelve areas, with the middle of the stage being a thirteenth. A director may tell actors to "cross from three to six."

The *thrust* (also called an *apron, open,* or *platform stage*) has a stage that juts into the audience so that spectators sit on three sides of the acting area. (See figure 6-3.) In back of the stage may be a wall or a stagehouse through which people, scenery, and props may enter and exit.

Environmental theatre has a free-form space that is shared by actors and audience who intermingle and interact. While this type of staging has not been used much for musicals, it was used for a 1974 Broadway revival of the musical *Candide,* as mentioned in chapter one. (See figure 1-6.)

Since musicals are performed today more frequently on a proscenium stage than any other kind, everything said about staging in the rest of this book will pertain to this type of stage.

Figure 6-2. Example of an arena stage.
(Courtesy of the Arena Stage in Washington, D.C. Photo: George de Vincent.)

Figure 6-3. Example of a thrust stage.
(Courtesy of the Stratford Festival, Ontario, Canada. Photo: David Cooper.)

Body Positions

If a director says to you, "Cross to down left and give me a one-quarter right," he is directing you to move to a specific area of a proscenium stage (described above) and take a particular body position. These positions are as follows:

FULL FRONT.   The actor is facing the audience. Normally when singing a solo onstage, this is your position. (See figure 6-4.)

ONE-QUARTER LEFT.   The actor turns to his left about half-way between full front and profile. This is often the position you assume when you are sharing a scene with another person, who will probably be in the opposite one-quarter position. Most duets are sung in one-quarter or full front. (See figure 6-5.)

PROFILE LEFT.   The actor faces left with his profile (i.e., the right side of his body) to the audience. Often a director will have two people in profile left and profile right positions when they are having an argument. (See figure 6-6.)

THREE-QUARTER LEFT.   The actor turns to a position half-way between the left profile and full back. (See figure 6-7.)

FULL BACK.   The actor has his back to the audience. (See figure 6-8.)

THREE-QUARTER RIGHT.   The actor is in a position half-way between full back and the right profile positions. (See figure 6-7.)

PROFILE RIGHT.   The actor faces right with his profile to the audience. (See figure 6-6.)

ONE-QUARTER RIGHT.   The actor is in a position half-way between profile right and full front. (See figure 6-5.)

Movements and Stage Pictures

While movements and stage pictures are normally the director's responsibility, all actors should have a basic knowledge about the following:

• If you are standing in a full front position and you are told to cross right, you should start walking to your right with your right foot; if told to cross left, begin with the left foot to walk to your left.

• If you are standing in a one-quarter position, your upstage foot will probably be slightly in front of the downstage foot. When you start to walk from this position, begin with the upstage foot.

• All movements onstage must be motivated. If you do not understand why your director has asked you to move to a certain place, ask. The director should be able to explain it to you. If by some chance you do not get a satisfactory answer, you must create a reason for yourself. Never move onstage without a purpose.

• If two actors are sharing a scene and both are equally important, you will probably be in opposite one-quarter or profile positions. However, if the director chooses to make one person more prominent because of a

Figure 6-4.   Full front body positions.
(Photo: Kimberly Harbour.)

Figure 6-5. One-quarter body positions.

(Photo: Kimberly Harbour.)

Figure 6-6.   Profile body positions.
(Photo: Kimberly Harbour.)

Figure 6-7. Three-quarter body positions.
(Photo: Kimberly Harbour.)

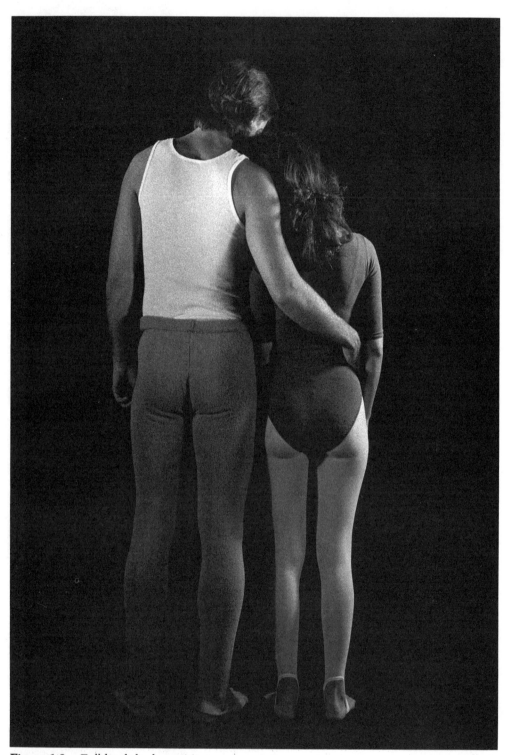

Figure 6-8. Full back body positions.
(Photo: Kimberly Harbour.)

lengthy speech or important business, the director may tell this actor to *take the stage* by assuming a one-quarter or full front position and direct the other actor to *give the stage* by taking a three-quarter or full back. Note that full front and one-quarter positions are usually much more attention-getting than three-quarter or full back, although the latter can be effective in certain situations.

- *Upstaging* is an unkind accusation in the theatre. This occurs when an actor, who wants more attention from the audience, deliberately moves upstage of another to a full front or one-quarter position and thereby forces the other actor to turn to a three-quarter position to talk with this person. No director should permit upstaging to occur.

- If two standing actors are sharing a scene and the director tells one to cross the other, the person moving will normally pass in front of (that is, downstage of) the stationary actor to the place specified by the director. The nonmoving actor may then have to *dress stage* or *counter* (that is, move slightly or change position in order to obtain again a balanced stage picture).

- A speaking character will normally cross in front of other characters, rather than behind them, in order to be heard and seen easily during the cross.

- Usually, you will cross on your lines and be still when others are speaking. However, if a line must be emphasized, you may want to move before or after delivering it, because moving on the line may lessen the impact.

- When moving, do not stop in front of another character so that you cover this person (unless there is some reason in the script for this).

- When blocking three or more actors, the director will often use triangular arrangements with the dominant character at the apex.

- Unless there is some good reason in the script or you are directed to do the following, avoid: Side-stepping or backing up onstage. Standing in straight lines or semicircles with other actors. Looking down too much while speaking. (Audiences like to watch faces, especially your eyes, so don't act to the floor—act to your fellow performers.)

Special Problems

Under this heading we will take up some violent actions, such as falling, fainting, fighting, slapping, firing a gun, stabbing, strangling, and hair pulling. All acts of violence must be carefully blocked and rehearsed so that no one gets hurt, and no actor should be permitted to deviate from the plans. Some nonviolent acts also need careful rehearsal, such as kissing, kneeling, gesturing, handling props, eating, drinking, curtsying, bowing, and delivering asides and soliloquies, so they too will be discussed in this section.

FALLING AND FAINTING. The easiest and safest way to fall onstage is to fall on your left or right side. First, get a mat to practice on; then remove any eyeglasses and be sure that your pockets do not contain something that will break or injure you. Remember to stay as relaxed as possible and to take your time in falling—a fall usually does not have to be fast. To fall to the left, put your weight on your right foot, bend your knees and gently fall to the side of your left leg, hip, torso, and shoulder. Finally, allow your head to touch the mat. Don't fall on the kneecap, don't put your hands out to break the fall as you might sprain a wrist (keep them close to your body), don't bump your head, and don't let your feet bounce. Most of the time you will want to land with your head downstage; if you end up with your feet downstage, your position may look funny to the audience. Of course, in playing a comedy scene, you can fall awkwardly with feet bouncing and arms away from the body.

You must consider *why* you are falling and act accordingly. If you are supposed to be struck or stabbed, you may want to grasp the wound, stagger a step or two, and slowly fall. If furniture is nearby, you can use it to break your descent. If you are supposed to faint, like, for example, the females who pass out on seeing Conrad perform in *Bye Bye Birdie,* you should relax the entire body and collapse to the floor or onto furniture. Being shot is the hardest fall to do realistically. With this one, you may react quickly as though you have received a tremendous blow of great force that knocks you back and down.

FIGHTING.   All fight scenes must be choreographed carefully and practiced frequently. In rehearsal, the combatants must learn to trust the others and to establish eye contact before any punch is thrown to assure each other that they are aware of what is about to happen. Also, rings and eyeglasses should be removed by combatants before the fight begins.

In *Kiss Me, Kate,* the script calls for Katharine to hit Petruchio in the stomach. A blow to the midsection may be concealed from the audience if it is done from upstage with the victim, who has his back to the audience, downstage of the hitter. She can start with a clenched fist, but immediately before contact she may pull her punch or open her hand so that her palm will make a sound when striking Petruchio, who reacts by grunting and bending over.

A blow to the head may be done with a downstage hitter, who has his back to the audience, covering the victim, who is upstage. The attacker's blow should miss his opponent's chin by about an inch. Bringing the hands in to protect himself, the victim can supply the sound by quickly clapping his hands together while groaning and jerking the head back and away.

A kick to the abdomen or groin can be done from upstage with the downstage victim concealing the movement with his body. The receiver puts his hands in front of him near his body. The kicker aims for the hands, and the recipient reacts as though in great pain.

Armed combat varies according to the historical period and the type of weapon used. Generally, if you must fight with a weapon onstage, your director will provide an expert to choreograph the fight. If not, you will have to research the subject yourself by consulting books on stage combat in your library (there are several listed under Suggested Reading).

SLAPPING.   When one character must slap another, as Katharine slaps Petruchio in *Kiss Me, Kate,* the slapper should remove rings, relax the striking hand, aim for the fleshy part of the cheek (avoiding the ear, eye, and nose), and hit with relaxed fingers. At the same time the person slapped turns his or her head away from the blow. Before striking another person, the slapper should practice hitting his or her own face until the right amount of force is determined.

FIRING A GUN.   Never shoot a prop gun directly at anyone onstage or at the audience; a gun loaded with a blank cartridge can discharge a wad that may injure or even kill. No one should have access to a gun except the actor firing it and the prop person responsible for it. Guns should never be left lying on a prop table for anyone to pick up and play with. When they are not in use, they should be locked up because they can and have killed people.

If the script demands that you fire a gun at someone, as Chino in *West Side Story* shoots Tony, aim upstage of the victim, who should be at least eight feet away. Be sure, also, that technicians and performers backstage have been warned to stay out of the line of firing. In this scene from *West Side Story* and in other musicals, such as *Annie Get Your Gun*, the performers may pretend to shoot onstage while a recording of gunshots is played or a prop gun is fired offstage by the property master or stage manager.

STABBING.   Performers have also been killed by using real knives on-stage. Always use a prop knife that is made of rubber or that is collapsible. In such musicals as *West Side Story*, *Oklahoma!*, and *Carousel*, the use of knives must be carefully blocked and controlled.

The easiest way to conceal a stabbing is to have the victim downstage of the stabber so that the receiver's body covers the movement. The attacker can raise his hand with the knife (to show it to the audience) and bring it down with force towards his opponent's chest. Just before reaching it, the assailant turns the knife under so that it is the back of his hand that hits the victim, not the knife.

STRANGLING.   The strangler places his hands on his opponent's shoulders near the neck. The victim puts his hands over the strangler's and does all of the moving, groaning, and gasping. The assailant appears to be applying pressure, but the victim is controlling the movement.

HAIR PULLING.   The puller grabs the victim's hair, but the latter holds the assailant's wrist. The victim may writhe and yell but is actually controlling the action.

KISSING.   For a standing kiss, two actors should move close together as though they were going to dance. If this is a serious, romantic scene, it is important that their feet be close together because, if their feet are apart and the actors lean in toward each other, their positions will look funny. The man's downstage arm can be around her waist with his upstage arm around her back. Her downstage arm can be on his arm or shoulder with her upstage arm around his neck. The man's head may be downstage of the woman's head as they tilt their heads to kiss. (Note the kisses in the scenes from *The Mikado*, *Kiss Me, Kate*, and *South Pacific* in chapter ten.)

If kissing while sitting on a sofa, the woman may put her head on his upstage shoulder as he bends to kiss her. Sometimes a hand to the face or hair of the other is a nice touch that can be done by either the man or woman.

In kissing a lady's hand, the man should raise her hand gently to his mouth, as he bends forward, and briefly touch the back of her hand with his lips.

KNEELING.   When kneeling onstage to a person, an actor will usually put the downstage knee on the floor, because this makes it easier for the kneeling character to cheat front so that his face may be seen and his voice heard. When kneeling to pray, usually both knees are on the floor.

GESTURING AND HANDLING PROPS.   Normally you should use the upstage hand in gesturing and handling props so as to avoid covering yourself. For instance, in using a telephone onstage, you should hold it in your upstage hand with the mouthpiece below your mouth. The important point is that you must be heard and seen.

EATING AND DRINKING.   There are two things to remember about eating and drinking onstage: do them as little as possible and time them so that you will not have to speak with your mouth full. If drinks are served in opaque containers, the audience will never know if you have drunk the liquid or not. You must, of course, look as though you are eating and drinking, while you are actually consuming small bites and sips.

If the script calls for an alcoholic beverage, the prop crew should provide water, tea, gingerale, or fruit juice, changed, if necessary, by food color to look like the intoxicating drink. As for food, don't be surprised if the prop crew substitutes easy-to-eat-and-prepare food for items that are difficult to fix or swallow.

CURTSYING.   A woman's curtsy has remained about the same for hundreds of years. The most common curtsy involves placing the ball of one foot in back of the other, keeping the weight on both feet. She should bend her knees while nodding her head or bending forward from the waist. (See figure 6-9.) Another type of curtsy involves stepping back with one foot, putting all of her weight on it as she bends the rear knee. She should point the toe of the front foot as she bends forward. The depth of the curtsy depends on whom she is greeting, with royalty receiving the deepest. Her hands may rest on her dress, may be crossed over her breast, or may be held out and back with palms turned to the front.

Maids of former years did "bob" curtsies as they entered or left rooms. This involves a slight bending of the knees as she nods her head.

BOWING.   Men's bows have changed a great deal through the years, but a stage bow that is good for all periods from the Middle Ages to the early nineteenth century involves the man stepping back with the toes slightly turned out on the rear foot. He should transfer his weight to the back leg as he bends his rear knee. His front leg is straight. He may nod his head or bend forward as he removes his hat and sweeps it to the rear or places

Figure 6-9. A curtsy.
(Photo: Kimberly Harbour.)

it over his heart. If he is not wearing a hat, he may put one hand over his heart, or his hand (with the palm up) may be extended forward and then down to the floor. (See figure 6-10.)

By the middle of the nineteenth century, a man usually put his heels together with his toes slightly turned out and nodded or bowed from the waist with his hands at his sides. This same bow serves as a male servant's bow for all periods from the Middle Ages to the present. It may also be used by both men and women for a bow at curtain call.

Figure 6-10.   A bow.
(Photo: Kimberly Harbour.)

ASIDES.   Some musicals, especially older ones, may contain asides—short remarks made by a character to the audience that other people onstage are not supposed to hear. To deliver an aside, the actor may simply turn toward the spectators from anywhere onstage or may move downstage to get closer to the audience. Other actors may turn away, freeze, or do some action so that they appear not to hear the aside. Then, after the aside is finished, all return to their previous positions. (Look at the aside used by Nanki-Poo in the excerpt from *The Mikado* in chapter ten.)

SOLILOQUIES.   A character who reveals his or her innermost thoughts and feelings while alone onstage is delivering a soliloquy. In musicals, a soliloquy may be spoken, or it may be sung. It may be directed to the audience, in which case the performer may move closer to the spectators, or it may be so reflective that it should appear as though the character is thinking out loud. The latter type may be delivered from any part of the stage while the performer looks toward or away from the audience. Each soliloquy should be carefully analyzed for meaning in order to determine the best way to handle it.

Exercises

1. To see if you understand the nine stage areas and the eight body positions, move as follows:
    a. Start in a one-quarter left at DL and cross to a one-quarter right at DR.
    b. From there, move to a three-quarter right at UR.
    c. Next move to full front in DC.
    d. From there, move to a three-quarter left at UL.
    e. Next move to full back in UC.
    f. Move now to profile right at R.
    g. Next move to profile left at L.
    h. End in full front at C.

2. Two actors should do the following movements:
    a. Stand in one-quarter positions in C as though you are sharing a scene. Actor A at the left should cross to R, and the other actor, B, should then dress stage (or counter).
    b. Actor A, now at R, should give the stage to Actor B who is in C, and B should take the stage.
    c. Actor A should now cross in front of Actor B to DL and end in a profile left.
    d. Actor B should cross and kneel to the right of A, who turns to B.

3. Using a floor mat for protection, practice the following as described in this chapter:
    a. Fainting.
    b. Falling because you have been shot.
    c. Falling because you tripped.

4. With another person, practice the following:
    a. A blow to the midsection of the body.
    b. A blow to the chin.
    c. A kick to the abdomen.
    d. Slapping.
    e. Stabbing.
    f. Strangling.
    g. Hair pulling.
    h. Standing kiss.
    i. Seated kiss.
    j. Kneeling and kissing a lady's hand.
    k. Curtsies and bows.

5. Practice the following asides from Gilbert and Sullivan's *The Pirates of Penzance*. In Act I, young Frederic is talking with Ruth, a middle-aged woman, when a chorus of girls is heard in the distance.

FREDERIC: Surely I hear voices! Who has ventured to approach our all but inaccessible lair? . . .

RUTH: (*Aside*) Confusion! it is the voice of young girls! If he should see them I am lost.

FREDERICK: (*Looking off*) By all that's marvellous, a bevy of beautiful maidens!

RUTH: (*Aside*) Lost! lost! lost!

6. In Act I of Gilbert and Sullivan's *The Mikado*, Ko-Ko, the Lord High Executioner of Titipu, is left alone onstage and delivers the following soliloquy:

KO-KO: This is simply appalling! I, who allowed myself to be respited at the last moment, simply in order to benefit my native town, am now required to die within a month, and that by a man whom I have loaded with honours! Is this public gratitude?

COMEDY TECHNIQUES

Because many musicals are comedies, it is necessary for the musical performer to understand some of the basic techniques for getting laughs. Even in musicals that cannot be called comedies because of their serious themes, such as *Cabaret* or *Camelot*, there may be some humorous characters and funny scenes, so studying comic techniques is a must for all musical performers. It is not an easy matter, though. Most actors agree that playing comedy is harder than acting serious plays, so let's look at some of the problems.

Analyzing a Comedy

First, you should know what a comedy is: an entertaining play that has a happy ending. Comedy is often based on surprise (the spectators expect one thing to happen and laugh when something else occurs), exaggeration, incongruity, or deviations from normality that provoke laughter. Both *Mame* and *Hello, Dolly!*, for instance, derive much of their humor from the unusual and amusing characters who are the protagonists, Mame and Dolly.

Often, we can define a comedy more specifically as a *satire* (or comedy of manners), *farce* (or situation comedy), or *romantic comedy*. When the show attacks a subject through ridicule, it can be termed a satire. *Guys and Dolls* is an example that presents a satirical portrayal of a group of New York gamblers. A musical like *A Funny Thing Happened on the Way to the Forum*, which places emphasis on wild, highly improbable physical activity, may be labelled a farce. If the comedy is concerned primarily with the humorous events that can happen when one or two couples are in love, as in *Annie Get Your Gun*, it is generally called a romantic comedy.

You must figure out what type of comedy you are playing and remember that there are wide differences among them. Slapstick farce needs a physical approach; satires may need a more intellectual one; and comedies that emphasize romance may need a more emotional approach. Ask yourself where the humor, the fun, the wit lie in this musical and who or what will get the laughs. Remember that in order for spectators to laugh, they must understand the words, the situation, and the objectives of the characters. If they do not comprehend these, they will not think the show is funny.

Next, examine your character's function in the comedy. Are you the hero or heroine, villain or villainess, top comedian or comedienne, best friend of one of the above, a funny servant, an eccentric person, or who are you? Are you supposed to get laughs? If so, will the laughs come from your overall characterization, from a funny voice, from witty lines, from the machinations of the plot, from humorous movements or business, or from bizarre props, costuming, makeup, or hairstyles? The answer may be any or all of the above.

In analyzing a comic character, you may find that he or she is pre-occupied intensely with one idea. For example, Dolly wants to marry Horace Vandergelder and that influences her actions throughout *Hello, Dolly!*. J. Pierrepont Finch in *How to Succeed in Business Without Really Trying* wants to be a top executive. Both characters are obsessed with their goals, and both are funny characters.

Perhaps you are not the lead but have an interesting smaller role, such as *Funny Girl*'s Mrs. Brice or Mrs. Strakosh, who are humorous because of their motherly advice, their butting into Fanny's business, their unusual vocal qualities, and their accents. Lina Lamont, the silent movie actress in *Singing' in the Rain*, gets laughs because of a high-pitched, strident, nasal voice; and Hedy La Rue, the office siren in *How to Succeed in Business*, can be played amusingly with a sexy, high-pitched, rather breathy voice. Don't overlook the possibility of creating a funny character by changing the pitch, rate, loudness, quality, or dialect or accent of your voice.

Are the laughs in your musical coming from the lines? Are there jokes? Mispronunciations? Extreme exaggerations? Incongruities? Surprises? Funny words, or words used in strange ways? Lines with double meanings? Puns? Malapropisms? In *Kiss Me, Kate*, one gangster says, "The minute a man signs an I.O.U. everything goes dark." The second gangster adds, "The doctors call it magnesia." (In substituting *magnesia* for *amnesia*, the gangster has used a malapropism, which is the use of an incorrect word for one that is similar in sound.)

You must analyze the dialogue for the jokes and learn to recognize a "straight line" or "feed line" that leads to a "punch line" or "laugh line." In the previous excerpt from *Kiss Me, Kate*, the first gangster has the straight line and the second has the laugh line. Another example from *Kiss Me, Kate* comes after an elder statesman, Harrison Howell, explains that he has reached a certain distinction in Washington by having his own park bench. Lois has the straight line when she asks, "One thing I've always wanted to know—what do you do about the pigeons?" Harrison's punch line is "Duck, my dear. Just duck."

Actors must know how to build to a laugh and to get it by "topping" the straight line or by "undercutting." The excerpt just given from *Kiss Me, Kate* is an example of topping because Harrison will undoubtedly say his line louder and at a higher pitch than the straight line. An instance of undercutting may be found in a speech by King Pellinore in *Camelot* when he is getting ready to depart from a garden party with his dog Horrid. He builds to this laugh with "Come along, Horrid. What a glorious day! There's even a hint of summer in the air. (*Looks at the dog*) Or is that you?" If Pellinore builds during the first three sentences to a loud tone and a higher pitch and if, after looking at the dog, he speaks quietly at a lower pitch, he should get a laugh—especially if he sniffs and uses a facial expression that indicates he has just smelled a bad odor.

Not all laugh lines should be punched out. Some can be almost thrown away and still get a laugh. Take this exchange between Meg and Jeff in *Brigadoon:* Meg is pursuing Jeff, who is resisting her advances. Sitting down on a hard cot, Jeff says, "What's under here—a rock garden?" Meg replies, "My father used to sleep on it." And Jeff (thinking that her father's first mistake was conceiving Meg) has a throw-away laugh line: "That was his second mistake." While the line itself may be taken at a lower level of loudness and pitch than the feed line, Jeff will still want to point up the word *second* because key words in laugh lines must be played up or "pointed" in order to get a reaction.

Does the humor come from the plot? Many of the laughs in *Promises, Promises,* for example, come from Chuck's lending the keys of his apartment to married executives who need a place to entertain girlfriends. This, of course, leads to all sorts of amusing situations.

Does the humor depend on comic movements, business, facial expressions, or props? Mazeppa and Electra appear in just one scene in *Gypsy* and Tessie Tura is in only two, yet these three strippers are well remembered. The laughs come from the gimmicks they employ in stripteasing, as they explain in a memorable song, "You Gotta Get a Gimmick": Mazeppa strips while blowing a bugle; Electra wears electric bulbs on her body that light as she bumps and grinds; and Tessie combines stripping with ballet dancing. (See figure 6-11.)

Do the laughs come from unusual costuming, makeup, or hairstyles? In *Kiss Me, Kate,* the two gangsters, who are trying to collect a debt from the star of a Shakespearean play, put on such ill-fitting Elizabethan costumes with droopy tights that the audience should laugh at their appearance.

Acting Comedy

No matter how stupid, foolish, or villainous your role is, you should like the character, understand the person, and be sympathetic to his or her foibles. Play up the eccentricities and exaggerations and have a good time while you are doing this, but don't be too obvious about trying to be funny—the audience may not find this amusing. After all, the character usually is not trying to be comic or is even aware that he or she is funny, so just play the role and let the peculiarities of the character, lines, situations, props, or costumes get the laughs.

Playing comedy involves being aware of your audience, listening to them, waiting for them to respond, and letting them laugh. A good audience reaction depends on the actors' timing, setting up a joke, building, springing the punch line at the right time, and holding for the laugh.

Figure 6-11.   Chotzi Foley, Maria Karnilova, and Faith Dane as the three strippers in *Gypsy*.
(Courtesy of the Billy Rose Theatre Collection, the New York Public Library at Lincoln Center, Astor, Lenox, and Tilden Foundations.)

How do you deliver a funny line? It varies according to the situation. But often the comedic effect can be improved by turning the laugh line out to the audience and playing it to the balcony. Key words must be pointed up, and the words must be spoken clearly and distinctly. If the listeners fail to hear or understand either the feed line or the laugh line, they will not laugh. Sometimes a slight pause before the punch line will help. And usually you will not cross on a punch line, as the movement may distract the audience from listening to the words.

After the punch line, you wait for them to respond. If a big laugh results, you freeze, unless your movement is causing them to continue to laugh. After the laugh passes its peak and you think you can be heard, speak your next line. If, however, the laugh never comes, quickly go on to your next line.

Don't laugh at your own joke, as the audience may not think it is funny if you do. And do not interfere with another actor's laugh by mugging, moving on the punch line, or distracting the audience's attention in any other way.

Playing farce requires a knowledge of physical comedy, sometimes called "low comedy." In this style we get into the old comedic devices that have been used to make audiences laugh since the beginning of the theatre. Here is a list of some that come up frequently in farce.

- The take or slow take: A slow, comic realization of what has been done or said, usually played with the comedian looking out at the audience.

- The double take: Another delayed reaction to a line or situation. Usually the comedian, who is looking at a person or situation, fails to find anything unusual and looks away; then he realizes what he has seen or heard, and quickly looks back.

- The burn or slow burn: Something bad happens to the comedian, but at first he doesn't react. Then, slowly, anger and fury build within him until he violently lets out his pent-up feelings.

- The sight gag: This is visual humor as the laughs come from a funny prop, costume, makeup, hairstyle, or movement.

- "Shtick": A repeated bit of comic business, routine, or gimmick used by a star performer.

- The running gag: Comic business that is repeated throughout a show.

- Deadpanning: Using an impassive manner with no facial expressions.

- Mugging: Using exaggerated facial expressions.

- Sudden changes in facial expression: Going quickly from happy to sad or vice versa.

- Hitting with boards, slapsticks, umbrellas, or canes.

- Chases.

- Tripping, slipping, and falling.

- Stepping on a nail or other sharp object.

- Getting fingers stuck on chewing gum, in a door, and elsewhere.

- Disguising as another character (often of the opposite sex).

- Chasing a hat by kicking it forward each time the comic bends over to pick it up.

- Throwing and receiving a pie or cake in the face.

- A man's trousers or a woman's skirt falling unexpectedly to the floor.

- A comic walking fast on his or her knees.

- Two, three, or more characters, lined up closely behind each other, walking in unison across the stage.

- Two people tugging on a rope until one lets go and the other falls.

- While a character is trying to speak or sing to the audience, the comedian stands in back making fun by mugging or imitating the person, who is not aware that the comic is there.

• After taking a drink, the comic hears something shocking and squirts water out of his mouth.

In playing all types of comedy, keep your energy level up. Overall, a comedy will probably be faster and louder than a serious play, although there will be many variations within any show. As with all other types of acting, you must keep up the illusion that this is the first time you have been in this situation. You must listen to the other actors, think, and respond as though you have just had the thought that prompts you to say these words.

Exercises

Read the book of a famous musical comedy and analyze it:

1. What type of comedy is it? Why do you give it this classification?
2. Choose a character that you might play, and answer these questions about this person:
   a. What is the character's function in the comedy?
   b. Is he or she obsessed with an idea?
3. Look for the following in your script, and give examples of those you can find:
   a. Unusual voices, dialects, or accents that are supposed to get laughs.
   b. Jokes, mispronunciations, extreme exaggerations, incongruities, surprises, funny words or words used in strange ways, lines with double meanings, puns, malapropisms.
   c. A straight line that leads to a punch line.
   d. Should the punch line in c. top or undercut the straight line?
4. Is the plot of the musical based on a funny situation?
5. Are comic movements, business, props, costuming, makeup, and hairstyles called for?
6. Take a joke from your script and practice delivering it for maximum effect. Are you pointing the key words? Are you saying the words distinctly?
7. Practice a take, double take, and slow burn. If there are no lines in your script that you can use for this, look at the following excerpt from *Kiss Me, Kate*. The situation is that Fred, a stage director, is instructing Lois, a former nightclub singer, in how to act on the stage:

FRED: I realize, Lois, that in nightclub work you don't have to cheat— (*Theatrical expression to cover actor's appearing to play scene with another actor but actually aiming his lines out to the audience*)

LOIS: (*Interrupting*) Oh, don't you though?

FRED: You don't have to cheat front, Miss Lane, but on stage when you're playing scenes with other people, you do. This is your first show, and I know it's hard for you.

LOIS: (*Almost baby-wise*) Do you mean thus—(*Of course* SHE *turns wrong*) or thus?

FRED: We'll thus it later.

Before Fred says his last line, he could do a take, a double take, or a slow burn. Try each one, or perhaps you can figure out a better way to react.

8. Is there a sight gag indicated in your script?

9. Is there a running gag or any of the other comedic devices listed in this section?

CONCENTRATION

Concentration is the process of gathering together your resources, your powers, and your efforts in order to direct your energies to your character's objective. When you are onstage playing a role, you must give your entire concentration to that objective despite the many distractions that may surround you. There may be performers and technicians standing in the wings; there may be actors onstage who are not concentrating; there may be people coughing in the audience—many things can keep you from absorbing yourself in playing your part. But you must train yourself to ignore these distractions and keep your mind focused on your performing. Otherwise you may find yourself forgetting lines, blocking, a costume change, a prop, or other things that will ruin your performance.

The great Russian director and teacher of acting, Constantin Stanislavski (1863–1938), wrote about the necessity for concentration in his fine books on acting (which are listed under Suggested Reading). By concentration he did not mean that you should forget that you are performing for an audience; however, you should forget everything that interferes with your creativity onstage so that you can immerse yourself in acting the part. (See the next chapter for more about the Stanislavski System.)

Exercises

To improve your ability to concentrate, work on the following:

1. Sit still and concentrate on the sounds around you. Block everything else out of your mind except the sounds and describe them.

2. Next, concentrate on odors. What can you smell at the moment?

3. Now, concentrate on your sense of touch. How do your clothes and shoes feel? What else is touching you? The floor? Your chair? The air? Describe these.

4. With your hands touch all of your outer garments from the soles of your shoes on up. Describe the differences in texture.

5. Can you taste anything at the present? Describe it.

6. What can you see? Look around you for a minute, then test your powers of observation by closing your eyes and trying to describe accurately everything you saw.

7. Take a small object from your purse, briefcase, or wallet: a coin, a pencil, a credit card, a picture, lipstick, comb, or something similar.

Give this article your full concentration for one minute, then put it away and see if you can describe it accurately.

8. Next, make up a story about this object; for example, how this valuable coin was lost by a coin collector and came into your possession. Use your imagination; see what sort of adventurous tale you can create.

9. Give this article to another actor who will hide it in the room or on a stage while you are not looking. Your objective is to find this object. Give this search your full attention and concentration as others call "cold," "warm," or "hot" to guide you. After you find it, leave the object where it is. Now return to the place where you began this exercise, and recreate as closely as you can what you were thinking and what you did during your search.

10. Write a letter to someone you love. Do this sitting onstage or at the front of the room before a group of other actors who will try to distract you from writing. The group may not touch you, but they may come near you, talk, whisper, or try to distract you in another way. Keep concentrating on your letter writing.

11. Sitting or standing in front of a group of other actors, tell them about the one to whom you were writing the letter. See this person in your mind's eye and describe him or her in detail. The group may provide typical audience sounds (moving in the chair, whispering, coughing, sneezing, a baby crying, and similar noises) to try to distract you.

IMPROVISATIONS

Improvisations are used by many acting teachers to develop actors' abilities to listen, concentrate, think on their feet, imagine, and create. When an improvisation requires the actor to recall a previous sensory or emotional experience, it may help the person to get in touch with feelings that can be used later onstage.

Some directors use improvisations at auditions to test the imagination and creativity of actors. While rehearsing a show, directors may use improvisations to help actors understand what has happened offstage before their entrances or what has occurred in incidents that are referred to in the script but not shown onstage. When working with a scene that has dialogue or a situation that is difficult to understand, directors may ask actors to improvise the scene, playing it in their own words, to help them comprehend the thoughts and emotions. Sometimes full-length plays and musicals for public performances are partially developed through actors' improvisations, so this is an important skill for performers to develop.

In a class improvisation, actors are usually told *who* the characters are or *what* the situation is or *when* or *where* the scene takes place or *why* the incident occurs or *how* it happens. Ordinarily you are not given all of this information so it is up to you to create what is not provided. When more than one actor is involved, the participants are generally given a few minutes to decide on the who, what, when, where, why, and how. Then they are asked to present their improvisation, devising their characterizations, dialogue, and actions extemporaneously.

The improvisation does not have to be long or funny, as some actors believe. You should stick to the subject, listen to the others, react spontaneously, and concentrate on staying in character and speaking as your character would in this situation. If you think that you are not good at doing improvisations, you probably just need to do them more often. Actors can usually improve their abilities to improvise by practicing.

Exercises

1. The following are improvisations for one person:
   a. You are sleeping when a strange noise awakens and scares you.
   b. You are reading in your room when a mouse runs across the floor.
   c. In trying to drive at night in a fog, you almost have a bad accident.
   d. It is your birthday, and you eagerly check the mailbox to discover that no one has sent you a card or letter.
   e. Because you drank too much at a party, you are now having difficulty opening the door to your home and getting to bed.
   f. You get a telephone call from your spouse telling you the marriage is over.
   g. You are trying to paint the walls of your apartment, but you are having trouble with the roller, dripping paint on furniture, stepping in the paint bucket, and so forth.
   h. You return home to discover that you have been robbed.
   i. You are trying to prepare an intimate dinner for two, but everything goes wrong: you burn the meat, the cake falls, you put too much salt on the broccoli, and so forth.
   j. By accident you are locked in a bank vault overnight.
   k. You are playing solitaire and watching television when you hear on the news that you are wanted for murder.

2. The following improvisations are for two people:
   a. One of you receives a telephone call that affects both of you.
   b. A husband and wife are having breakfast the morning after he embarrassed her at a party.
   c. A shoplifter is caught and interrogated by a department store guard.
   d. One of you wants something that the other one has.
   e. An employer fires an employee who has been with the company for thirty years.
   f. A customer arrives at a garage sale and discovers that the seller was a close college friend.
   g. A lawyer advises a client who is accused of murder.
   h. Two people are waiting to be interviewed for one job.
   i. A customer returns a defective product to the manager of a store.
   j. One of you wants a divorce from the other.
   k. A grandparent tries to tell a grandchild what sort of profession the young person should go into.

3. The following are group improvisations for three or more people:
   a. One of you is a travel agent and the others arrive to book trips.
   b. You are a group of college students travelling in a bus to see a musical performance in a nearby city when the bus runs off the road and into a creek.

c. You are members of a family who are waiting at the airport for a relative to arrive from abroad whom you have never seen.

d. One of you is a talk show host and the others are celebrities invited to be interviewed on television.

e. You are attending the twenty-fifth annual reunion of your college class.

f. One of you is a steward or stewardess and the rest are passengers on an airplane when you hit turbulence.

g. One of you sees a UFO, but the others do not see it.

h. One of you is the receptionist and the others are patients with various ailments who are waiting to see a doctor.

i. You are a group of rock musicians travelling on a bus to your next engagement. One of you has lost a large sum of money and suspects everyone else on the bus.

j. You are a group of actors who are taking off your makeup and getting dressed after a bad performance of *Oklahoma!* You are all tired, disgruntled, and inclined to blame everyone else for the poor show.

k. You are elderly residents of a nursing home who are discussing the illness of one of your friends.

7

PREPARING A MUSICAL ROLE

EVE [an actress]:   I couldn't have done it without you.

BILL [a director]:   (*Surprised*) Without *me?* Come *on* . . . I stopped by and gave you a five-minute pep talk before the curtain went up . . .

EVE: Something you said made the whole difference. Without it, I might have been just plain embarrassing.

BILL: Really? What was that?

EVE: You said, "The one thing that makes an audience uncomfortable is to see an actor pressing—sweating to make good." You said, "If you feel you're losing them, don't panic. Hold very still inside. Don't go after them; make them come to you."

—from *Applause*

Bill gave Eve some good advice, and in this chapter we'll consider more suggestions and ideas about how to prepare a part for a musical, starting with how to analyze the script and role. Then, we shall take up rehearsing, creating a character, and preparing songs and dances.

ANALYZING THE MUSICAL AND ROLE

First of all, read the script carefully to learn about the plot, characters, thoughts, words, songs, and dances. A good analysis will provide the foundation you need for preparing your part.

Plot

Your director should discuss with the entire cast the following questions plus his or her concept of the musical. Your individual study should focus on how you can contribute to the director's interpretation. Look in your script for answers to the following:

- Where and when do the scenes take place?
- What is the plot all about?
- Is there a conflict? Between whom?
- Is there a subplot? Who is involved in it?
- Where are the minor and major climaxes?
- Is the musical a comedy, satire, farce, romantic comedy, drama, melodrama, tragedy, fantasy, or something else?
- What is the style of the show? All musicals are presentational in style, but some are more realistic than others: *My Fair Lady,* for example, is more realistic than *Stop the World—I Want to Get Off,* which is highly theatrical with no attempt at illusion. How realistic will your production be?

Characters

Examine the characters, paying particular attention to the one you are playing. You should know your character so well that you can write a biography that covers the period from birth to the time of the show. For information about your character, look at the following:

1. Your character's first entrance to see if the writer provides a description of this person.
2. Other stage directions for information about your character's movements, stage business, attitudes, thoughts, and feelings.
3. What other characters say about the person you are playing.
4. What your character says about him- or herself.
5. What actions he or she does during the play.
6. How your character changes during the play.

If the author does not provide everything you need to know about your character, you must use your imagination and make some educated guesses based on what is given to you by the bookwriter, so that you can compile a complete biography.

You should also know the answers to the following:

- Who are the characters? How are they related?
- What is your character's function in the play? Is your character the protagonist, antagonist, friend or relative of one of these, comedian, member of the singing or dancing chorus, or what?
- What is your character's nationality? Ethnic origin? How has your character been influenced by his or her family?
- What should your character look like? What is your character's physical appearance, age, weight, height, and color of hair?
- How would you describe your character's posture, movements, stage business, and rhythm of movement and speech?
- What should your character's speaking voice be like? What dialect or accent do you need for this part?

- What are the intellectual characteristics and education of your character? Emotional characteristics? Personality? Social and economic status? Occupation? Hobbies? Religion? Politics?

- What kinds of costumes should you wear to play this character? Shoes? Makeup? Hairstyles?

- Does your character use any unusual props?

- What is your character's main objective or major goal for the entire play? For example, in *My Fair Lady* Eliza's major goal is to better herself.

- What has happened to your character immediately before every scene your character is in? To figure out your character's objective on entering, you must know what has taken place earlier. To help actors determine this, directors may ask them to improvise occurrences that are not in the show but affect the characters' attitudes, thinking, and feeling at their entrances. In Eliza's case, before Act I, Scene 1 opens, she has been preparing her violets and selling them on the street.

- What are your character's objectives and motivations for every scene your character is in? In *My Fair Lady*, Eliza's objective at the beginning of the first scene of Act I is to sell flowers, and her motivation is her need for money. To figure out an objective for your character, ask yourself, "*What* do I want? And express the objective using a verb after "I want"; for example, "I want *to sell* flowers." For the motivation, ask yourself, "*Why* do I want this?" The answer in Eliza's case is: "I want to sell flowers because I need money."

- What actions does your character do to achieve the objectives? The actress playing Eliza should answer that her action in Scene 1 is to ask people to buy flowers.

- What obstacles prevent your character from achieving the objectives? At the beginning of *My Fair Lady*, Eliza meets an obstacle: Freddy, a well-to-do young man, who accidentally knocks her down and ruins her violets. So how can she overcome this obstacle? Her objective is still to sell flowers but now they are spoiled. Another obstacle occurs when a bystander tells her that a "bloke" (Higgins) is recording every word she says. When she hears this, her objective changes; it is now "I want to defend myself." Her motive? To stay out of jail. Her action is to get the crowd to sympathize with her and help her. And so it goes throughout the play. Eliza's objectives, motives, and actions change according to the obstacles and events.

- What is your character's attitude toward every other character with whom he or she is involved? What is your character's emotional state? What is he or she thinking? Analyze Eliza's attitude when she enters in Act I, Scene 1. She needs money, and she has come to sell her flowers to the rich people who are leaving the opera house and waiting for taxis. She is not afraid of these wealthy people—she knows that she has the right to sell her flowers there—and when Freddy accidentally knocks her down and ruins her flowers, she talks to his mother about paying for them. The mother dismisses her without giving her money, so Eliza asks Pickering to buy a flower. Emotionally, she is anxious (she wants to sell some flowers) and angry (she was knocked down and her flowers were stepped on). She is thinking that she must get someone to buy these flowers or she will not make as much money for the night as she should. After she realizes that a man is recording her words, these factors change. Her attitude toward Higgins becomes fearful; emotionally, she is terrified; she is thinking that she must defend herself. And so, her attitudes, emotions, and thinking will change throughout the play with each new event.

- Is your character different at the end of the play than at the beginning? In what ways has your character changed? Eliza progresses during *My Fair Lady* from a poor cockney street vendor to a self-assured, poised young woman who is the match of her mentor, Higgins.

Thoughts

Your stage director should also discuss with the cast the ideas in the musical. Investigate the following:

- What is the theme or message of the musical?
- What other major ideas are expressed?
- How are the ideas expressed? In dialogue, actions, songs, dances, or signs on the stage?

Words

Examine the text; that is, the words of the dialogue and lyrics. If you don't know what a particular sentence means, look up the words in a dictionary. Usually this will suffice, but not always, for the following reaons:

1. There may be several meanings listed for each word, and you may not be able to figure out which meaning the author had in mind.

2. Some words or meanings may not be in standard dictionaries because they are obsolete, archaic, colloquial, substandard, or foreign.

3. A meaning may not be listed in a dictionary because it is connotative, which is an emotional, implied meaning that is suggested by the literal meaning of the word. By using connotations, a character may show his or her feelings or attitude. For example, when Higgins calls Eliza a "squashed cabbage leaf," he is revealing his emotions and point of view towards this cockney girl.

To be sure that you understand the musical, ask yourself the following:

- Do you understand every word and sentence of the text? If not, research them, or ask your director to explain them.
- Do you understand the sensory images (words that stimulate the senses)? For instance, when Higgins orders Eliza not to "sit there crooning like a bilious pigeon," the writer's words create visual and aural images in our minds. Sensory images may appeal to our sense of sight, hearing, taste, touch, or smell. To interpret these well, you must understand the image, then see it in your mind's eye or feel it within your body before saying the words.

- Do you understand the figures of speech, such as the *simile* (a comparison that is often introduced by *like* or *as*), *metaphor* (a comparison that is made when a word or phrase is used in place of another), and *allusion* (a reference to a place, a person, or an event)? "Crooning like a bilious pigeon" is an example of a simile, and in the following sentence, Higgins uses three metaphors followed by an allusion: "Yes, you squashed cabbage leaf, you disgrace to the noble architecture of these columns, you incarnate insult to the English language: I could pass you off as the Queen of Sheba."
- Do you understand the jokes in the script? The puns, malapropisms, extreme exaggerations, and other comic devices? Do you have straight lines or punch lines? (If so, read Comedy Techniques in chapter six.)
- Do you understand the subtext of your scenes? On your first examination of the words in the script, the true meaning may not be immediately apparent because a character may be saying one thing while he or she actually has something else in mind. Sometimes the writer may describe in a stage direction what the character is really thinking, but other times the writer may not give the actor this help. In this situation, the stage director should decide on the interpretation to be given the scene and discuss it with the performers. Constantin Stanislavski wrote that spectators come to the theatre to hear the subtext—they can read the text at home. In other words, the audience wants to see how the performers interpret the text.

Songs and Dances

Next, pay particular attention to the songs and dances, analyzing the dramatic or comic function of these numbers and their meanings. (See chapter two for types of songs and dances.) Ask yourself the following:

- What kinds of singing and dancing numbers does my character do? With whom?
- What type of accompaniment will there be? (Full pit orchestra, small combo, two pianos, or what?)
- What ideas are expressed in these songs and dances?
- What is the function of each song or dance number you are in? Is it to provide a climax to the scene? To add humor? To delineate character? To reveal what a character is thinking or feeling? To demonstrate the change in a character, the passing of time, or a shift in place? To progress the plot? To give exposition? To set the mood of a scene? To tell a story? To foretell the future? To state the theme or a main idea? Or is it primarily to show off your talents?

REHEARSING

The rehearsal period for a musical is usually about four to ten weeks. In summer theatres, however, rehearsals may be much more abbreviated, sometimes as short as one week.

If you sing, dance, and act in the show, you will be called to singing rehearsals with the musical director, dancing rehearsals with the choreographer, and acting rehearsals with the stage director. It is entirely possible that you may rehearse parts of one scene, in which you sing, dance, and act, on different days with various directors. So how do you cope with the fragmentary nature of these rehearsals? You do this by keeping your analysis of the show and your character firmly in mind. You know your character's objectives, motivations, and actions for each scene, and these should guide you through your different rehearsals whether you are acting, singing, or dancing. Also, when you are rehearsing at home, you can practice them in the proper sequence to get used to the continuity of the scene. Eventually, at least by the time of run-throughs, you will be permitted at rehearsal to put the three elements together as called for in the script. At this point you can begin to concentrate on staying in character throughout the show.

Remember that rehearsal is the place to experiment, to take chances, to make mistakes, to try new and different interpretations. Do not be afraid to fail! Not everything you try will work wonderfully, but your director, choreographer, and musical director should be watching to correct you if you err, to help you achieve a great performance, and, above all, to encourage you.

Your stage director represents the audience. Most of the time he or she sits in the theatre and tries to improve every element of the show so that the audience will understand, believe, and appreciate it all. You must listen carefully to your director because this person is looking at the whole production—not just your role—and is trying to be sure that your character fits into the total concept.

The following are the types of rehearsals you will have with the stage director. (In chapter eight you will find more suggestions for proper behavior at rehearsals and performances.)

Reading

The rehearsal process traditionally begins with one or more reading rehearsals in which the stage director, producer, musical director, choreographer, stage manager, cast, and others assemble to read the dialogue, listen to the music, and discuss the musical. If it is a new show, the bookwriter, composer, and lyricist may also be present. (See figure 7-1.) Subjects for discussion may be the director's concept; the style; the theme and thoughts; the structure and meaning of the plot; the objectives, motivations, and actions of characters; character relationships; the text and subtext of scenes; and plans for the songs, dances, scenery, costumes, lighting, and sound.

Theatre Games and Improvisations

Some directors like to take time for theatre games to get the cast acquainted and to build trust among the performers. Sometimes improvisations may be done, such as the following:

- Improvisations of what characters were doing immediately before each scene. This may help actors to begin each scene with a clear objective in mind and the right attitude, thoughts, and feelings. It may also promote an appropriate response to the stage environment. For this, consider how differently a character will react if he or she is very familiar with a place or is entering it for the first time.

- Improvisations of events that are spoken of but are not shown onstage. For example, in the scene from *My Fair Lady* in chapter ten, it is mentioned that Higgins gave Eliza a ring in Brighton. That day might be the subject of an improvisation that would give the actors a better idea of their relationship.

Figure 7-1. Robert Goulet, Julie Andrews, Richard Burton, and other performers at a reading rehearsal of *Camelot*.

(Courtesy of the Billy Rose Theatre Collection, the New York Public Library at Lincoln Center, Astor, Lenox, and Tilden Foundations.)

Blocking

After discussing plans for the scenery and properties, the stage director and performers block the show; that is, they decide on the major movements in the dialogue scenes and the songs, unless the latter are to be staged by the choreographer. Some directors are more dictatorial about blocking than others; some dictate every movement while others allow the performers to move as they feel like it.

Many actors will at this point start to wear shoes to rehearsals that are similar to those they will wear in the show, because they believe that shoes are a good key to the character.

Developing

During developing rehearsals the director and performers work on characterization, line interpretations, learning lines, voice, dialect or accent, articulation, projection, stage business, and adjustment of the blocking. After songs and dances have been choreographed and rehearsed, they will be integrated with the dialogue.

Some rehearsal techniques that may be used are:

- Speaking out loud what Stanislavski called the "inner monologue," which is what your character is thinking and feeling. Your director may ask you to say your character's thoughts softly and then the line from the script as you normally say it. Then, you keep alternating thoughts and lines throughout the scene. This is a good way for the director to determine if you do understand what the character is thinking and feeling.

- Reversing roles with your partner(s) to see if this brings you a deeper understanding of the characters and the situation by letting you see the problems from the point of view of the other(s).

- Playing opposite values. In other words, if your character is supposed to hate someone, act as though you love that person. If your character is angry, play the scene calmly. Because we vacillate in life in our feelings toward others, this exercise can help you to explore the different facets of your character's emotions and keep you from playing on just one level throughout a scene. What you do in this exercise may not be what you decide to use for performances, but it may open up some choices for you.

If you must wear a long skirt, hat, sword, cane, glasses, or other items that may present problems in handling, it is customary to begin, as soon as you have the script out of your hands, to use substitute garments and props until the ones designed for performances are available. If you wear glasses but your character does not, rehearse without them as soon as you learn your lines.

Polishing

In polishing run-throughs, the director works on the tempo of scenes, the pace of the show as a whole, concentration, ensemble playing, and the "illusion of the first time." In a run-through, the show is not stopped unless absolutely necessary; rather, the director, musical director, choreographer, and stage manager take notes to give to the performers at the end of a scene, an act, or the entire rehearsal.

Technical

Near the end of the rehearsal period, the scenery, props, lights, sound, and curtains are added to the show. The emphasis in "tech" rehearsals is on perfecting technical work and cues. Two other important events may occur around this time: the dress parade, where performers put on their finished costumes for the costume designer, director, and others to approve, and the performers' first rehearsal with the orchestra.

Dress

At dress rehearsals, costumes, makeup, and hairstyles are worn, and the show is performed with full orchestral accompaniment and all technical elements. Notes are given at the end of the rehearsal.

CREATING A CHARACTER

While doing your analysis of the musical and your role in it, you must begin to plan your characterization. There are three principal ways to prepare a characterization: you can approach the role "internally" or "externally" or you can use a combination of the two.

Performers who prepare internally are sometimes known as emotional, intuitive, or representational actors. Working from the inside to the out, emotional actors concentrate primarily on the character's inner thoughts and feelings. One of the first to popularize this method was Constantin Stanislavski, who founded the Moscow Art Theatre in 1898. Through his books his system has spread throughout the world. In the United States, different versions of the Stanislavski System are used, all of which are usually referred to as "the Method."

Stanislavski advocated a thorough analysis of the play and the character to discover an inner as well as an outer truth. The goal is to reach a state of creativity for acting truthfully. To achieve this, actors must develop their voices and bodies to be responsive to the demands of performing, and they must be concerned with both inner preparation and valid external physical actions.

While the Stanislavski System was developed for playing realistic and naturalistic plays, it has been used successfully for other styles, including presentational musicals. Stanislavski directed operas and was well aware of the problems that musical performers face. Musical artists must not only act with truth, they must also sing and dance truthfully. To this end, the Stanislavski System can be very helpful to you.

Some performers, however, prefer to prepare externally. These people are sometimes called technical, presentational, or mechanical actors.

Working from the outside to the inside, technical actors pay more attention to the outer manifestations of emotions and thoughts than to the inner experience of them. They carefully analyze the part and decide on the appropriate posture, movements, business, facial expressions, manner of speaking, costumes, makeup, and hairstyles. Although they may not consciously try to think the thoughts or feel the emotions, the planned external actions may stimulate their inner feelings. The great English actor Laurence Olivier once said that after he decided how to hold his mouth for a particular part the rest of the characterization fell into place. Peter Sellers commented that once he found the right voice for a character he was working on, he then had the characterization he wanted.

Many actors, however, use the best ideas from both approaches, and this is what I suggest that you do. Because inner emotional experiences and their external expressions are invariably linked together, actors can work from the inside to the outside or from the outside to the inside. From your analysis of the musical and your role, you should have ideas about the external and the internal characteristics of your part that will provide the base from which you can work during the rehearsal period. As you gather material through your research, observations, personalization, imagination, and physicalizations, your first concept of the character will probably change. It may change more after you explore further your character's objectives, motivations, actions, obstacles, attitudes, emotions, thoughts, and physical and vocal characterization. Also, working with your director and fellow performers should provide additional insights.

Further Research

If you are in *Camelot,* your research may involve reading the source for this musical, which is T. H. White's novel, *The Once and Future King;* if you are in *My Fair Lady,* you should read George Bernard Shaw's play, *Pygmalion,* on which this musical was based. The authors of these sources may give you ideas and background material about the characters that would never occur to you if you only studied the musicals.

Other information you may want to know is who wrote the musical, when it was written, who starred in the first Broadway production, and how it was received by the critics.

For someone playing Eliza in *My Fair Lady,* research may involve discovering what a cockney dialect is or what life in London in 1912 was like. You may want to research costumes, shoes, hairstyles, manners, bows, curtsies, and many other things to make you more familiar and comfortable with the time period or place in which your musical is set. Some reference books on manners and customs are given in Suggested Reading.

If available, you may want to listen to a recording of the musical by a Broadway cast or watch a videotape, film, or live performance. Some directors may not want you to see or listen to another production for fear it will stifle your creativity, but many directors will encourage you to do so with the hope that it will give you ideas for playing the part.

Observation

Do you know someone who is similar to your character in age, personality, occupation, or in some other significant way? If so, you may want to study this person, without his or her knowing it, to get ideas you can use. Perhaps you can discover something for stage business, such as how she handles a handkerchief or how he keeps adjusting his glasses, or ideas for costumes, makeup, hairstyling, posture, movements, dialect, accent, or manner of speaking.

If you do not know someone to observe, consider going to a place where a similar person might be. Actors playing detectives often go to the local police force for help; those playing nurses may go to a hospital. Sometimes you can even get ideas from watching animals—perhaps one character might move like a cat and another like a monkey. Astute observations can help you achieve a realism in your portrayal that may be otherwise lacking.

Personalization

Stanislavski taught that you should "go from yourself" in creating a role. You should use your own memories—both sensory and emotional—in preparing to act any part. Think about the experiences that you have had in life that are close to your character's. Have you ever been as much in love as Nellie and Emile are in *South Pacific?* Have you ever hated a parent as Mordred hates Arthur in *Camelot?* Have you ever mourned the death of a loved one as Maria does in *West Side Story?* If you have had a comparable experience to one depicted for your character, make use of it as you are preparing your role. It will help you achieve in your acting a realistic, believable sincerity.

Imagination

Sometimes in preparing a part you cannot find the right person to observe, there is no experience in your past life to assist you, and your research is of no help. What should you do then? Stanislavski said to use the "magic if." Ask yourself what would you do *IF* you were this person in this situation. In other words, use your imagination. Think about your character, taking into consideration everything you know about the role, and then imagine how this person would react when faced with this event. Try the "magic if."

Physicalization

After you have a good idea of what your character should be like, your next problem is to determine how you can make your audiences understand this person. This is done through physicalization (i.e., physical expression) of psychological traits (e.g., shyness, boldness, vanity, insecurity) and physical elements (e.g., a crippled leg, a stiff neck, a good body alignment, a lisp). These traits affect the way you talk, walk, and stand, your stage business, your facial expressions, your rhythm, and your manner toward other people. How are you going to communicate to an audience the brashness of Mama Rose in *Gypsy?* Or the timidity of Motel when he is in the presence of Tevye in *Fiddler on the Roof?* You do this through the expressions of your voice and body. Get inside the character's skin, feel and think like this person, and your voice and body should make the audience understand your role.

Vocal Characterization

In analyzing your character, you should have thought about how this person speaks. Is the pitch range different from yours? The rate of talking? The overall loudness level? The quality of the sound? The articulation? Is your character's dialect or accent different from yours? If so, study and practice until you have your vocal characterization the way you want it.

As mentioned in chapter five, if you must learn a dialect or accent, try to find someone who speaks this way to help you, go to a dialect coach, or read about it in a dialect/accent book and listen to the accompanying tapes. (See Suggested Reading for some titles.) After you become proficient in your vocal characterization, you must next determine if you can be understood. Your director should help you with this because it is his or her job to make sure that the meaning of the lines will be clear to the audience.

If the director cannot hear or understand you, the trouble may be that your dialect or accent is too strong, your articulation is not distinct enough, or you are not projecting. If you find that your voice is becoming tired or strained at rehearsals, you may be tensing the throat and neck muscles too much. Review the exercises in chapter five.

Learning Your Role

After the dialogue scenes have been blocked by the stage director, you should start to learn your lines. Some actors arrive at the first rehearsal with their dialogue and songs memorized, but most wait until the movements of the acting scenes have been planned so that they can learn lines and movements together.

As for songs, most stage directors prefer that they be rehearsed by the musical director and committed to memory before blocking. For dances, the choreographer will urge you to practice the routines and master them as soon as possible.

Some actors can learn their parts easily during the repetitions at rehearsals, but those who have large roles will have to spend hours outside of rehearsals learning lines, movements, songs, and dances accurately. Paraphrasing is not permitted in the professional theatre—you must say the lines exactly as written—and directors of amateur productions should also not permit any deviations.

As soon as possible you must try to act without your script and music because you cannot begin to concentrate fully on acting the role until you do.

Stage Business

This is the term for the small, detailed activities (not major movements) that you do to communicate your characterization or your character's emotional state, like smoking a pipe, having a drink, swinging a cane, or using a fan. The script or your director may stipulate certain motions, but often the actor is expected to create his or her own business.

Today we hear much about "body language" and how our movements can subtly communicate ideas to our viewers. When we are acting onstage, we must be sure that our gestures, facial expressions, and other movements are communicating the right ideas about our characters to the audience.

Interacting with Fellow Performers

When you have the script out of your hands, you can begin to listen to other actors, think about what you have heard, and respond. Is there true communication among you, or are you just waiting to hear your cue and then reciting your lines? Are you playing off your partners, or are you anticipating what is supposed to happen and responding *before* the other actors provide the stimulus for your reaction?

Please, get into character and keep your concentration on what your character should be thinking and feeling at that moment. Don't let your mind wander! Some of the best ideas you will get about line interpretations, stage business, or characterization will probably come in rehearsal when you are deeply absorbed in being the character and responding to the others.

Acting has been likened to a game of catch. Your partner throws a line to you; you think about it, react, and throw a line back. You *give* to your fellow actor energy and sincerity; if you have a good partner, you *receive* the same, and this interaction can suggest new insights into these characters, new objectives, motivations, actions, tempos, and rhythms.

Tempo, or the rate of speed that you play a dialogue scene, is the responsibility of all of those in it. The stage director may call for an overall fast, medium, or slow rate, but there will, or course, be many variations within any scene.

Ensemble playing, or group creativity, should be the goal of all performers in a production. To achieve this, actors must depend on and trust each other to do the right thing. All must work together harmoniously to present the best performance of which they are capable.

Speaking over Underscoring

There are many places in musicals where actors must speak over musical underscoring. These involve careful timing of the words, business, and movements so that they are done at exactly the right moment to fit with the music. If you are not using a microphone, it may also require more vocal projection in order to be heard over the accompaniment.

These parts of the show must be carefully blocked and rehearsed with the conductor and the music. If the timing is exceptionally difficult, you may want to record the accompaniment so that you can work at home on coordinating your lines and movements with the music.

These sections are often transitions from the dialogue to a song or dance, and you therefore have the added task of making these changes seem logical. In many cases the emotions will build during the transition to the point where the character must break into song or dance. This is what happens in the scene from Act I, Scene 5 of *Cabaret* (which you will find in chapter ten). Sally has lines to say through the first page of the song "Perfectly Marvelous" that must build and be carefully timed so that she is ready to sing as soon as she has finished speaking. If she talks too quickly, she will have an awkward pause until the singing cue comes. If she speaks too slowly, the accompanists will have to wait for her.

When actors do sing, they must do so in character with the same dialect or accent that is used in speaking. You cannot sound like one person while speaking and another while singing.

Emotional Scenes

To act an emotional scene (crying, laughing, hating, loving, fearing, and the like) try working from the inside to the outside. To play a scene in which your character cries, for example, you may start with thinking about what has happened to make this character feel so sad. This should lead to the physical response of crying.

As mentioned previously, some actors achieve the inner emotion by remembering their own similar experiences and using these as a springboard to feeling the character's emotions. In other words, you may remember an occasion when you were unhappy and cried, and this memory may help you to understand the character and the emotion. (See the emotional memory exercises in chapter four.)

If you find it difficult to play an emotional scene by working from the inside to the outside, take the technical approach and work from the outside to the inside. Start by doing the movements associated with the emotion. If your character is supposed to be angry, look and sound like angry people you have observed: scowl, speak sharply, tense your muscles, and walk belligerently. If your character is sad, breathe erratically, sniffle, cry, and wipe away tears. You may find that if you do the physical motions, the inner feeling may thereby be triggered.

Remember, however, if you have to sing during an emotional scene, you cannot become so aroused emotionally that your breathing is affected adversely. Singing in emotional situations requires that you prepare technically, showing the outer manifestations of the emotion, as you have observed them in yourself or in others.

Playing Heroes and Villains

If you are cast as a leading sympathetic character, the audience must get to like you, care about what happens to you, and worry about you if you get into difficulties. As Eliza in *My Fair Lady* or King Arthur in *Camelot*, you are playing this type of character, and it is your responsibility to create the charisma, appeal, and attractiveness of the role.

On the other hand, some of the most interesting parts are villains. As Mordred in *Camelot* or Eve in *Applause*, you are definitely an unsympathetic character. But even though the audience is supposed to hate the character, you as the actor must get to know the character, understand him or her, and figure out the reasons why the person does such evil things. Remember that villains do not consider themselves bad; they can always justify their actions. Villains like themselves, so you, the actor, must like your character.

Acting in the Chorus

If you are playing a chorus role, you too must find your characterization. Unfortunately for chorus members, writers rarely give as much information about chorus parts as they do for the larger roles. Therefore, you may be on your own to decide on your characterization, objectives, actions, attitudes, stage business, and other important points discussed above. If you cannot determine these, ask your stage director to help you.

Stanislavski once said that "there are no small parts, there are only small actors." Remember that everyone onstage is important and that just one person who is out of character can ruin a scene. If you have been given the chance to play a chorus part, give it thought, time, and energy. It deserves no less than your best effort. Another quotation from Stanislavski says it all: "Today Hamlet, tomorrow an extra, but even as an extra you must become an artist."

Illusion of the First Time

At each rehearsal and performance you as an actor must strive to forget that you are hearing and saying lines that have been written in a script by an author—lines that you have rehearsed, perhaps, for weeks. You must believe that this is the first time you have been in this situation because it *is* the first time for your character. So listen to the others, think about what they are saying as your character should, and respond as though you just got this idea that causes you to say and do what the script stipulates. And at every rehearsal and performance, you must go through the same process: listen, think, and respond.

PREPARING SONGS

In preparing songs for a show, you will work with the musical director, composer (if available), conductor, choral and vocal directors, and rehearsal pianists on the singing and with the stage director and choreographer on the movement and dancing in the numbers. To start this process, begin with your own analysis.

Analysis

Before singing a note, you should analyze for each song the character and the situation; you should understand what has happened in the plot and why the authors have inserted a song at this particular place in the show. What is the function of this number? (See the questions earlier in this chapter under "Analyzing the Musical and Role.")

What happens immediately before the song? Does the song grow out of the mood of the preceding dialogue? Does the emotion grow within you during the dialogue to the point where you must sing to express yourself? For instance, in Act I, Scene 2 of *Brigadoon* (part of which is in chapter ten), Tommy is becoming interested in Fiona, and this develops easily into his singing "The Heather on the Hill."

Analyze the structure of the song. Songs, like plots, are often constructed to start slowly and then build to a big climax. There are many examples of this, but one of the best is "Rose's Turn" in *Gypsy*, which builds not only to a song climax but also to the climax of the show.

There are, of course, other types of construction. Consider a short reprise that Rose sings earlier in *Gypsy* after Herbie has left her. She sings just a few lines of "Small World" as she is in a daze, thinking about her situation. The song is like a soliloquy, in which a character shares thoughts and feelings with the audience while alone onstage.

Is the song a funny one that should get laughs, such as "Matchmaker, Matchmaker" from *Fiddler on the Roof?* (This may also be found in chapter ten.) Does the song lead in to a dance number, like Margo's "But Alive" in *Applause?* Is the song broken off by important plot action? In *Camelot* Guenevere sings almost eight lines of "I Loved You Once in Silence" when she is stopped by Lancelot's embrace.

You should next analyze the lyrics. What do they mean? Do you understand all of the words? Is there a subtext? What is your character's objective in singing this song? What motivates your character? What action should your character take to reach the objective? What is your character's attitude toward the others onstage? What emotions should your character be feeling as you sing this song? What is your character thinking?

Learning Your Songs

The first rehearsals that you have with the musical director and rehearsal pianist will probably involve learning the music accurately until you can sing your songs easily. At this time you may want to record the piano accompaniment so that you can study and rehearse them at home.

As you sing the lyrics, be certain that you are saying the words distinctly enough to be understood by the audience. Some voice teachers seemingly work on acquiring a good tone in singing vowels while diminishing the importance of consonants, but if the listeners hear only vowel sounds, they will not understand you and will quickly lose interest. It is vital that you learn to articulate all sounds clearly. When Hodel sings the words "Make me a match" in the song "Matchmaker, Matchmaker" (see chapter ten), she must not omit consonants. If she sings "May e a ma," the audience will not understand her. She should put a *k* sound on the end of *make* and an *m* at the beginning of *me*. For *match*, she should sing the initial consonant and vowel (*ma*) for almost the full number of beats indicated in the music, then quickly add the final consonants of *tch*. The purpose of sustaining the vowel sound is to open the mouth as much as possible to let the sound out.

For the same reason, you will want to exercise care in singing diphthongs. As mentioned in chapter five, diphthongs are two vowel sounds blended together, such as [aɪ] in the word *my*, [aʊ] in *vow*, and [ɔɪ] in *toy*. Because the first vowel of a diphthong is more open that the second vowel, you will want to give the first vowel more importance and quickly sing the second vowel. For example, the diphthong [aɪ] in *my* is composed of an *ah* sound and an *ee* sound. In singing *my*, you will want to sing *mah* for almost the full length of time indicated by the note and then quickly add the *ee* sound.

Dialects and accents may present problems. When Maria sings in *West Side Story*, she should use the slight Puerto Rican accent that she has while speaking. Eliza and her father in *My Fair Lady* should both use a cockney dialect when they speak and sing "Wouldn't It Be Loverly? and "With a Little Bit of Luck." Any dialect or accent, however, cannot be so authentic that the listeners cannot understand you. Your first consideration should be that the audience comprehends the words and the meaning of the song.

Personalization, Observation, Imagination

Next, work on interpreting the lyrics. Try personalizing; that is, relate the lyrics to your own life. Have you had any experiences that are similar to those expressed in the song? If so, how did you feel at that time? Look at a part of "I Have a Love," a song that Maria sings to her friend Anita about her love for Tony in *West Side Story*. The lyrics are:

> I have a love, and it's all that I have.
> Right or wrong, what else can I do?
> I love him; I'm his,
> And everything he is
> I am, too.
> I have a love, and it's all that I need,
> Right or wrong, and he needs me too.

Have you ever felt this way? Can you recreate how you felt? If you have not had any experiences in your life to help you, you will have to rely on your observations or your imagination. Try Stanislavski's "magic if"; ask yourself, "What would I do *if* I were this person in this particular situation?"

Physicalization

Try saying the lyrics as a long speech or soliloquy. You know who the character is, the situation, the mood, the character's attitude toward others present, and the ideas and emotions of the words. As you recite the lyrics, physicalize your character's traits, thoughts, mood, and feelings; that is, express them in physical motions. Let your body respond to the meanings of the words and the imagery. But here is a warning: don't act out every sentence literally, and don't get into the habit of pointing to yourself on the word *I*. It is probably a good idea to avoid pointing on *all* pronouns: *I, she, he, we, you,* and the rest.

Remember that you must get your entire body involved in singing a song. You don't sing only from the neck up—you sing with the whole body. From the feet to the head, every part of your body should be working. Forget about such things as "I don't know what to do with my hands" or "I don't know how to stand." Give yourself a good base from which to work; start with your feet twelve to eighteen inches apart and your weight equally divided. Then, concentrate on the thoughts and emotions of your song. The words should inspire images in your mind's eye and your body should move spontaneously in reaction to the words and music.

Phrasing

Melodies are divided into musical phrases, and these must be considered in planning where to breathe. Phrasing may be according to the demands of the music or the lyrics, but when you pause—for effect or to breathe—you have ended a phrase (a thought-unit). Normally, you do not want to pause in the middle of a word or phrase to inhale, because if you do the meaning will not be clear. Proper phrasing helps to get the sense of the song over to the audience. Obviously, though, you cannot sing indefinitely without pausing (you do have to take air into your body), so the object is to breathe where you will not harm the meaning or the melody.

As mentioned earlier in chapter five, some marks of punctuation are helpful in determining phrases: you will often pause at a period, question mark, exclamation point, semicolon, colon, and a dash. A comma may or may not indicate the end of a phrase. Probably you will want to pause about every two to four bars, but the exact placement of pauses must be decided on the basis of the musical structure and the sense of the words.

In phrasing the above excerpt from "I Have a Love," you might decide that you want to breathe at the period in the first line, but some singers do not breathe until the comma in the second line. Then they repeat this phrasing in the last two lines of the excerpt, so that the phrasing is as follows (the asterisk indicates the end of a phrase):

I have a love, and it's all that I have.
Right or wrong,* what else can I do?*
I love him;* I'm his,*
And everything he is*
I am, too.*
I have a love, and it's all that I need,
Right or wrong,* and he needs me too.*

You may not agree with this phrasing, and that's all right. You should try various possibilities to see what is the most effective phrasing for you.

A lot depends on your breath control. If you cannot sing many words on one breath, you will have to find more logical places to pause for breathing, because you must not let the sound die out before the end of a thought-group and you must never gasp for air.

Singers sometimes take tape recorders to rehearsals to record their singing. Then they listen objectively for faults, including poor phrasing. Another way to learn phrasing is to listen to the experts. If the song or the entire musical is on record, film, or videotape, you may get ideas for phrasing and interpretation by hearing it.

For help and guidance in determining phrasing, tempos, interpretation, articulation, and singing the notes as they are written, consult your singing teacher, musical director, vocal director, or rehearsal pianist.

"Talking" a Song

As Henry Higgins in the original 1956 production of Lerner and Loewe's *My Fair Lady*, Rex Harrison spoke many of the lyrics in such songs as "Why Can't the English." Other actors who are not trained singers have also used this style that involves partially speaking and partially singing a song. While talking to music, the performer adheres to the rhythm and varies the pitches to suggest the melody of the music but actually sings only a few lines or words.

In 1960, while writing *Camelot*, Lerner and Loewe again called for this type of rendition for parts of Arthur's solos. This role was written for Richard Burton, another fine actor who was not noted for his singing ability but for his outstanding speaking voice and articulation. Look at the musical notes for the first four words of the song "Camelot" in chapter ten. These x-shaped note heads indicate that the words should be spoken with approximate pitches.

Those of you who are not trained singers should keep this in mind because you may wish to select a song for auditions that will permit you to speak many of the lines and thus avoid having to sing difficult passages. If you do, remember that your speaking voice, articulation, and stage presence must be excellent.

"Belting" a Song

Many singers feel that they have two registers: a "head" voice or higher register and a "chest" voice or lower register. When you use your chest voice in a forceful style, this is called belting. Ethel Merman was well known as a belter, and songs written for her like "Everything's Coming Up Roses" in *Gypsy* demand this power and punch. Nell Carter belted in *Ain't Misbehavin'*; and when Jennifer Holliday sang "And I Am Telling You I'm Not Going" in *Dreamgirls*, she was acclaimed for her ability to belt a song.

If you want to develop this style, you should work with a vocal teacher or coach who will see that you do not injure your voice by straining and tensing the throat muscles. You must be careful because belting, which

body in a place that will not show. The microphone is generally clipped to your clothing close to the throat. The microphone may be hidden from the view of the audience, but it should not be covered.

If, while you sing, you are to hold a microphone, either wired or wireless, the sound designer should tell you how close to your mouth you should place the mike and whether you need to vary this distance according to the loudness and softness of your voice. Be sure to hold the mike low enough so that the audience can see your facial expressions, and handle the mike properly so that it will not distract from your singing. Don't swing it around, strike it against something, or drop it!

If you are to walk while singing, maneuvering the cord efficiently will also take some practice. You will probably want to have the mike in one hand while you hold the wire loosely in the other hand so that you can move it as needed. You must, of course, be aware of where the cord is so that you don't trip on it.

The sound designer should also give any needed instructions for the use of floor, overhead, and standing mikes. He or she will undoubtedly point out that microphones are delicate instruments that must be handled carefully, that dust, sweat, and saliva must be kept away from them, and that no one should ever blow into a microphone to test it.

Watching the Conductor

The conductor and the orchestra are an important part of any musical number, and you must coordinate your efforts with theirs. While singing onstage, performers need good peripheral vision. You must watch your conductor much of the time, but you cannot let the audience know you are doing this. You have to be aware of the tempo set by the conductor and other signals this person may give you, yet appear to be completely in character, absorbed in singing your song and projecting it to the audience.

PREPARING DANCES

When you dance in a musical, you will work closely with the choreographer and his or her assistants. The choreographer will create the dances, deciding for each number the dance steps, combinations, and arrangements of performers to suit the music, the space involved, the purpose of the dance, and the people who must be in it.

Most of the time in the professional theatre, the choreographer will work with accomplished dancers who can learn a routine quickly. From an early age professional dancers are trained in ballet, modern, jazz, tap, and other types. Most dancers continue studying while they are dancing professionally. The result is that today's professional dancers are amazing and versatile athletes. In shows like *A Chorus Line* and *Dancin'* the physically strenuous dances surprise and astound audiences.

In the amateur theatre, however, the choreographer will often have to work with untrained people. The choreographer's job then is to get them to move as well as possible. Often, in this case, the choreographer will build dances around movements that most people can do, such as walking, running, turning, skipping, kicking, social dancing, cheerleading or majorette steps, aerobic exercising, and the like. Movements to accompany songs may involve such motions as swaying, walking, turning, kicking, kneeling, arm and hand gestures, and easy dance steps. While these movements may be simple enough for those without dance training to do, those with dance training will do them better; if you aspire to work professionally in musicals, dance training is a must.

Normally, dances are taught by the choreographer or an assistant who demonstrates the steps. Then, while the choreographer corrects and helps, makes changes, and adjusts the groupings, the dancers repeat the steps until the desired effect is reached. However, even though your dancing is carefully controlled by the choreographer, you should do some individual work in analyzing the character, situation, and the dances you are in.

Analysis

When you dance in a musical, you are a specific character who is dancing for a particular purpose. This is different from being in a dance recital or concert where in some numbers you may not assume a characterization. To analyze a musical part, ask yourself the questions at the beginning of this chapter under "Analyzing the Musical and Role." Be sure you know the following:

- What is your role in the musical? What sort of a character are you?

- What has happened in the plot immediately before each dance you are in?

- What is the meaning and function of each dance? Does it tell a story? Or is it nonnarrative? Does it carry the plot forward? Is it a substitute for realistic action? Is it supposed to be funny? Does it establish the mood of a scene? Does it show the personality of a character or a change in character? Does it indicate the passing of time or a change in locale? Does it enhance a song? Does it give a visual interpretation of the accompanying music?

- What is your character's objective during each dance? Motivation? Action? Is there an obstacle to achieving this objective?

- What emotions is your character feeling? What is your character thinking?

- What kind of dance is involved? Jazz, ballet, tap, modern, folk, or some other type?

- Do you dance solo or with others? If the latter, what is your character's relationship to the others and attitude toward them?

- What will the set and costumes be like? The lighting? Props? How much space will you have for the dance? What kind of shoes will you wear, or will you be barefoot? Hairstyle? Makeup?

Now let's take a dancing part and analyze the first dance this character does. Imagine that you are playing in *West Side Story* the role of Riff, who is described as the intelligent, driving, but slightly whacky leader of the Jets. His friends are Tony, the Jets, and their girls; his enemies are the Sharks, their girls, Lieutenant Schrank, and Officer Krupke. Riff's first dance is in the prologue, which is a condensation of the growing rivalry between two teenage gangs, the Sharks, who are Puerto Ricans, and the Jets, who are of other American backgrounds.

The prologue begins with the Jets in control of an area (a street, an alleyway, and a brick wall) on the West Side of New York City. At first, only Bernardo, the Sharks' leader, enters, but the Jets get rid of him. Bernardo returns with other Sharks, but they too are driven off. Then, mild warfare between the two gangs erupts leading to an all-out free-for-all that is stopped by Krupke and Schrank.

The function of this dance is to give exposition, showing how the enmity between the Jets and the Sharks developed over a period of time. This dance tells a story, advancing the plot; it is a substitute for realistic action; it establishes the mood of the musical; and it shows the personalities of many of the boys in the two gangs.

Riff's objective in the prologue is to beat the Sharks and protect his friends, the Jets. His motivation is that he wants the Jets to control this area. His actions are to fight and outwit his enemies. The obstacles to be overcome are the Sharks, who also want this territory. Riff's attitude toward the Sharks is hatred, which dominates his thinking and feeling.

The kind of dance involved is basically jazz, but it is a dance strongly rooted in realistic movements because this dance substitutes for realistic action. This dance, which involves all of the Jets and the Sharks (about twenty male dancers), shows the enmity between the two gangs.

The street set, with a workable brick wall, should allow as much space as possible for the twenty to dance. The only prop indicated in the script is a flour sack, but choreographers may introduce other props, perhaps weapons such as a chain, a stick, or a piece of pipe. The clothes should be what typical teenage gangs of New York City might wear including sneakers and jackets that give the name of their gang (Jets or Sharks). The script indicates that the boys should have sideburns and long hair.

Observation, Personalization, Imagination, Physicalization

Dancers have as much need as actors and singers to observe, personalize, imagine, and physicalize. Please see the preceding sections in this chapter on these skills.

To continue with the example of Riff, suppose you were cast in this role and you had nothing in your background to help you work out the characterization needed for Riff. You might get some usable ideas by observing members of an urban teenage group from a poor section of a city. Or, if you do have experiences with gangs to draw upon, use personalization: try to remember your own sensory and emotional experiences that are similar to Riff's, think about how you acted and felt in those circumstances, and incorporate these feelings into your dancing. With either observation or personalization, you will want to use also your imagination to flesh out the characterization.

For dancers, physicalization involves getting across to an audience the thoughts, feelings, and the physical and psychological traits of the character through dance movements. If you were playing Riff, how would you move to tell the audience that Riff is a bright, street-smart, aggressive leader who hates the Sharks?

Dance Rehearsals and Performances

If your only function in a musical is to dance, you will work primarily with the choreographer, his or her assistants, the rehearsal pianist, and dance arranger until the dances have been learned and polished. Then the dances will be integrated into the show, and you will rehearse with the stage director, musical director, and other performers present.

Normally you will be accompanied by the rehearsal pianist or a recording of the accompaniment until late in the rehearsal period, when you will rehearse with the orchestra for the first time. As with singers, the change from piano to orchestral accompaniment can be stimulating or frustrating, depending upon how well your choreographer and rehearsal pianist have prepared you for this change. There should be no difficulties so long as the choreographer and conductor agree on tempos, but these are often matters of dispute.

During the final week of rehearsals, you will wear your costumes, makeup, wigs, and hairstyles for the first time, and this too can be an exciting experience. Now you will find out where your difficult costume changes are and how to make them quickly.

Like everyone else in the musical, you face the problem of keeping your performance fresh. Although you may have done your routines hundreds of times, remember that this is the first time these spectators have seen you dance in this musical and you have an obligation to give them a good show.

Dancer-Singer-Actor

For some musical roles, such as Riff in *West Side Story*, you must be not only an expert dancer but also a singer and actor. If you are cast in a role in which you do all three, you will rehearse your dances with the choreographer, your songs with the musical and vocal directors, and your dialogue with the stage director.

Some stars who started as dancers who have successfully learned to do it all are Gwen Verdon, Chita Rivera, Ann Reinking, Ben Vereen, and Tommy Tune, to mention only a few. If you are a trained dancer who aspires to do more in musicals than just dance, you too must study singing and acting. At both the amateur and professional levels, you are more likely to be cast if you can do all three well.

EXERCISES

1. As mentioned in this chapter under "Rehearsing," you should know what your character has been doing before an entrance so that you can begin with the right attitude, thoughts, emotions, and response to

the stage environment. As an exercise, look at the scene from *Company* in chapter ten and improvise what Sarah, Robert, or Harry was doing for five minutes before this excerpt begins.

2. You must respond to the stage environment as your character would. While you rehearse without scenery, furniture, stage lighting, or sound effects, you must be able to imagine these and react to them appropriately. As an exercise, look at the scene from *Funny Girl* in chapter ten, and improvise what Nick did when he entered this private dining room for the first time. The excerpt shows Fanny's entrance and her reaction. Disregarding the actual lines of the scene, improvise her response to the room.

3. Improvising events that are spoken about but are not shown onstage is a good way for actors to understand what happened during that incident. In the scene from *Grease* in chapter ten, Patty refers to Danny's being at her house one night. If you are playing Patty or Danny, you should know what took place; as an exercise, improvise what Patty and Danny did that evening.

4. Select one of the scenes in chapter ten that has a role you would like to play. Find a partner or partners to act the scene with you, and then follow the suggestions given in this chapter for preparing a part. In doing scenes, performers are usually their own director, musical director, and choreographer. Normally, scenes are presented without scenery, stage lighting, sound effects, or stage makeup, but some props and suitable clothes, shoes, and hairstyle can help you feel like the character. If your scene has a song, you will also need an accompanist and a piano. For more information about how to do a scene, look at the instructions that precede the scenes in chapter ten. Note especially the tenth suggestion on experimenting in rehearsal: Try improvising the events that occurred immediately before your scene and any incidents that may be talked about but are not shown onstage; also, try speaking the inner monologue, reversing roles, and playing opposite values.

5. Select a solo from a musical to perform before others. If suitable, you may use a song from chapter ten.
   a. Analyze the song. Find out what happened in the plot immediately before the song. What is the meaning and function of the number? What kind of person is your character? What is your character's objective in singing? What motivates your character to sing? What action should your character take to obtain the objective? What is your character's attitude toward everyone else onstage? What is your character thinking and feeling during this song?
   b. In rehearsal, recite the lyrics of the song as though it were a soliloquy or speech from a play. Do you understand what all of the words mean? Have you ever had similar sensory or emotional experiences?
   c. Physicalize the traits, thoughts, and emotions of your character as you recite the lyrics. Can you picture the images in your mind's eye?
   d. Rehearse with an accompanist as you work on articulation, phrasing, interpretation, tempo, movements, energy, and communication.
   e. While you will probably not have scenery, furniture, or stage lighting

for your performance, imagine what these should be like; and do wear clothes, shoes, and a hairstyle that are similar to what your character might wear.

6. If you are a dancer, work with an accompanist to plan a solo dance for a musical, and present it before others. Choreograph it yourself, or work with a choreographer. If an accompanist is not available, you may use recorded show music.

   a. Find out what sort of character does this dance, what has happened in the plot immediately before this dance, and the meaning and function of the number. Is the dance narrative or nonnarrative?

   b. What is your character's objective, motivation, and action? What is your character's attitude toward others in the scene? What is your character thinking and feeling while dancing?

   c. While you will probably not have any scenery or stage lighting when you perform your dance, determine from analyzing the script how much space is available for your dance and what the stage and lighting should be like.

   d. When you perform your dance, use a hairstyle, clothes, and shoes that are similar to what your character should wear.

8

BEHAVIOR AT REHEARSALS AND PERFORMANCES

BILL [a director]: Star, I have a few notes for you. (SHE *droops*) Absolute perfection! . . . (SHE *glows and goes to him*) Except you lost your biggest laugh in Act Two, dope, by moving on your own line, and—

—from *Applause*

Usually, at the beginning of the rehearsal period, singing, dancing, and acting rehearsals are held separately until the dialogue has been blocked and learned, the songs have been staged, and the dances have been choreographed. Then the acting, singing, and dancing are put together. After that, the technical elements and the orchestra are added, dress rehearsals are held, and the show is on. (For a description of the different types of rehearsals, see chapter seven.)

Normally, a Broadway musical will either have an out-of-town tryout in cities like Boston and Philadelphia or preview performances in New York. Because of the great expense of taking a show on the road, previews are the usual choice today. Previews give the producers, writers, lyricists, composers, directors, performers, and designers an opportunity to perfect the show by presenting it before audiences for a week or more before the announced opening. On opening night, though, the critics arrive, and then their reviews are broadcast or published. If the reviews are favorable, the show will usually run; if unfavorable, it will probably close almost immediately, and then everyone must seek work elsewhere.

When you go to rehearsals and performances, you will be expected to know how to behave, so this chapter has some common sense rules that performers should follow.

REHEARSALS

The following suggestions pertain to both amateur and professional performers. First of all, you should prepare for rehearsals. At home, you should study and rehearse your lines, blocking, songs, and dances, paying particular attention to the notes and directions that have been given to you. Unless you know that there will be an extensive warm-up at rehearsal, warm up physically and vocally at home. Then, always arrive early, and spend the time until the rehearsal starts warming up or studying your role.

If you must be late for or be absent from a rehearsal, notify the one you have been told to contact in this situation (probably the stage manager or the person holding the rehearsal) as far in advance as possible. If you wish to invite a friend to watch a rehearsal or if you want to leave a rehearsal before it is finished, ask the stage manager for permission.

Listen carefully to your directors and stage managers. Always take your script, music, and a pencil (with an eraser) to every rehearsal, including dress rehearsals, and record in your material or in a notebook all blocking and directions given to you. You must write down these instructions, your own ideas, and times of rehearsals and other appointments—do not rely on your memory. If you are using rented material that must be returned at the end of performances, write lightly so that you can erase all of your marks before giving the books back. Some notes and announcements that pertain to you may be placed on the callboard, so remember to check often the place where calls, messages, and the company rules are posted.

Obey your director's, stage manager's, or the theatre's rules with regard to smoking, eating, and drinking. In general, do not smoke, eat, or drink unless others are, and if you do, put your rubbish in a trash can. Be careful where you put out your cigarette—never stamp it out on a stage floor. Don't chew gum during rehearsals, unless your character is supposed to chew it. (An exception to this may be made for singers who want to use gum, a cough drop, lozenge, or mint to keep their throats moist during long rehearsals.) Never take an intoxicating drink, marijuana, tranquilizers, or other drugs before or while you are working. If you are under a doctor's orders to take medication, discuss with your doctor how you can avoid having the medicine affect your work in the show, and notify the stage manager of your medical problem.

Never be late for an entrance. When offstage, wait quietly for your next appearance. If it is a short wait, stay in character and think about your next scene—don't distract yourself and others by talking. If it is a long wait, put the time to good use by practicing your lines, songs, or dances—if you can get far enough away from the rehearsal so that you will not disturb those who are rehearsing. Before doing so, however, let the stage manager know where you will be in case you are needed. If you would like to go into the house to watch part of a run-through or dress rehearsal, ask the stage manager first if this is permitted.

Never direct your fellow performers. If you have a problem with another performer, ask the stage director or stage manager to solve it if it involves acting, the choreographer if it is about dancing, and the musical director if it concerns singing.

Dress appropriately for rehearsals: wear clothes and shoes that will permit you to move as your character should. As noted in chapter seven, if you have difficult costumes to wear or props to handle, you should devise some substitutes until the ones to be used in performances are available. For example, rehearsal pictures of *Cats* show the performers in rehearsal clothing with "tails" attached so that they could get used to them before the actual costumes arrived.

Think about your costumes and makeup before dress rehearsals. If you are expected to supply any item of costuming, be sure that you understand exactly what it is. In a Broadway production, all parts of the costume, including shoes, hairpieces, beards, and wigs, are provided and kept clean by the wardrobe staff. The producer must also supply all unusual makeup. Performers, however, are expected to furnish and apply their own ordinary, conventional makeup, so it is essential that all actors, singers, and dancers study and practice the art of stage makeup. If you are doubtful about what kind of makeup to do, ask your stage manager or director. (Under Suggested Reading, you will find the titles of several books on stage makeup.)

Think about your hairstyle(s) before dress rehearsals. On Broadway, a performer may not be required to cut or change the style or color of hair unless this is agreed to at the time of signing the contract. In these cases, the producer must pay for the expense of this change, its upkeep during the run of the show, and the return to the hair's original color at the close. If you do not know what kind of hairstyle is wanted, ask your stage manager or director. If it is a difficult one, the producer should arrange for an expert to style it for performances.

Don't bring valuables, such as money, a watch, or jewelry, to the theatre and leave them in an unlocked dressing room during rehearsals or performances as they may be stolen. If you must bring them to the theatre, give them to the stage manager who will put them in a safe place until the rehearsal or performance is over.

Check your props before rehearsals or performances begin to be sure that they are there, but leave them on a prop table until they are needed onstage. After using them in the show, return them to the prop table or to the person who has been designated to receive them.

Check your costumes before a dress rehearsal or performance begins. Be sure you are ready for any fast changes. If you need a dresser, ask the wardrobe supervisor for help. You will often have to share dressing facilities, so it is necessary that you be considerate of others by cleaning up your makeup and hanging up your clothes and costumes. If your costumes become soiled, ask the wardrobe supervisor about getting them cleaned. Personal cleanliness is a necessity as you must work in close contact with other performers, staff, and crews.

Don't get in the way of the stage and prop crews when they are trying to change the set. If you do not know where to wait during a scene change, ask your stage manager.

Cooperate with your producer, director, choreographer, musical director, stage manager, and other members of the staff. If you want to be cast again, show them what a good, reliable performer you are. Be considerate of others, and stay cheerful and healthy.

PERFORMANCES

By requirement of Actors' Equity Association, professional actors must be at the theatre no later than a half hour before a performance, perform their services to the best of their abilities, care properly for their costumes and props, respect the property of the production and the theatre, and abide by all reasonable rules and regulations of the producer that are not in conflict with Equity's rules.

Conscientious professionals sign in well before the half-hour deadline in order to take time with their makeup and hairstyle, to dress, and to warm up physically and mentally.

In a professional production, if a performer is late for the "half hour" call or appears unable to perform because of intoxication or a similar cause, the producer may replace the person for that performance or may dismiss the performer. In such cases, Actors' Equity Association has a precise and detailed procedure to follow.

As for amateur performers, from time to time they often need to be reminded of some common sense suggestions such as the following:

Eating before performances is a personal matter, but many actors prefer not to eat or drink anything for several hours before going onstage. Be careful especially of drinking carbonated beverages because they may make you belch onstage. Also, stay away from nuts, popcorn, and other foods that may stick in your throat. As for smoking, theatres have definite regulations about where you may smoke, so before you light up, be sure to ask where the smoking areas are.

In the amateur theatre, the call for performers is usually forty-five minutes or one hour before performance time, but you may want to arrive earlier if you have a difficult makeup or you need to do an extensive warm-up. Be sure to check in as soon as you arrive at the theatre so that the stage manager will know you are there. The directors and/or stage manager may hold a meeting with the cast before the performance to stimulate the performers, give them notes, or do a group warm-up.

Keep your stage makeup and hairstyle(s) exactly as they were when they were approved by the stage director at dress rehearsals. Don't change them unless you get permission from the stage manager to do so.

Refrain from all contact with the audience after you are in costume or stage makeup. Don't go through the lobby or halls where the audience can see you before the show, at intermission, or after the show. Discourage friends from trying to come backstage before the show or at intermission. Tell them where you will meet them after the performance.

Treat your costumes with care. If one should become torn or damaged, see the wardrobe supervisor immediately. Watch how and where you sit in a costume (in some companies you may be asked not to sit in certain garments), and be careful not to lose any parts of your outfit, such as gloves, handkerchief, or stockings.

Handle props carefully. While backstage, never play with the props or eat prop food. If a prop should become damaged, report it to the property master.

Once the house is open and the audience is entering the theatre, you must be quiet backstage. During performances you must be very quiet in the wings and in the areas near the stage.

Don't stand in the wings of the stage to watch the show; go to the wings shortly before your entrance. While there, stay out of the way of those who are trying to get offstage (stage exits must remain open), and be sure that the audience cannot see you. If you can observe people sitting in the theatre, they can see you. Spend the time until your entrance thinking about your character and your character's objective, motivation, and action; don't ruin your concentration—and that of others—by talking.

During performances, keep your blocking, stage business, line interpretations, songs, and dances as they were on opening night. If you have an idea for improving these, discuss it with the stage manager, but don't make any changes without the stage manager's approval. Directors who return to check up on musicals several weeks after the opening are often appalled at the number of "improvements" that have crept into the show. Usually, performers are told to cut them out.

While onstage, if anything unusual happens (an actor misses an entrance, a prop is not in its place, and the like), stay in character and adapt to the changed circumstances. If you must ad-lib, do so in character until such time as you can return to the dialogue of the script.

If a prop or part of a costume inadvertently falls to the floor, pick it up if you are nearby. A dropped article will attract and hold an audience's attention until somebody removes it.

If the line preceding one of your lines gets a big laugh, wait until the laugh is almost out before delivering your next line. (See "Comedy Techniques" in chapter six.)

If you forget your dialogue or lyrics, it is better to ad-lib than to wait to be prompted. If you make a mistake onstage (such as forgetting your lines), don't worry about the error during the show or it will affect the rest of your performance. Keep your concentration on what you are doing at the moment. Then, after the performance is over, review what happened so that it will never occur again.

Avoid "in-jokes" (jokes that the performers understand but the audience does not). Performers in long runs may develop such jokes as a way to combat boredom, but if they are concentrating on staying in character and doing the best work of which they are capable, they should not get bored.

9

PREPARING A MUSICAL AUDITION

FANNY BRICE: Listen, Mr. Keeney, I've had a lot of experience—honest! I've been on the stage since I was ten! Amateur contests, Gottliebs' Southern Rep— professional companies! Last season I doubled six parts! I played a daughter and her own father. How do you like that—a sixty-year-old Indian chief! So why don't you give me a chance? Maybe you don't like me in the chorus. Why don't you let me audition for that specialty tomorrow? Huh?

—from Funny Girl

To get a role in a musical, you must audition. This is true of college, community, summer, regional, off-Broadway, and Broadway productions. Only rarely does it happen that someone is given a role without an audition, and that someone is usually a well-known performer whose work is highly respected.

Auditions may take place in a theatre, rehearsal room, classroom, studio, or office. They may be tryouts for a specific musical or general auditions for several future productions; and they may be for acting, singing, or dancing roles or a combination of these. In this chapter you will find suggestions for all of these plus ideas for interviews, photographs, résumé, and where to find notices of auditions.

First of all, let's look at some general suggestions that pertain to most kinds of auditions.

ALL TYPES OF AUDITIONS

If auditioning frightens you, it will not be consoling to learn that this feeling will probably never disappear completely; however, with experience it usually lessens. Therefore, my first suggestion is to audition as often as possible, always performing as well as you can. Even if you are not cast, you have nothing to be sorry about if you have done your best, because you will have learned from the audition experience.

Since many musical roles today demand singing, acting, and dancing, my second suggestion is to study all three and be prepared to audition for all of them.

My third suggestion is to get acquainted with the stage director, producer, bookwriter, composer, lyricist, musical director, choreographer, casting director, stage manager, star of the show, or whoever is casting the musical. It is a recognized fact that directors would rather cast someone they know and like than an unknown; however, if you are an unknown, there are certain things you can do to improve your chances. Consider the following.

Before the Audition

Start early to think about what the audition will probably be like, and plan to cope with it in order to make the best possible impression. Analyze and rehearse your material until you know it thoroughly. If you can arrange it, have your audition videotaped so that you can see exactly how you look and sound. View this tape objectively and analytically. What are your weaknesses? How can you improve?

In addition to videotaping, practice your audition before several friends. Ask them to give you criticism. If there is a time limit for your audition, have them time your work to make sure you are within the limits. You may want to repeat this mock audition several times to be sure that you will not fold under pressure. The better prepared you are, the less chance there is that fright will adversely affect your audition.

YOUR CLOTHES.   For an acting or singing audition, dress to suit the character you are most interested in playing—within reason and within the limits of your own wardrobe. If you have been unable to look at a script and do not know the characters, if you are interested in many characters, or if you are auditioning for a period piece (*period* means a show that does not use contemporary dress), wear nice-looking, comfortable, clean clothing that flatters you and reveals your personality. Dress as you would if you were going to a business interview for an office job. Look the best you can but not overdressed or weird, unless that describes the part you want.

Usually you will want to wear clothes that do not attract attention to themselves so that the auditioners will give you their full attention and not your garments. However, if you are going to a large audition, where several hundreds may be trying out, you may want to wear something that will distinguish you from the crowd, such as a flower in your lapel, a bright scarf, a hat, or an unusual belt. If you are called back to a second audition, wear the same clothes and hairstyle so that you have a better chance of being remembered. One young actress wore a bright red sweater to an audition at which about eight hundred were competing for parts. Later at callbacks and interviews, to which she wore the same sweater, she found that directors remembered "the girl in the red sweater," and she credited this sweater with helping her get a role.

Women: Usually you should select a dress, blouse or sweater and skirt, or suit that shows your legs—unless you have bad-looking ones or the character you want to play would wear pants or jeans.

Men: Wear a jacket and slacks (or suit) and a shirt with or without a tie. In warm temperatures and in less formal situations, such as college and community auditions, you may want to omit the jacket and dress more casually. In cold weather you may prefer turtleneck, pullover, or cardigan sweaters.

Men and women: Don't wear anything that is uncomfortable or restrictive of your movements. Be especially careful about wearing a hat, headscarf, or sweat band that may conceal your face or hamper head or facial movements. Select shoes that fit well, look good, and are easy to move in without clomping.

If you think that you will have to do a dance audition immediately after an acting or singing audition, you should either bring dancewear that you can change into quickly or devise one outfit for all auditions. For example, women may wear a skirt over a leotard and tights for an acting or singing audition and then remove the skirt for the dance audition; men can do the same with jeans or slacks over their dance clothes.

For a dance audition, you will want to wear flattering dancewear and bring suitable shoes (jazz, sneakers, oxfords, character, ballet, *pointe*, tap, acrobatic, or modern) for the types of dancing in the show.

YOUR MAKEUP AND HAIRSTYLE. Women: You should make up judiciously to flatter your best features. If you are auditioning onstage in a theatre, you can wear more makeup than if you are trying out in a small room; but don't look overly made up or bizarre unless you are auditioning for that type of character.

Both men and women should dress their hair in a way that is appropriate for the character they are most interested in. If you do not know anything about the characters or are interested in several of them, be sure that your hair is clean and attractively styled and that it will not cover your face as you try out.

WARMING UP. Before going to the audition take the time to loosen up vocally and physically. Do some of the exercises from chapters four and five, and rehearse your songs again.

At the Audition

Plan to arrive *before* the announced time of starting (or your appointment) so that you will have a few minutes to compose yourself and check your appearance. Take with you a pen, because you may have to fill out an information card or sheet, and your photo, résumé, and portfolio of pictures in case you are asked for them. (See the section on "Photographs and Résumé" in this chapter.)

Listen carefully to announcements about the casting and the musical. Observe the whole situation: What is the procedure? How are the auditioners responding to those trying out? Where is the best lighting for you to stand in for your audition? Becoming familiar with the whole situation may help to alleviate any stage fright you may be feeling.

If you have the chance to watch the auditions, see what you can learn from them. Some may be bad, but others may be excellent. Stay as long as you can, and come back to other auditions if you are allowed to. Appear very interested in being in the production, and be courteous, cooperative, and kind to everyone.

STAGE FRIGHT.   If nervousness is a problem for you, remember that almost all of us have stage fright at auditions to some degree, largely because we are afraid we will not do well. The best way to deal with fright is to be well prepared. The worst way is to take a sedative, alcohol, or some other substance that will slow down your reflexes and make you less alert. You don't need these "crutches"; you can handle stage fright without them.

Talk yourself out of being nervous: tell yourself that everyone is feeling this way, that you know what you are doing, and that you will do it well. Convince yourself that being excited is good and that you will give a better audition because it will make you more energetic and dynamic.

Get your mind off the situation by forcing yourself to concentrate on something else, for example, your breathing or the tension in your body. Breathe in while you mentally count slowly to four, hold your breath as you count again to four, then breathe out to a slow count of four. If you feel tense in the throat or neck, massage these muscles with your hands. Drop your head forward, then move it slowly with your eyes closed to the left, back, right, and let it drop in front again, trying to feel as relaxed as possible. Yawn as you bring your head up to a good posture. Consciously tense and relax various muscles of the body, and do other relaxation exercises from chapters four and five.

YOU'RE ON!   When your name is called to audition, walk to the designated place with poise and stand in the best light. You will project more confidence to your spectators if you can give a friendly smile and hold your head up in a good alignment. Looking down nervously will tell your auditioners that you are unsure and unprepared.

Remember that as soon as you are in sight of the auditioners your audition has begun, because they are evaluating your appearance, demeanor, clothes, walk, posture, and state of tension before you have opened your mouth. If you are asked questions, answer graciously with humor (if possible) and good eye contact. If you give an introduction to your selection, say this directly to your viewers. But once you begin to perform your material, avoid watching them to see how they are reacting. It will make them uncomfortable if you stare at them for the whole time. Instead, if you are supposed to be talking or singing to one or more people, look over the heads of your spectators and play to imaginary characters behind your viewers at the back of the room or theatre.

While auditioning, try to stay relaxed, and don't allow yourself to think about how well or badly you are doing. If you make a mistake, don't worry about it. Concentrate on staying in character and going on as well as you can.

After the audition, the way you leave the stage or room will also contribute to the impression you make on your viewers. Remember that the audition is not over until you are out of their vision.

IMPROVISATIONS.   Some directors like to use improvisations as part of an audition. If you are asked to do one, listen carefully to the instructions, get into character, and let your imagination go. If you find improvising difficult, you need to practice this skill. Most actors find that it becomes easier with experience, so work at it. See the section on "Improvisations" in chapter six.

ACTING-SINGING-DANCE AUDITIONS.   If you are being considered for an acting or a singing or a dancing role, the chances are that you will be asked to demonstrate that you can do the other two. Actors and dancers should be prepared to sing at least sixteen bars of two different songs. Singers and actors will probably have to show that they can dance or at least move well; and any dancers and singers who are being considered for a speaking part will have to read a scene or two from the script. As mentioned earlier, your best bet is to be prepared to audition for all three.

AUDITION ON VIDEOTAPE.   In some situations, you may be asked to submit an acting, singing, or dance audition on videotape. If so, get professional help to record your audition; be certain that the lighting, camera work, and sound are of top quality. Follow the instructions carefully about length and types of material. If there are no instructions, prepare contrasting pieces that total five to ten minutes.

Now let's consider suggestions for different types of auditions that you may attend.

SPECIFIC AUDITIONS FOR ACTORS

Auditions for an acting role in a specific musical usually consist of reading one or more scenes from the script either by yourself, with other actors, or with someone on the production staff such as the stage manager. Evaluating your work will be the director, casting director, or others from the staff. To do your best, think about the following.

Before the Audition

The producer, director, casting director, or an agent may be able to lend you a script for a few days. If it is a published work, your public library may have a copy. If you can get hold of a script, study it carefully. Analyze the plot and the characters you are interested in, and practice major speeches of those roles. Unless you are instructed otherwise, you do not need to memorize anything, but for an important audition many actors will study the script to the point where they know many of the lines.

If you are told ahead of time which scene will be used for your audition, give it special attention. Ask yourself:

- Where and when does the scene take place?
- What has happened to your character immediately before his or her first line?
- What is your character's objective, motivation, and action in this scene?
- What is your character's attitude toward others in the scene?
- What is your character feeling and thinking?

At the Audition

Even though you have studied the whole script, you will sometimes not know the scene you are to read at the audition until you get there; then you must hastily determine the answers to the above five questions. If you have been unable to read the script, the best idea is to inquire if you may have time to read through the scene. Usually you will be given at least a few minutes to glance at it and make a few decisions about it. If you don't understand the scene, ask some questions—if this is possible and appropriate.

If you are told to read the copy cold, with no chance to look at it, be gracious, project a positive attitude, and do the best you can. If you cannot quickly figure out a characterization, let them know what *you* are like. Project vitality, enthusiasm, energy, and your voice. The ability to read cold can be improved with practice, so it is something that all actors should work on.

Stand in a good body alignment unless this would be unsuitable because the character should have a poor one. Your posture, movements, gestures, and facial expressions should be appropriate for the character. If the scene demands action, you may indicate it within reason. If chairs are provided, you may sit, rise, and walk around, but all movement should have a purpose. Don't let your nervous excitement cause you to wander aimlessly about the stage or room.

When reading from the script, hold it high enough so that your head is upright, unless you are playing a character whose head is always bent over. You will get your best voice quality if your neck and head are relaxed and in a good alignment. Do not, however, hold your script so high that your face is concealed; let the auditioners see your eyes and facial expressions and hear your voice. Project your voice for the size of the theatre or room so that the listeners can hear and understand you. Use a vocal quality and dialect or accent that is suitable for the character with adequate variety of loudness, rate, and pitch.

Get away from the script as much as possible. Develop the ability to see a phrase, think the thoughts your character should be thinking, and look up as you speak. If you find that you lose your place easily, mark it with a finger so that you can spot the next phrase quickly as you repeat the process: look at a phrase, think, and communicate it. At first, you may be able to see only a few words at a time, but with practice you should be able to increase the number of words that you can handle. This is a technique used by television newscasters, public speakers, and oral interpreters. It is also a useful technique for actors at auditions because it gets your eyes away from the script as you say the words.

If you are reading alone, look over the heads of your listeners as you speak. If you are reading with the stage manager or one or more actors, listen to them, look at them when this is appropriate, or look away to think. Communicate with them, and react to them as your character should.

GENERAL AUDITIONS FOR ACTORS

The following suggestions cover general auditions at which you may be auditioning for more than one director, for a season of several musicals, for an agent, or to enter an acting school or university theatre department. You, therefore, are not trying for one specific musical or part. Sometimes a general audition is held to select those who will be given a specific audition.

For a general audition, you are usually asked to prepare one or two monologues with a one- to five-minute time limit. The usual meaning attached to the word *monologue* is a dramatic sketch performed by one actor. For audition purposes, this normally means an excerpt from a musical or play in which a character talks to one or more other characters, addresses the audience, or delivers a soliloquy.

Sometimes for a general audition you may be asked to do a short scene from a musical or play with a partner of your choice. In this case, select a good actor to work with; a poor partner will make the scene bad and make you look bad. To prepare a scene, follow the suggestions in chapters seven and ten. It is much more common, though, to do monologues rather than a two-person scene at general auditions, so the rest of this section pertains to preparing and presenting monologues.

Before the Audition

Many actors think that finding the right monologues is the hardest part of a general audition because it takes a lot of time and reading to select good material. Start early to find it so that you will have at least two weeks to rehearse and learn it before the tryouts.

YOUR MATERIAL.   Your goal is to find selections that you like and understand, that show off your abilities and versatility, and that are right for your age and physical appearance.

You should choose excerpts from less common plays and musicals because directors and agents are tired of hearing the well-known ones. If you are permitted only one monologue, select a contemporary one in a realistic style (unless the instructions stipulate otherwise). If you may do two selections, get contrast in the roles; for example, take one from a drama and the other from a comedy, or one from a modern and another from an old play. The characters should be different in personality, temperament, intellect, emotions, and rhythm to show your range as an actor.

If you cannot find in a musical or play one speech of the desired length to use as a monologue, you can join together several short speeches of one character. Sometimes you will have to do some editing or rewriting so that the joined speeches make sense. You can pause briefly and react as though another character has spoken to you, but do not pause too long.

If you can only do one monologue, you should probably do a selection that requires Standard American speech and avoid other dialects and accents. The reason is that more American musicals and plays use Standard American than any other; if you do an excerpt that needs another dialect, such as southern or Brooklyn, the directors may think that you cannot speak Standard American.

Try to find a monologue that will permit you to begin energetically to attract the auditioners' attention; but, in general, avoid the big climactic moments of a play that call for a lot of yelling.

Usually at general auditions a chair will be available for your use, but don't count on it. Get a selection that you can do standing if no chair is there.

ANALYSIS AND REHEARSAL.   Read and analyze the entire work. You cannot do justice to an excerpt if you do not know and understand the whole script. Be sure to figure out where and when the scene takes place and what has happened immediately before your monologue so that you can begin with the right objective, motivation, and action in mind and appropriate attitude, thoughts, and feelings.

Project your voice so that your auditioners will hear and understand every word you say. Use an appropriate vocal quality for the character and good variety of loudness, rate, and pitch. Don't let stage fright make you rush your material. Use the posture, gestures, and movements that your character should use. And do move when you have a purpose for moving! Use as much of the lighted area as you need.

At the Audition

Be certain your name is known to the people doing the casting. If this is a large audition, you may have to say your name and a number both at the beginning and at the end of your audition. State them loudly and clearly.

Don't give a lengthy introduction to your material. At the most, state, with good eye contact to your auditioners, the title of the play and name of the character; but when you are under a severe time limitation, you don't need any introduction.

Where you look during a monologue depends on the type you are doing. If you are addressing one or more imaginary characters, place these people either downstage of you or behind your auditioners at the back of the room or theatre. The latter will let you focus on a spot that is over the heads of your listeners. If you are addressing the audience, let your eyes sweep the room; but don't make your auditioners uncomfortable by watching them for reactions. If you are delivering a soliloquy, probably some lines should be said reflectively as though you are speaking your thoughts aloud and others as though you are talking to the audience. A careful analysis of your material is needed to determine where to look.

In performing two monologues, take just a moment after the first one to get your mind focused on the second. You may want to lower your eyes or head until you are in character.

SINGING AUDITIONS

Usually at both general and specific auditions for singers, you are asked to sing one song of your choice. If you do well, you may be given the chance to perform immediately a second song of a different type, or you may be requested to prepare a particular song for a later audition. The following are some suggestions for these situations.

Before the Audition

Even though the announcement of auditions may say to prepare one song, you should get ready at least two different types of songs of about one to three minutes each and rehearse them until you can do them properly and easily.

YOUR SONGS.   Select songs you do well that are reasonably similar in style to the musical you are auditioning for. Your two choices should, however, be different in mood and tempo to show off your versatility. The standard combination is an up-tempo number, like "Always True to You in My Fashion" from *Kiss Me, Kate,* and a ballad, such as "Almost Like Being in Love" from *Brigadoon.* If you can "belt," you may prepare one number of this type and another to show off your head voice.

Many students want to know, "Should I sing something from the show I'm auditioning for?" Unless you have been asked to do this, most experts say no. The reason is that, if you do not do the number as the director envisions it, the director may think that you cannot be taught to do it as he or she wants it. For the same reason, if the composer and lyricist are present, do not sing anything by them.

If the roles and ranges are publicized, select songs from different musicals that have about the same range and are sung by characters that are similar to the part you are interested in. If you are not aiming for one particular role, select songs that allow you to project your personality. In either case, start early to prepare your audition so that you will have sufficient time to rehearse it.

Try to find songs that others will not be singing at the audition. Avoid the current hits, but choose songs that will display the best aspects of your voice at the beginning. The reason is that sometimes you will be told to stop after only a few bars.

Do not use a patter song, but if you tend to get very nervous at auditions, select songs with moderately fast tempos.

Some songs, such as "The Heather on the Hill" from *Brigadoon,* can be sung by either sex. Other songs, like "I'm in Love with a Wonderful Guy" from *South Pacific,* are supposed to be sung by a woman while some, such as "There Is Nothing Like a Dame," also from *South Pacific,* were written for men to sing. Be sure that the lyrics are appropriate for you.

YOUR MUSIC.   Get the sheet music for your selections, and rehearse with a pianist or coach. If the songs are not in a good key for you, you will have to transpose them or get a copyist or other musician to do this. Never hand music to an accompanist and ask him or her to transpose it on the spot. If a stranger plays for you at an audition, you must be sure that the music is legible and that any special instructions, such as changes in tempo, repeats, and cuts, are clearly indicated.

Keep the music sheets clean and flat—do not fold or wrinkle them. If the music is on thin pages that fall off the piano rack easily, you should devise some way to help the accompanist keep them on the piano. If the music is on only one side of the paper, you can tape the sheets onto cardboard or tape them together (tape the right edge of page one to the left side of page two, the right edge of page two to the left edge of page three, and so on). When you finish, your two to five taped-together sheets should stay on the piano rack, and the accompanist should be able to read them easily without having to turn pages. If the pianist must use music in a book or music that you have put into a loose-leaf notebook, make certain that the pages will lie flat and can be turned easily.

ANALYSIS AND REHEARSAL.   Be sure you are singing the notes correctly and articulating the lyrics distinctly. The auditioners must understand every word you say. Remember, though, that you must go beyond this: you must interpret the song and act it as though you are a character in a musical production singing to a large audience. Those of you who suffer from stage fright while singing as yourself may find that your nervousness may be less if you concentrate on getting into the role and thinking and feeling like the character.

If your character is singing to someone, as in "You'll Never Get Away From Me" from *Gypsy,* imagine that this person is standing at the back of the room or theatre, and play to this character. If singing a number that in a show would be directed to the audience, such as "Let Me Entertain You" from *Gypsy,* let your gaze roam about the theatre or room as it would in a production. But avoid singing directly to your auditioners for very long.

Don't plan to stand in back of the accompanist to read the music over his or her shoulders. And don't hold the music or lyrics in your hands—you must memorize your material. Don't decide to sit down during your audition because a chair may not be available. And don't close your eyes too much while you sing because your eyes are an important way to communicate your feelings to an audience.

Start in a good body alignment with your weight on both feet placed about a foot to a foot and a half apart. As you sing, get involved in the song and let it excite you. Your gestures should flow naturally and your movements should appear spontaneous. If, however, you find it difficult to gesture naturally, consider holding a prop, such as a hat, cane, scarf, shawl, handkerchief, or some object you are singing about. If a prop is out of the question, you can let your hands hang relaxed at your sides for a while or clasp them lightly in front of you at your waist. If you wear a jacket, you can put one hand in the pocket and the other at your side or at your waist. But your goal should be to forget about your body and focus on the meaning of the lyrics. Then you may be able to move spontaneously in response to the music and words.

You should plan to move during any passages where the accompanist is playing but you do not sing (termed "air"), in order to hold your auditioners' attention until you sing again. You can walk downstage or to left or right stage, staying in lighted areas, of course. You must also decide on your posture for your final note: where should your hands and arms be during the rideout (the music used for your last word and the following music)? Are your arms rising above your head or to shoulder height? Or have they been up in the air on the previous line and are coming down on the rideout? There are numerous possibilities for the final pose: two arms up in the air or out to the side or down at your sides; one arm up in the air and the other down; fists clenched or hands opened; head back or bent over; a bow or a curtsy. Whatever you decide, make the ending special; it's the last thing they hear and see, and it may be the way they remember you.

YOUR ACCOMPANIMENT.   Find out if an accompanist will be provided at the audition; if not, get your rehearsal pianist to go with you or use a tape recording of instrumental music with no singing on it. Don't sing without accompaniment unless specifically requested to do so. Generally, it is not a good idea to plan to accompany yourself on piano or guitar because auditioners will want to see how you move while singing.

At the Audition

When you hand your music to an accompanist provided by the show, explain where to start and stop, the tempo, and any special instructions. Then go to the best lighted part of the stage or room. When you and your auditioners are ready, nod to the pianist to begin.

When you retrieve your music from the accompanist, remember to thank this person; aside from considerations of politeness, he or she may have a say about casting. Also, thank the others from the show who are present.

DANCE AUDITIONS

It has been noted that dancers are the most overworked and underpaid people of the theatre. Broadway's chorus dancers—called gypsies—work the longest hours with the least recognition, and careers are notoriously short. But if you still want to be a dancer, here are a few suggestions for coping with both general and specific auditions.

Before the Audition

Usually you do not have to prepare a routine in advance since normally the choreographer or an assistant will teach all dancers at the audition a combination that you will perform in small groups or alone. Occasionally, though, you may be asked to do a short dance of your own. If so, devise a routine ahead of time that shows off your abilities in the type(s) of dance they need for the show. Plan for your own musical accompaniment: If an accompanist will be provided, bring your sheet music; if not, bring your own pianist or a tape recording and player.

If you pass the dance audition, you will probably be asked to sing sixteen bars of a song, so go to the audition prepared to do at least two different types of songs. If singing makes you nervous, select songs with a medium fast tempo, move while you sing, and concentrate on being a character in a show who is energetically selling the song. (See "Preparing Songs" in chapter seven.)

Before going to any dance audition, warm up at home or in a dance class. Warm up again immediately before the tryout. There may be no place for this, but you must make a place whether it be in the wings, hallway, or rest room. Dancing without warming up, particularly while under stress at an audition, can result in injuries.

At the Audition

While auditioning, project an energetic, dynamic personality. Most show dancing is highly presentational, and choreographers generally look for dancers who can "fill the stage" with their energy.

When appropriate, smile. Do not audibly count the beats. And if you forget the steps, do something—don't stop. At a group audition, don't try to copy someone else's style. Concentrate on doing the routine to the best of *your* ability.

INTERVIEWS

There are times when an agent or a director, casting director, or other member of a production's staff will want to interview you to see if you should be given the chance to audition or just to find out more about you before deciding on casting. Professionally, if you are a member of Actors' Equity Association, you may attend specially scheduled interviews for principal roles. If you are selected to audition, you will then be given a specific time to return to try out.

While interviews can be stressful, the best strategy is to try to relax, be friendly, confident, cheerful, and talk about whatever is suggested by the interviewer. You are almost certain to be asked to give a summary of what you have done in the theatre, so be sure you have a good answer ready. Look at the interviewer, and communicate with that person clearly, concisely, and courteously. At the end, remember to thank those conducting the interview, the receptionist, doorkeeper, and others. You never know who may have input into casting.

PHOTOGRAPHS AND RÉSUMÉ

If auditioning professionally (and many times at nonprofessional auditions), you will need to submit an eight-by-ten-inch black-and-white photograph in glossy, semimatte, or matte finish. Good pictures are a necessity. You must have a flattering headshot that looks like you and conveys the image you want to project; it should be reasonably recent.

To the back of the picture, you should attach (with tape, paste, or staples) a one-page typed résumé cut down to the size of the photograph. To prepare your résumé, select from figure 9-1 the items that pertain to you (for example, if you do not belong to a union, omit "Union Affiliations"), and arrange them attractively on the page. You must include a telephone number at which you can be reached, but you should be careful to whom you give your home telephone and address. It is wise to use only your agent's telephone and address. If you do not have an agent, list only an answering service or a phone with an answering machine. If you have a post office box or a business address at which you can receive mail, you may want to list this as your mailing address, but usually you should not give your home address.

In addition to the picture to accompany your résumé, you should acquire photographs of yourself in other poses that indicate your abilities to play different types of roles and pictures of you in various theatrical productions. Arrange these in a portfolio with your favorable reviews, in case an interviewer asks to see your "book."

YOUR NAME

Union Affiliations: (If any.)

Agent: (If you have one.)   Height:

Agent's phone: (If you don't have an   Weight:
agent, give your answering service or
phone with an answering machine.)   Color of hair:

Agent's address: (If you don't have an   Color of eyes:
agent, you should probably *not* list an
address.)   Vocal range: Soprano, tenor, etc. If you
                                            can belt, add the word *belt*.)

                                            Dance skills: (List types you do well.)

Theatre experience: (Include acting, singing, and dance experience for this and
the next two items. Put your best credits first, listing name of show, role, and
where you performed it.)

Film:

Television:

Commercials: (If you have done these, put "list available on request" but don't go
into detail here.)

Training: (List teachers, if well known.)

Special talents: (Languages, dialects, accents you do well; other musical skills,
such as pianist or guitarist; athletic abilities; circus skills; and the like.)

Awards: (If applicable.)

Figure 9-1.   Résumé form.

If you are sending your picture and résumé by mail to ask for an interview or audition, you will need to write a cover letter that is typed on attractive stationery. Take time to compose a short, interesting letter that mentions the names of any mutual friends and states your request succinctly.

After an audition or interview, you should follow up by writing a note to thank the person for his or her consideration. Postcard-sized photos of you that include your name and telephone are handy to send to important people to tell them what you are doing and remind them of what you can do.

NOTICES OF AUDITIONS

Where do you learn the time and place of auditions? If you are in New York or Los Angeles, you should watch the theatrical trade papers as well as the theatre pages of newspapers. The trade papers in New York are *Back Stage* and *Show Business;* in Los Angeles, *Drama-Logue, The Hollywood Reporter,* and *Hollywood Variety.* In addition, *Variety* is sold in most cities and can be found in many libraries. Theatrical agents also receive information about auditions, and dance studios often post notices of dance auditions. Members of Actors' Equity Association may look at announcements in the offices of the union, but anyone may visit the office of the Theatre Communications Group in New York to find out about auditions for regional theatres. Knowing other performers is a help too, because a lot of casting news is spread by word-of-mouth.

Outside of New York and Los Angeles, the theatre sections of newspapers, *Variety,* and the local offices of the Actors' Equity Association are your best sources of information. Another way is to call or write the theatrical organizations with which you would like to perform. You may send your picture and résumé and ask to be notified about their next auditions. Be sure to enclose a stamped, self-addressed envelope for a reply.

The Theatre Communications Group can provide you with a list of regional theatres for a small fee. From the Actors' Equity Association you can obtain the names of Equity-approved theatrical agents, but a more complete list of agents, plus casting directors and other information, may be found in *Ross Reports Television,* which is a monthly publication of Television Index, Inc., in New York. The yellow pages of phone books may also contain a list of theatrical agents in the area covered by that book. In addition, Lawrence S. Epstein's *A Guide to Theatre in America,* which your public library should have, provides lists of agents, producers, and theatres that produce their own shows.

EXERCISES

1. Following the suggestions in this chapter, prepare for a general acting audition by finding two one-minute monologues from musicals or plays. Rehearse the material; then present it before others at a mock audition.

2. Prepare a one-minute singing audition, following the guidelines in this chapter. Rehearse the song with an accompanist or with taped instrumental music, and perform it before others for their criticism.

3. Prepare a one-minute dance audition using piano accompaniment or taped music. Choreograph and rehearse your routine; then present it at a mock audition.

10

SCENES FROM MUSICALS FOR REHEARSAL

JULIAN [a producer-director]: Best? That's not good enough! I want better than your best, I want sheer, unadulterated brilliance!

—from *42nd Street*

In this chapter you will find sixteen short excerpts from famous musicals for you to study, rehearse, and use to demonstrate your "unadulterated brilliance." The following is a brief summary of the suggestions given in chapter seven for preparing your role:

1. Read the entire script and answer the questions under "Analyzing the Musical and Role" in chapter seven. Examine your character's main objective for the whole show and the objectives, motivations, and actions for your scene. Determine your character's thoughts, feelings, and attitudes toward others in the excerpt, and study the meanings of the words of the text.

2. Research the musical to give yourself a good background for working on this part. Find out about the bookwriter, lyricist, and composer, the source, the New York production, and the times and places depicted in the show.

3. Observe people who are similar to your character in age, personality, occupation, or in some significant way; then, at home, recreate what you saw. Did you obtain any ideas for your character from these observations?

4. Personalize the character by examining your own sensory and emotional experiences that are similar to your character's. Do these help you to understand why the character behaves as she or he does?

5. Use your imagination to flesh out the details of your characterization. Try Stanislavski's "magic if"; ask yourself, "What would I do *if* I were this person in this situation?"

155

6. With your partner(s), plan the blocking of your scene; then, learn your lines and movements together.

7. Prepare externally for your character by working on your voice, posture, stage business, and movements. Are you trying to physicalize the psychological and physical traits of your character? How would you describe the rhythm of the character in movement and speech?

8. Pay particular attention to your vocal characterization. Are you using the right dialect or accent? Should the pitch range, rate of speaking, overall loudness level, quality of tone, articulation, or rhythm be different from your usual way of speaking? Can you be heard and understood? Do you have an appropriate variation of pitch, rate, loudness, and quality?

9. Prepare internally by trying to think the thoughts and feel the emotions of the character as you rehearse and perform. Listen to your partner(s), think about what they say, and respond to them.

10. Experiment in rehearsal. Be sure that you and your partner(s) know what the stage, scenery, properties, lighting, and sound should be like even though you may be working in a bare room with just a couple of chairs and no sound effects. Imagine your environment and respond to it as your character would. Do an improvisation of what has happened to your character immediately before your scene starts, and consider how these happenings affect your attitude, thoughts, and feelings at the beginning of the excerpt. Try improvising events that are spoken of in your scene but are not shown onstage, and experiment with speaking the inner monologue, reversing roles with your partner(s), and playing opposite values. (See "Rehearsing" in chapter seven.)

Ten of the following scenes have songs and music. While only a few call for dancing, all need coordinated movement. In addition to the above suggestions, if you sing and dance in your scene, you should also do the following:

1. As you recite the lyrics of the song, physicalize the traits, thoughts, and emotions.

2. Work with an accompanist on articulation, phrasing, interpretation, tempo, energy, and communication of the song.

3. Consult with your partner(s) about the movements or dancing needed during the song.

For scenework, you do not need a director, musical director, choreographer, scenery, stage lighting, sound effects, or stage makeup. If there is a song in your scene, you will need an accompanist and a piano. For some scenes you may need a few chairs and a table. Hand props (such as the jewelry, ring, and slippers in the scene from *My Fair Lady*) should be used if they are easy to obtain. If any unavailable props are called for in a scene, you can pantomime handling them or use substitute props. Wear clothing, shoes, and a hairstyle that are similar to what your character might wear, and use or do not use eyeglasses according to what your character would do.

SCENE FOR THREE MEN FROM
ACT II OF *IOLANTHE* (1882) BY W. S.
GILBERT AND ARTHUR SULLIVAN

CHARACTERS: *The Lord Chancellor*
   Earl of Mountararat
   Earl Tolloller

SETTING: *The palace yard at Westminster. Westminster Hall is left and a clock tower is upstage.*

TIME: *Night.*

SITUATION: *All three of the gentlemen in this scene are attracted to Phyllis, a beautiful ward of the Lord Chancellor. But the Lord Chancellor feels that he cannot apply to himself for permission to marry her. After singing about his unrequited love for Phyllis, he has fallen exhausted onto a seat as Mountararat and Tolloller enter. They have decided that their friendship with each other is more important than feuding over Phyllis, so in this scene they convince the Lord Chancellor that he may, indeed, approach himself for permission to marry Phyllis.*

COMMENTS: *The Lord Chancellor is described as a kindly old gentleman, and all three are depicted as rich and plain. Mountararat and Tolloller may be dressed in appropriate peers' clothing: swallow-tail coat, knee breeches, stockings, long robe, and coronet. The Lord Chancellor wears his official robe.*

PUBLISHED TEXTS: *Gilbert, W. S., and Arthur Sullivan.* The Complete Plays of Gilbert and Sullivan. *New York: The Modern Library, 1936.*
   Gilbert, W. S. The Savoy Operas. *2 vols. London: Oxford University Press, 1962.*

(LORDS MOUNTARARAT *and* TOLLOLLER *come forward*)

LORD MOUNTARARAT: I am much distressed to see your Lordship in this condition.

LORD CHANCELLOR: Ah, my Lords, it is seldom that a Lord Chancellor has reason to envy the position of another, but I am free to confess that I would rather be two Earls engaged to Phyllis than any other half-dozen noblemen upon the face of the globe.

LORD TOLLOLLER: (*Without enthusiasm*) Yes. It's an enviable position when you're the only one.

LORD MOUNTARARAT: Oh yes, no doubt—most enviable. At the same time, seeing you thus, we naturally say to ourselves, "This is very sad. His Lordship is constitutionally as blithe as a bird—he trills upon the bench like a thing of song and gladness. His series of judgments in F sharp minor, given *andante* in six-eight time, are among the most remarkable effects ever produced in a Court of Chancery. He is, perhaps, the only living instance of a judge whose decrees have received the honour of a double *encore*. How can we bring ourselves to do that which will deprive the Court of Chancery of one of its most attractive features?"

LORD CHANCELLOR: I feel the force of your remarks, but I am here in two capacities, and they clash, my Lord, they clash! I deeply grieve to say that in declining to entertain my last application to myself, I presumed to address myself in terms which render it impossible for me ever to apply to myself again. It was a most painful scene, my Lord—most painful!

LORD TOLLOLLER: This is what it is to have two capacities! Let us be thankful that we are persons of no capacity whatever.

LORD MOUNTARARAT: Come, come. Remember you are a very just and kindly old gentleman, and you need have no hesitation in approaching yourself, so that you do so respectfully and with a proper show of deference.

LORD CHANCELLOR: Do you really think so?

LORD MOUNTARARAT: I do.

LORD CHANCELLOR: Well, I will nerve myself to another effort, and, if that fails, I resign myself to my fate!

(*Trio*—LORD CHANCELLOR, LORDS MOUNTARARAT *and* TOLLOLLER)

LORD MOUNTARARAT:

If you go in
You're sure to win—
Yours will be the charming maidie:
Be your law
The ancient saw,
"Faint heart never won fair lady!"

ALL:

Faint heart never won fair lady!
Every journey has an end—
When at the worst affairs will mend—
Dark the dawn when day is nigh—
Hustle your horse and don't say die!

LORD TOLLOLLER:

He who shies
At such a prize
Is not worth a maravedi,
Be so kind
To bear in mind—
Faint heart never won fair lady!

ALL:

Faint heart never won fair lady!
While the sun shines make your hay—
Where a will is, there's a way—
Beard the lion in his lair—
None but the brave deserve the fair!

LORD CHANCELLOR:

I'll take heart
And make a start—
Though I fear the prospect's shady—
Much I'd spend
To gain my end—
Faint heart never won fair lady!

ALL:
    Faint heart never won fair lady!
      Nothing venture, nothing win—
      Blood is thick, but water's thin—
      In for a penny, in for a pound—
      It's Love that makes the world go round!
            (Dance, and exeunt arm-in-arm together)

HE WHO SHIES AT SUCH A PRIZE

Words by W. S. Gilbert   **(From *Iolanthe*)**   **Music by Arthur Sullivan**

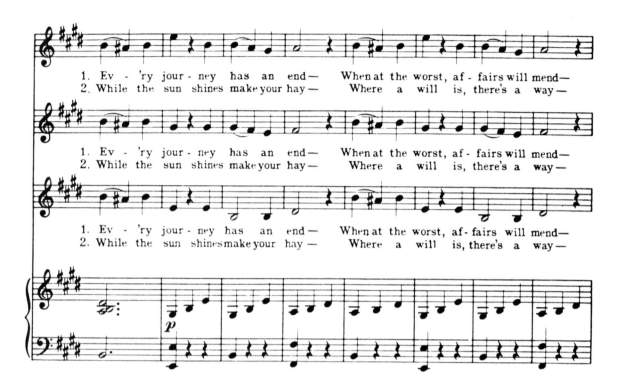

1. Ev - 'ry jour - ney has an end— When at the worst, af - fairs will mend—
2. While the sun shines make your hay — Where a will is, there's a way—

1. Ev - 'ry jour - ney has an end— When at the worst, af - fairs will mend—
2. While the sun shines make your hay — Where a will is, there's a way—

1. Ev - 'ry jour - ney has an end— When at the worst, af - fairs will mend—
2. While the sun shines make your hay — Where a will is, there's a way—

Dark the dawn when day is nigh— Hus-tle your horse and don't say die!
Beard the li - on in his lair— None but the brave de-serve the fair!

Dark the dawn when day is nigh— Hus-tle your horse and don't say die!
Beard the li - on in his lair— None but the brave de-serve the fair!

Dark the dawn when day is nigh— Hus-tle your horse and don't say die!
Beard the li - on in his lair— None but the brave de-serve the fair!

Ld. Chan.

I'll __ take heart   And make a   start—   Though I

fear   the pros - pect's sha - dy__   Much I'd spend   To   gain __ my

end—   "Faint   heart   nev - er   won   fair   la - dy!"

in for a pound— It's Love that makes the world go round!_____

in for a pound— It's Love that makes the world go round!_____

in for a pound— It's Love that makes the world go round!_____

*(Dance, and **exeunt arm-in-arm** together.)*

SCENE FOR ONE MAN, ONE WOMAN
FROM ACT I OF *THE MIKADO* (1885) BY
W. S. GILBERT AND ARTHUR SULLIVAN

CHARACTERS: *Nanki-Poo, son of the Mikado of Japan*
Yum-Yum, ward of Ko-Ko, Lord High Executioner of Titipu

SETTING: *Courtyard of Ko-Ko's official residence in Titipu, Japan.*

TIME: *The morning of the day when Yum-Yum is to marry Ko-Ko.*

SITUATION: *A year earlier Nanki-Poo, disguised as a wandering minstrel, met and fell in love with Yum-Yum, but because she was engaged to her guardian Ko-Ko, Nanki-Poo left town in despair. However, when he heard that Ko-Ko was condemned to death for flirting, he hurried back hoping to marry Yum-Yum but found that Ko-Ko had been given a reprieve and made the Lord High Executioner.*

COMMENTS: *Both Yum-Yum and Nanki-Poo—who is still disguised in this scene as a minstrel—are good-looking, young, and in love. While their manners, costumes, and hairstyles may suggest those of Japan in the late nineteenth century, the diction and spirit of this scene is that of British comic opera.*

PUBLISHED TEXTS: *Gilbert, W. S., and Arthur Sullivan.* The Complete Plays of Gilbert and Sullivan. *New York: The Modern Library, 1936.*
Gilbert, W. S. The Savoy Operas. *2 vols. London: Oxford University Press, 1962.*

(*Enter* NANKI-POO)

NANKI-POO: Yum-Yum, at last we are alone! I have sought you night and day for three weeks, in the belief that your guardian was beheaded, and I find that you are about to be married to him this afternoon!

YUM-YUM: Alas, yes!

NANKI-POO: But you do not love him?

YUM-YUM: Alas, no!

NANKI-POO: Modified rapture! But why do you not refuse him?

YUM-YUM: What good would that do? He's my guardian, and he wouldn't let me marry you!

NANKI-POO: But I would wait until you were of age!

YUM-YUM: You forget that in Japan girls do not arrive at years of discretion until they are fifty.

NANKI-POO: True; from seventeen to forty-nine are considered years of indiscretion.

YUM-YUM: Besides—a wandering minstrel, who plays a wind instrument outside tea-houses, is hardly a fitting husband for the ward of a Lord High Executioner.

NANKI-POO: But—(*Aside*) Shall I tell her? Yes! She will not betray me! (*Aloud*) What if it should prove that, after all, I am no musician?

YUM-YUM: There! I was certain of it, directly I heard you play!

NANKI-POO: What if it should prove that I am no other than the son of his Majesty the Mikado?

YUM-YUM: The son of the Mikado! But why is your Highness disguised? And what has your Highness done? And will your Highness promise never to do it again?

NANKI-POO: Some years ago I had the misfortune to captivate Katisha, an elderly lady of my father's Court. She misconstrued my customary affability into expressions of affection, and claimed me in marriage, under my father's law. My father, the Lucius Junius Brutus of his race, ordered me to marry her within a week, or perish ignominiously on the scaffold. That night I fled his Court, and, assuming the disguise of a Second Trombone, I joined the band in which you found me when I had the happiness of seeing you! (*Approaching her*)

YUM-YUM: (*Retreating*) If you please, I think you Highness had better not come too near. The laws against flirting are excessively severe.

NANKI-POO: But we are quite alone, and nobody can see us.

YUM-YUM: Still, that doesn't make it right. To flirt is capital.

NANKI-POO: It *is* capital!

YUM-YUM: And we must obey the law.

NANKI-POO: Deuce take the law!

YUM-YUM: I wish it would, but it won't!

NANKI-POO: If it were not for that, how happy we might be!

YUM-YUM: Happy indeed!

NANKI-POO: If it were not for the law, we should now be sitting side by side, like that. (*Sits by her*)

YUM-YUM: Instead of being obliged to sit half a mile off, like that. (*Crosses and sits at other side of stage*)

NANKI-POO: We should be gazing into each other's eyes, like that. (*Gazing at her sentimentally*)

YUM-YUM: Breathing sighs of unutterable love—like that. (*Sighing and gazing lovingly at him*)

NANKI-POO: With our arms round each other's waists, like that. (*Embracing her*)

YUM-YUM: Yes, if it wasn't for the law.

NANKI-POO: If it wasn't for the law.

YUM-YUM: As it is, of course we couldn't do anything of the kind.

NANKI-POO: Not for worlds!

YUM-YUM: Being engaged to Ko-Ko, you know!

NANKI-POO: Being engaged to Ko-Ko!

(*Duet*—YUM-YUM *and* NANKI-POO)

NANKI-POO:

Were you not to Ko-Ko plighted,
   I would say in tender tone,
"Loved one, let us be united—
   Let us be each other's own!"
I would merge all rank and station,
   Worldly sneers are nought to us,
And, to mark my admiration,
   I would kiss you fondly thus—

(*Kisses her*)

BOTH:

    I   } would kiss {you} fondly thus—(*Kiss*)
    He }   { me }

YUM-YUM:

    But as I'm engaged to Ko-Ko,
    To embrace you thus, *con fuoco,*
    Would distinctly be no *gioco,*
    And for that I should get toco—

BOTH:

    Toco, toco, toco, toco!

NANKI-POO:

    So, in spite of all temptation,
      Such a theme I'll not discuss,
    And on no consideration
      Will I kiss you fondly thus—
              (*Kissing her*)
    Let me make it clear to you,
    This is what I'll never do!
      This, oh, this, oh, this, oh, this—
              (*Kissing her*)

TOGETHER:

    This, oh, this, etc.

          (*Exeunt in opposite directions*)

WERE YOU NOT TO KO-KO PLIGHTED

Words by W. S. Gilbert   **(From *The Mikado*)**   **Music by Arthur Sullivan**

(Exeunt in opposite directions)

SCENE FOR ONE MAN, ONE WOMAN FROM ACT I, SCENE 2 OF *BRIGADOON* (1947) BY ALAN JAY LERNER AND FREDERICK LOEWE

CHARACTERS: *Tommy Albright*
               Fiona MacLaren

SETTING: *MacConnachy Square in the Scottish village of Brigadoon. A fair is in progress in this Highland town that has the look of an eighteenth-century community. Booths and carts are onstage with some chairs and benches.*

TIME: *About 9 A.M. of a day in May.*

SITUATION: *Tommy and his friend, Jeff, both Americans, have come to Scotland to hunt game and have wandered into this village that is not on their map. (Later in Scene 5 they will discover that two hundred years ago a man asked God to make Brigadoon vanish into the mist and return just as it was for one day every hundred years.) Tommy has met Fiona and has been invited to the wedding supper for her sister and Charlie to be held that evening. By the beginning of the following excerpt, most of the townspeople have departed, leaving only a few who are quietly shopping upstage. Tommy's first line refers to Charlie, who has just exited.*

COMMENTS: *Tommy, from Georgia, is about thirty, virile looking with an attractive, sensitive face. He is dressed in tweeds. Fiona, about twenty-two, is attractive, bright, frank, and direct. She is in simple Scottish peasant garb. This is a good scene for two actors to use to practice the American southern and Scottish dialects.*

PUBLISHED TEXTS: *Lerner, Alan Jay, and Frederick Loewe.* Brigadoon. *New York: Coward-McCann, Inc., 1947.*

Richards, Stanley (ed.). Ten Great Musicals of the American Theatre. *Radnor, PA: Chilton Book Company, 1973.*

TOMMY: (*Smiling*) He's a nice kid.

FIONA: Aye. He is that.

TOMMY: It's wonderfully refreshing to see a fellow so enthusiastic about getting married.

FIONA: Is it so unusual?

TOMMY: I think it is. Look at me. I'm not bubbling over like Charlie. And next month I'm facing the minister.

FIONA: Ye're gettin' married?

TOMMY: Yes.

FIONA: Oh!

TOMMY: Oh—what?

FIONA: I'm very surprised. Somehow ye dinna look like the sort of lad who would want to settle down.

TOMMY: I didn't say that. I just said I was getting married.

FIONA: If ye feel that way, why are ye?

TOMMY: Because the girl wants to.

FIONA: Is that reason enough?

TOMMY: Sure. I don't know how it is in the Highlands, but in my neighborhood if you've been going with a woman for a while and she decides she wants to get married, you'd better agree right away and save yourself a lot of trouble.

FIONA: Why?

TOMMY: Because if you don't, she'll either torment you so you'll marry her for relief, or she'll be so sweet about it you'll feel guilty and your conscience will make you do it.

FIONA: I mus' say it dinna sound like ye love her very much.

TOMMY: It doesn't, does it?

FIONA: An' it also sounds like a very peculiar land ye come from.

TOMMY: Well, believe me, lass, this isn't the usual hamlet off the highway either. What was that business about Charlie and the man who postponed the miracle?

FIONA: Oh, that. (*Thinks a moment*) I'm sorry. I canna say.

TOMMY: But you said you'd tell me later.

FIONA: I know. But I canna say.

TOMMY: That's fine. You know, if I hang around this town very long I'll probably discover that everybody in it is slightly nutty. Is that possible?

FIONA: I canna say.

TOMMY: Why not?

FIONA: I dinna know what "nutty" means.

TOMMY: It means slightly insane.

FIONA: (*Turning on him suddenly*) Well, then I can assure ye we're all far from insane. We're a most blessed group of people. An' I·never realize how fortunate we are until I meet someone from the outside—I mean, a stranger to Brigadoon. I dinna know anythin' about ye, but from the little ye've said I'm quite certain that everythin' ye think I think differently about, an' I'm also quite certain that what I think is much more . . . (*She begins to calm down*) . . . well . . . pleasant. An' now I'm sorry I said all that, but ye angered me when ye called us insane.

TOMMY: (*Quite surprised and a bit sheepish at the outburst*) Hey, you don't like me very much, do you?

FIONA: That's the odd part. I like ye very much. I jus' dinna like anythin' ye say.

TOMMY: (*After a moment*) Fiona . . .

FIONA: Aye?

TOMMY: If I stuck around here today, would you take me to the wedding this evening?

FIONA: Why do ye suddenly want to go?

TOMMY: (*Imitating her*) I canna say.

FIONA: Well, I'll take ye. An' I'll be highly pleased ye'll be there.

TOMMY: You will? Why?

FIONA: Because of what I jus' told ye. I like ye very much.

TOMMY: (*Amused and a little bewildered*) That's right. You did say that, didn't you?

FIONA: Now I'll show ye some place where ye can lie down an' rest.

TOMMY: What are you going to do?

FIONA: Gather some heather for the weddin.'

TOMMY: Where do you do that?

FIONA: On the hill—where the heather is.

TOMMY: May I go with you?

FIONA: No. I'll do it much faster alone.

TOMMY: (*Coming close to her*) I won't bother you. Really. Maybe I'm the one who's slightly nutty, but . . .
    (FIONA *walks away from him. The music begins.*)

TOMMY: (*Sings "The Heather On The Hill"*)
    Can't we two go walkin' together,
    Out beyond the valley of trees,
    Out where there's a hillside of heather
    Curtseyin' gently in the breeze?
    That's what I'd like to do:
    See the heather—but with you.

    The mist of May is in the gloamin',
    And all the clouds are holdin' still,
    So take my hand and let's go roamin'
    Through the heather on the hill.

    The mornin' dew is blinkin' yonder;
    There's lazy music in the rill;
    And all I want to do is wander
    Through the heather on the hill.

    There may be other days as rich and rare.
    There may be other springs as full and fair.
    But they won't be the same—they'll come and go;
    For this I know:

    That when the mist is in the gloamin',
    And all the clouds are holdin' still,
    If you're not there I won't go roamin'
    Through the heather on the hill;
    The heather on the hill.
    (*The music continues under*)

FIONA: (*A little disconcerted*) Ye see. Ye can say nice things when ye want to.

TOMMY: It almost sounded like I was making love to you, didn't it?

FIONA: Oh! There's a difference between makin' love an' jus' bein' sentimental because ye're tired.

TOMMY: Is that what I'm being—sentimental because I'm tired?

FIONA: I believe so. But 'tis very agreeable.
    (*Sings*)
    The mist of May is in the gloamin',
    An' all the clouds are holdin' still,

So take my hand and we'll go roamin'
Through the heather on the hill.

The mornin' dew is blinkin' yonder;
There's lazy music in the rill;
An' 'tis a lovely time to wander
Through the heather on the hill.

There may be other days as rich an' rare.
There may be other springs as full an' fair.
But they won't be the same—they'll come an' go.

TOMMY *and* FIONA:

For this I know:
That when the mist is in the gloamin',
And all the clouds are holdin' still,
If you're not there I won't go roamin'
Through the heather on the hill;
The heather on the hill.

(*The music stops and* TOMMY *and* FIONA *stand looking at each other*)

THE HEATHER ON THE HILL

Words by Alan Jay Lerner   (From *Brigadoon*)   **Music by Frederick Loewe**

Cue: **TOMMY:**   May I go with you?

FIONA: No. I'll do it much faster alone. (*The music begins*)

TOMMY: I won't bother you. Really. Maybe I'm the one who's slightly nutty, but...

B REFRAIN

The mist of May is in the gloam-in'; And all the clouds are hold-in' still.

So take my hand and let's go roam-in' Through the

heath - er on the hill. The morn-in' dew is blink-in'

yon - der; There's la - zy mu - sic in the rill;

SCENE FOR ONE MAN, ONE WOMAN FROM ACT I, SCENE 3 OF *KISS ME, KATE* (1948) BY COLE PORTER AND SAMUEL AND BELLA SPEWACK

CHARACTERS: *Lilli Vanessi*
Fred Graham

SETTING: *Two dressing rooms at the Ford Theatre in Baltimore. Fred's room at the right is drab and sparsely furnished. Lilli's room at the left is elaborately decorated. The following excerpt takes place in her room.*

TIME: *Thirty minutes before the opening of a musical version of Shakespeare's* The Taming of the Shrew *in which Fred and Lilli star.*

SITUATION: *Divorced from Fred for one year, Lilli has become engaged to a presidential advisor, Harrison Howell. Rehearsals for the* Shrew *have not been pleasant as the two stars have been fighting.*

COMMENTS: *Fred is a writer, director, and actor. His former wife, Lilli, is a motion picture star who is returning to the stage for this production. They are both in dressing gowns as they are getting ready for opening night. During this scene, Fred and Lilli waltz to "Wunderbar." If you cannot waltz, look at the instructions in chapter four under rhythm exercise 2.*

PUBLISHED TEXTS: *Spewack, Samuel and Bella, and Cole Porter.* Kiss Me, Kate. *New York: Alfred A. Knopf, 1953.*

Richards, Stanley (ed.). Ten Great Musicals of the American Theatre. *Radnor, PA: Chilton Book Company, 1973.*

(LILLI *displays resplendent ring for* FRED's *benefit*)

FRED: I see it! I see it! What is it? The Hope Diamond or Aly Khan's emerald?

LILLI: Did I show you the star sapphire Harrison sent me? It was his mother's engagement ring.

FRED: His mother must have worn it on her big toe.

LILLI: (*Beaming pridefully*) And now it's mine! (*Sits on couch*)

FRED: Congratulations!

LILLI: Do you know what day this is, Fred? Our anniversary, and you forgot.

FRED: What anniversary?

LILLI: (*Sweetly*) The first anniversary of our divorce.

FRED: If you must know, I was thinking of sending you a cactus. But, no money. I know you're rolling in it.

LILLI: Every night before I go to bed, that's exactly what I do. Roll in my money. Wonderful for the hips. (*She pats one and moves to sit at dressing table*)

FRED: (*Bitterly*) Hollywood—swimming pool—avocado ranches. While I—I put every penny I could scrape, borrow, or steal into my *Cyrano* in Paris. My magnum opus! But I was a huge success.

LILLI: (*Looking into mirror*) And you closed on Saturday? Four glorious performances!

FRED: I'll have you know, there was a general strike!

LILLI: (*With mock sympathy and looking right at* FRED) Oh, you couldn't have been that bad!

FRED: Same old Lilli! (*Picks up photo on dresser*) Who's this little monster? Harrison Howell?

LILLI: That's you at the age of two—bottoms up!

FRED: Cute little fellow. Mind if I keep it?

LILLI: No. And you can have this, too. (*Holding up cork and rising*)

FRED: What's this? A cork?

LILLI: Our first bottle of champagne.

FRED: Our wedding breakfast?

LILLI: Yes, in my apartment.

FRED: You mean that one room of yours over the Armenian bakery?

LILLI: You're a fine one to complain. You didn't even have a room.

FRED: Why do you think I married you? (*Sits on couch*)

LILLI: (*Thinking back*) That was the season we played the Barter Theatre in Virginia and they gave you a ham.

FRED: (*Stung*) Well, we lived on that all winter, you forget!

LILLI: *You* forget I got a job reading tea leaves in a Gypsy tea room opposite Macy's. (*Sits on couch beside him*)

FRED: And *you* forget *I* demonstrated shaving soap in Woolworth's.

LILLI: (*Suddenly remembering*) That's right. That's how I spent my honeymoon—at Woolworth's. Watching you shave.

FRED: We weren't married then?

LILLI: (*Nodding*) Oh yes, dear, we were. Mother was coming to stay with us. It was right after we closed on the road in a little British makeshift of a Viennese operetta that for some reason was laid in Switzerland. But the costumes were Dutch.

FRED: And so were those salaries. I could have sworn it was right after that flop revival of the *Prince of Potsdam.* Yes, I was understudying the lead. I was the youngest understudy in the business.

LILLI: No, dear. We were both in the chorus. (*Music starts*) There was a waltz in it. Remember? Something about a bar. (*She starts to hum*)

FRED: (*Rises*) Ja! Madame, you are ravishing tonight . . . You have made me the happiest of men.

LILLI: (*Rising, goes to* FRED) Your Highness. (*Both suddenly remember and speak*)

FRED: *Wunderbar!*

LILLI: *Wunderbar!*

FRED and LILLI: (*Sing "Wunderbar"*)

SHE: *Wunderbar.*

HE: *Wunderbar.*

SHE: There's our fav'rite star above.

HE: What a bright-shining star!

BOTH: Like our love, it's *wunderbar!*

(FRED, back of lounge. LILLI sits on lounge)
(Verse)

HE: Gazing down on the Jungfrau

SHE: From our secret chalet for two,

HE: Let us drink, *Liebchen mein,*

SHE: In the moonlight benign,

BOTH: To the joy of our dream come true.

(*Refrain*)

BOTH: *Wunderbar, wunderbar!*

(*He takes her hand*)

HE: What a perfect night for love,

SHE: Here am I, here you are, (*Rises*)

HE: Why, it's truly *wunderbar!*

BOTH: *Wunderbar, wunderbar!*

HE: We're alone and hand in glove,

SHE: Not a cloud near or far,

HE: Why, it's more than *wunderbar!*

SHE: Say you care, dear,

HE: For you madly.

SHE: Say you long, dear,

HE: For your kiss.

SHE: Do you swear, dear? (*Turns and takes his hand*)

HE: Darling, gladly,

SHE: Life's divine, dear,

HE: And you're mine, dear!

(*Embrace*)

BOTH: *Wunderbar, wunderbar!*

HE: There's our fav'rite star above,

SHE: What a bright-shining star!

BOTH: Like our love, it's *wunderbar!*

(*They waltz a bit*)

HE: And you're mine, dear!

(*Embrace*)

BOTH: *Wunderbar, wunderbar!*

(*Sway*)

HE: There's our fav'rite star above,

BOTH: What a bright-shining star!
     Like our love, it's *wunderbar!*

(*They kiss at end of song*)

WUNDERBAR

(From *Kiss Me, Kate*)   Words and Music by Cole Porter

cue: LILLI: No, dear. We were both in the Chorus!

SCENE FOR ONE MAN, ONE WOMAN FROM ACT I, SCENE 7 OF *SOUTH PACIFIC* (1949) BY RICHARD RODGERS, OSCAR HAMMERSTEIN II, AND JOSHUA LOGAN

CHARACTERS: *Ensign Nellie Forbush*
Emile de Becque

SETTING: *A beach on an island in the South Pacific where some sailors have erected a makeshift shower.*

TIME: *A day during World War II.*

SITUATION: *In the first scene, Emile told Nellie that he had left France twenty-five years ago because he had killed a man. Later, she was asked by her commanding officer to spy on Emile so that the U.S. Navy could learn more about him; but by this scene she has decided to break off with him and has sung "I'm Gonna Wash That Man Right Outa My Hair" to her friends as she washed her hair onstage. While drying her hair, she became aware of Emile's presence and went back into the shower to put a jersey over her wet shorts and halter. As the following begins, she comes out, carrying a towel, and says "Hello" as though she is surprised to find Emile there. Her friends have just exited to leave them alone.*

COMMENTS: *Nellie, an optimistic, vivacious young lady from Little Rock, Arkansas, is a Navy nurse who is stationed on this island. Emile, who owns a nearby plantation, is a charming, middle-aged man, with a slight French accent.*

PUBLISHED TEXTS: *Rodgers, Richard, Oscar Hammerstein II, and Joshua Logan. South Pacific. New York: Random House, 1949.*

Rodgers, Richard, and Oscar Hammerstein II. Six Plays by Rodgers and Hammerstein. New York: Random House, 1963.

NELLIE: Hello!

EMILE: Hello. . . . That song . . . is it a new American song?

NELLIE: It's an American type song. We were kind of putting in our own words. (*Looking around*) Where *is* everybody?

EMILE: It is strange with your American songs. In all of them one is either desirous to get rid of one's lover, or one weeps for a man one cannot have.

NELLIE: That's right.

EMILE: I like a song that says: "I love you and you love me . . . And isn't that fine?"

NELLIE: (*Not very bright at the moment*) Yes . . . that's fine.

EMILE: I left a note for you at the hospital. It was to ask you to my home for dinner next Friday.

NELLIE: Well, I don't think I'll be able to come, Emile, I—

EMILE: I have asked all my friends. The planters' colony.

NELLIE: (*Determined to wash him out of her hair*) A big party. Well then, if I can't come, you won't miss me.

EMILE: But it is *for* you. It is for my friends to meet you and—more important—for you to meet them; to give you an idea of what your life would be like here. I want you to know more about me . . . how I live and think—

NELLIE: (*Suddenly remembering her promise to "spy on him"*) More about you?

EMILE: Yes. You know very little about me.

NELLIE: That's right! (*Getting down to business*) Would you sit down? (EMILE *sits.* NELLIE *paces like a cross-examiner*) Do you think about politics much . . . And if so what do you think about politics?

EMILE: Do you mean my political philosophy?

NELLIE: I think that's what I mean.

EMILE: Well, to begin with, I believe in the free life—in freedom for everyone.

NELLIE: (*Eagerly*) Like in the Declaration of Independence?

EMILE: C'est ça. All men are created equal, isn't it?

NELLIE: Emile! You really believe that?

EMILE: Yes.

NELLIE: (*With great relief*) Well, thank goodness!

EMILE: It is why I am here . . . Why I killed a man.

NELLIE: (*Brought back to her mission*) Oh, yes. I meant to ask you about that too . . . I don't want you to think I'm prying into your private life, asking a lot of questions. But . . . I always think it's interesting why a person . . . kills another person.

(EMILE *smiles understandingly.*)

EMILE: Of course, Nellie. That has worried you. (*He turns away to compose his story. Then he begins by stating what he considers the explanation and excuse for the whole thing*) When I was a boy, I carried my heart in my hand. . . . So . . . when this man came to our town—though my father said he was good—I thought he was bad. (*With a shrug and a smile*) I was young . . . He attracted all the mean and cruel people to him. Soon he was running our town! He could do anything—take anything . . . I did not like that. I was young. (NELLIE *nods, understanding*) I stood up in the public square and made a speech. I called upon everyone to stand with me against this man.

NELLIE: What did they do?

EMILE: (*Letting his hands fall helplessly to his side*) They walked away!

NELLIE: Why?

EMILE: Because they saw him standing behind me. I turned, and he said to me, "I am going to kill you now." We fought. I was never so strong. I knocked him to the ground. And when he fell, his head struck a stone and . . . (*He turns away and lets* NELLIE *imagine the rest*) I ran to the waterfront and joined a cargo boat. I didn't even know where it was going. I stepped off that boat into another world . . . (*He looks around him, loving all he sees*) where I am now . . . and where I want to stay. (*He turns to* NELLIE *and impulsively steps toward her, deep sincerity and anxiety in his voice*) Nellie, will you marry me? . . . There are so few days in our life, Nellie. The time I have with you now is precious to me . . . Have you been thinking?

NELLIE: I have been thinking.

(*Singing, thoughtful, considering*)

Born on the opposite side of the sea,
We are as different as people can be,

EMILE: It's true.

NELLIE:

And yet you want to marry me. . . .

EMILE: I do.

NELLIE:

I've known you a few short weeks and yet
Somehow you've made my heart forget
All other men I have ever met
But you . . . but you . . .

EMILE: (Sings)

Some enchanted evening
You may see a stranger,
You may see a stranger
Across a crowded room,
And somehow you know,
You know even then
That somewhere you'll see her
Again and again. . . .

NELLIE:

Who can explain it?
Who can tell you why?

EMILE:

Fools give you reasons,
Wise men never try . . .
Some enchanted evening,
When you find your true love,
When you feel her call you
Across a crowded room,
Then fly to her side
And make her your own,
Or all through your life you may dream all alone!

NELLIE: (Clinging to him)

Once you have found him
Never let him go.

EMILE: Once you have found her
Never let her go.

(They kiss)

Will you come next Friday?

NELLIE: (Somewhere, from out of the ether, she hears her voice murmur an
inarticulate but automatic assent) Uh-huh.

(EMILE kisses her again and leaves)

Intro to: SOME ENCHANTED EVENING

Lyrics by Oscar Hammerstein II   (From *South Pacific*)   **Music by Richard Rodgers**

Cue: EMILE: "*... and where I want to stay.*"

EMILE

NELLIE

yet you want to mar-ry me. I do. _____ I've

known you a few short weeks and yet Some-how you've made my heart for-get

All oth-er men I have ev-er met but you, but you.

poco rall.

Reprise: SOME ENCHANTED EVENING

Lyrics by Oscar Hammerstein II   (From *South Pacific*)   **Music by Richard Rodgers**

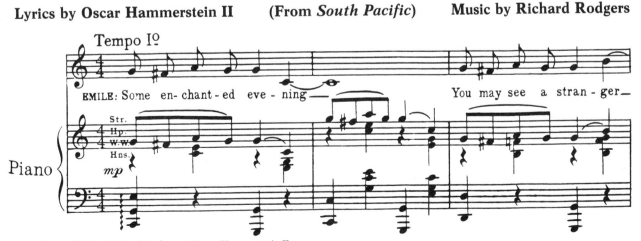

Tempo Iº

EMILE: Some en-chant-ed eve-ning _____ You may see a stran-ger_____

Piano

SCENE FOR ONE MAN, ONE WOMAN FROM
ACT II, SCENE 1 OF *MY FAIR LADY* (1956) BY
ALAN JAY LERNER AND FREDERICK LOEWE

CHARACTERS: *Henry Higgins*
Eliza Doolittle

SETTING: *Higgins's study in London, England. It has a sofa, easy chair, desk, stool, recording apparatus, and a staircase at one side that leads up to a landing.*

TIME: *3 A.M., following a ball; 1912.*

SITUATION: *After months of training, Higgins and Colonel Pickering have taken Eliza, a poor flower girl, to a ball and passed her off as a duchess. Things have gone well, and Higgins is elated, though sleepy. Eliza, however, is glum.*

COMMENTS: *Higgins is a vital, energetic man of forty or so, who is outspoken, but likeable. Eliza is about nineteen, a spirited girl from an impoverished section of London who has been taught by Higgins to speak and act like an upper-class lady. In this scene, they have just returned from the ball and are still dressed in evening clothes. The dialect used by both is Standard British.*

PUBLISHED TEXT: *Lerner, Alan Jay, and Frederick Loewe.* My Fair Lady. *New York: Coward-McCann, Inc., 1956.*

HIGGINS: Goodnight, Pickering. Oh, Mrs. Pearce! (*But she is gone*) Oh damn, I meant to tell her I wanted coffee in the morning instead of tea. Leave a little note for her, Eliza, will you? (*He looks around the room*) What the devil have I done with my slippers? (*The slippers are by the desk.* ELIZA *tries to control herself, but no longer can. She hurls them at him with all her force*)

ELIZA: There are your slippers! And there! Take your slippers, and may you never have a day's luck with them!

HIGGINS: (*Astounded*) What on earth? (*He comes to her*) What's the matter? Is anything wrong?

ELIZA: (*Seething*) Nothing wrong—with you. I've won your bet for you, haven't I? That's enough for you. I don't matter, I suppose?

HIGGINS: You won my bet! You! Presumptuous insect. *I* won it! What did you throw those slippers at me for?

ELIZA: Because I wanted to smash your face. I'd like to kill you, you selfish brute. Why didn't you leave me where you picked me out of—in the gutter? You thank God it's all over, and that now you can throw me back again there, do you?

HIGGINS: (*Looking at her in cool wonder*) So the creature is nervous, after all? (ELIZA *gives a suffocated scream of fury and instinctively darts her nails in his face.* HIGGINS *catches her wrists*) Ah! Claws in you, you cat! How dare you show your temper to me? (*He throws her roughly onto the sofa*) Sit down and be quiet.

ELIZA: (*Crushed by superior strength and weight*) What's to become of me? What's to become of me?

HIGGINS: How the devil do I know what's to become of you? What does it matter what becomes of you?

ELIZA: You don't care. I know you don't care. You wouldn't care if I was dead. I'm nothing to you—not so much as them slippers.

HIGGINS: (*Thundering*) *Those* slippers.

ELIZA: (*With bitter submission*) Those slippers. I didn't think it made any difference now.

(*A pause.* ELIZA *hopeless and crushed,* HIGGINS *a little uneasy*)

HIGGINS: (*In his loftiest manner*) Why have you suddenly begun going on like this? May I ask whether you complain of your treatment here?

ELIZA: No.

HIGGINS: Has anybody behaved badly to you? Colonel Pickering? Mrs. Pearce?

ELIZA: No.

HIGGINS: You don't pretend that I have treated you badly?

ELIZA: No.

HIGGINS: I'm glad to hear it. (*He moderates his tone*) Perhaps you're tired after the strain of the day? (*He picks up a box of chocolates*) Have a chocolate?

ELIZA: No. (*Recollecting her manners*) Thank you.

HIGGINS: (*Good-humored again*) I suppose it was natural for you to be anxious, but it's all over now. (*He pats her kindly on the shoulder. She writhes*) There's nothing more to worry about.

ELIZA: No, nothing more for you to worry about. Oh God, I wish I was dead.

HIGGINS: (*In sincere surprise*) Why, in Heaven's name, why? Listen to me, Eliza. All this irritation is purely subjective.

ELIZA: I don't understand. I'm too ignorant.

HIGGINS: It's only imagination. Nobody's hurting you. Nothing's wrong. You go to bed like a good girl, and sleep it off. Have a little cry and say your prayers; that will make you comfortable.

ELIZA: I heard your prayers. "Thank God it's all over!"

HIGGINS: (*Impatiently*) Well, don't you thank God it's all over? Now you are free and can do what you like.

ELIZA: (*Pulling herself together in desperation*) What am I fit for? What have you left me fit for? Where am I to go? What am I to do? What's to become of me?

HIGGINS: (*Enlightened, but not at all impressed*) Oh, that's what's worrying you, is it? (*Condescending to a trivial subject out of pure kindness*) Oh, I shouldn't bother about that if I were you. I should imagine you won't have much difficulty in settling yourself somewhere or other—though I hadn't quite realized you were going away. You might marry, you know. You see, Eliza, all men are not confirmed old bachelors like me and the Colonel. Most men are the marrying sort, poor devils. And you're not bad-looking. It's quite a pleasure to look at you at times. (*He looks at her*) Not now, of course. You've been crying and look like the very devil; but when you're all right and quite yourself, you're what I should call attractive. Come, you go to bed and have a good night's rest; and then get up and look at yourself in the glass; and you won't feel so cheap. (*Peering into the box of chocolates, in search of a creamy one. In the process, a genial afterthought occurs to him*) I daresay my mother could find some chap or other who would do very well.

ELIZA: We were above that in Covent Garden.

HIGGINS: What do you mean?

ELIZA: I sold flowers. I didn't sell myself. Now you've made a lady of me, I'm not fit to sell anything else.

HIGGINS: Tosh, Eliza, don't insult human relations by dragging all that cant about buying and selling into it. (*Not finding a creamy one, he puts the chocolates down*) You needn't marry the fellow if you don't want to.

ELIZA: What else am I to do?

HIGGINS: Oh, lots of things. What about that old idea of a florist's shop? Pickering could set you up in one. He's lots of money. (*Chuckling*) He'll have to pay for all those togs you've been wearing; and that, with the hire of the jewelry, will make a big hole in two hundred pounds. Oh, come! You'll be all right. I must clear off to bed; I'm devilish sleepy. By the way, I was looking for something. What was it?

ELIZA: Your slippers.

HIGGINS: Yes, of course. You shied them at me.

(*He picks them up and is starting for the stairs when she rises and speaks to him*)

ELIZA: Before you go, sir—

HIGGINS: (*Stopping, surprised at her calling him "sir"*) Eh?

ELIZA: Do my clothes belong to me or to Colonel Pickering?

HIGGINS: (*Coming back to her as if her question were the very climax of unreason*) What the devil use would they be to Pickering? Why need you start bothering about that in the middle of the night?

ELIZA: I want to know what I may take away with me. I don't want to be accused of stealing.

HIGGINS: (*Deeply wounded*) Stealing? You shouldn't have said that, Eliza. That shows a want of feeling.

ELIZA: I'm sorry. I'm only a common, ignorant girl; and in my station, I have to be careful. There can't be any feelings between the like of you and the like of me. Please will you tell me what belongs to me and what doesn't?

HIGGINS: (*Very sulky*) You may take the whole damned houseful if you like. Except the jewels. They're hired. Will that satisfy you? (*He turns on his heels and is about to go in extreme dudgeon*)

ELIZA: (*Drinking in his emotion like nectar and nagging him to provoke a further supply*) Stop, please! (*She takes off jewels*) Will you take these to your room and keep them safe? I don't want to run the risk of their being missing.

HIGGINS: (*Furious*) Hand them over!

(*She gives him the jewels, he crams them into his pocket, unconsciously decorating himself with the protruding ends of the chains*)

If these belonged to me instead of the jeweler, I'd ram them down your ungrateful throat.

ELIZA: (*Taking a ring off*) This ring isn't the jeweler's; it's the one you bought me in Brighton. I don't want it now. (*He throws the ring violently across the room and turns on her so threateningly that she crouches with her hands over her face, and exclaims*) Don't you hit me.

HIGGINS: Hit you! You infamous creature, how dare you accuse me of such a thing? It is you who have hit me. You have wounded me to the heart.

ELIZA: (*Thrilling with hidden joy*) I'm glad. I've got a little of my own back, anyhow.

HIGGINS: (*With dignity, in his finest professional style*) You have caused me to lose my temper, a thing that has hardly ever happened to me before. I prefer to say nothing more tonight. I am going to bed. (*He starts up the stairs*)

ELIZA: (*Pertly*) You'd better leave your own note for Mrs. Pearce about the coffee, for it won't be done by me!

HIGGINS: (*Stopping about halfway up the stairs*) Damn Mrs. Pearce! And damn the coffee! And damn you! And damn my own folly in having lavished my hard-earned knowledge and the treasure of my regard and intimacy on a heartless guttersnipe! (*He marches up the stairs with impressive decorum and spoils it by tripping on the top step. He successfully recovers but while looking to see if she noticed his awkwardness, he runs into the table and inadvertently turns on the machine. Guttural vowel sounds come pouring through the speaker. He turns it off violently and with a slam of the door, disappears.*)

(ELIZA *runs to the ring on the floor and picks it up*)

SCENE FOR ONE MAN, ONE WOMAN FROM ACT I, SCENE 7 OF *GYPSY* (1959) BY JULE STYNE, STEPHEN SONDHEIM, AND ARTHUR LAURENTS

CHARACTERS: *Rose*

           Herbie

           Waitress (no lines)

SETTING: *A section of a gaudy Chinese restaurant in New York.*

TIME: *Evening; in the early 1930s.*

SITUATION: *Rose, the mother of Louise and June, has managed her daughters' vaudeville career since they were very young. Tomorrow they are going to audition for Mr. Grantziger at the Palace Theatre, and Rose has just sent the girls back to the hotel to get their beauty sleep. Like the girls, Rose is wearing a coat made from hotel blankets.*

COMMENTS: *Rose is an aggressive stage mother who is determined that June will be a star. Their agent, Herbie, is a nice, sensible man who loves Rose and wants to marry her. They are both middle-aged.*

PUBLISHED TEXTS: *Laurents, Arthur, Jule Styne, and Stephen Sondheim.* Gypsy. *New York: Random House, 1960.*

    Richards, Stanley (ed.). Ten Great Musicals of the American Theatre. *Radnor, PA: Chilton Book Company, 1973.*

ROSE: I'll cold-cream their faces and be right back.

HERBIE: The hotel is two doors away! Honestly, you behave as though those girls—Rose! (*This because she is collecting silverware and is about to put it in her bag*)

ROSE: We need new silverware. (*Stops, then puts down the silver. Quietly*) Herbie, how long is it going to take you to get used to me?

HERBIE: How long did it take me to get used to those coats?

ROSE: What's the matter with them? They're real stylish! Louise is very talented with a needle. Herbie, as the good Lord says: an eye for an eye, a tooth for a tooth—(*On this, she sweeps the silver into her bag*) And it serves them right for overcharging. (*Starts to go.* HERBIE *hands her a knife, which she also takes. But then she stops and returns*) They can skip the cold cream for one night. (*Automatically, he gets up and helps her off with her coat.* ROSE, *admiringly*) All this time we've been together, and you still stand up for me!

HERBIE: It's instead of standing up *to* you.

ROSE: O.K., you say we're never alone. I wanted to have dinner tonight, just the two of us, but what was I going to do with the girls? They're babies.

HERBIE: Rose, no matter how you dress 'em, no matter how you smother 'em, they're big girls. They're almost young women—

ROSE: They're not and they never will be!

HERBIE: I'm embarrassed in front of them! When are you going to marry me, Rose?

ROSE: Don't forget to take our scrapbooks to Mr. Grantziger's tomorrow.

HERBIE: When are you going to quit stalling?

ROSE: We got to show him proof that we headlined on the Orpheum.

HERBIE: Rose—

ROSE: All right: so it was a long time ago.

HERBIE: (*Gets up*) Rose, if I walk out, you'll be stuck with the check! (ROSE *pulls* HERBIE *back into the chair*) Honey, don't you know there's a depression?

ROSE: Of course I know! I read *Variety*.

HERBIE: Don't you know what it's doing to vaudeville? Don't you know what the talkies are doing to vaudeville? Don't you know I love you?

ROSE: You think I'd be unfaithful to my husbands if you didn't? But I have to think of my girls and their happiness.

HERBIE: Louise is very happy being the front end of a cow!

ROSE: It's better than being the rear end! Anyway, she loves animals.

HERBIE: She and June should both be in school—

ROSE: And be just like other girls; cook and clean and sit and die! (*To a passing waitress, sweetly*) Honey, could I have a spoon to stir my tea? . . . Herbie, I promised June I'd make her a star and I will. I promised I'd get her on the Pantages Circuit and I did. I promised I'd get her on the Orpheum Circuit and I did.

HERBIE: *I* did! And you promised me that after I did, you'd marry me.

ROSE: I promised her she'd headline on Broadway and—

HERBIE: Didn't you hear what I said?

ROSE: Yes, but I'm ignoring it. (*To the waitress, for the spoon*) Thanks, honey. Herbie, it isn't very polite for a gentleman to remind a lady that she welched. There was no date on that promise—

HERBIE: ROSE, STOP HANDING ME—

ROSE: Your stomach! (*Quickly handing him a pill*) Herbie, why don't you get angry outside, instead of letting it settle in your stomach?

HERBIE: I'm afraid.

ROSE: Of me?

HERBIE: Of me.

ROSE: What do you mean?

HERBIE: If I ever let loose, it'll end with me picking up and walking.

ROSE: Only around the block.

HERBIE: No.

ROSE: Don't say that. (*Sings*)
    You'll never get away from me.
    You can climb the tallest tree,
        I'll be there somehow.
    True, you could say, "Hey, here's your hat,"
    But a little thing like that
        Couldn't stop me now.
    I couldn't get away from you
    Even if you told me to,
        So go on and try!

Just try,
And you're gonna see
How you're gonna not at all get away from me!

HERBIE: What is it? What do you want? There are better agents.

ROSE: Not for me.

HERBIE: And even weaker men.

ROSE: Not for me.

HERBIE: Then what?

ROSE: You. Oh, Herbie, just help me like you been helping. Just let me get June's name up in lights so big, they'll last my whole life.

HERBIE: Rose, what you expect—

ROSE: I'll *get!* And after I get it, I promise I'll marry you. (HERBIE *moves away from the table*) I even promise to keep my promise. (*Silence*) Please, Herbie. I don't want to upset anything before the audition tomorrow. Including your stomach.

HERBIE: (*Singing*)
Rose, I love you,
But don't count your chickens.

ROSE: (*Singing*)
Come dance with me.

HERBIE:
I warn you
That I'm no Boy Scout.

ROSE:
Relax a while—come dance with me.

HERBIE:
So don't think
That I'm easy pickin's—

ROSE:
The music's so nice—

HERBIE:
Rose!
'Cause I just may
Some day
Pick up and pack out.

ROSE:
Oh no, you won't,
No, not a chance.
No arguments,
Shut up and dance.

You'll never get away from me,
You can climb the tallest tree—
I'll be there somehow!

True, you could say, "Hey, here's your hat,"
But a little thing like that
Couldn't stop me now.

BOTH:

> I couldn't get away from you
> Even if I wanted to—

ROSE:

> Well, go on and try!
> Just try—

HERBIE:

> Ah, Rose—

ROSE:

> And you're gonna see—

HERBIE:

> Ah, Rose—

ROSE:

> How you're gonna not at all
> Get away from me!

(The lights fade)

YOU'LL NEVER GET AWAY FROM ME

Words by Stephen Sondheim   (From *Gypsy*)   **Music by Jule Styne**

Cue: ROSE: Your stomach!

SCENE FOR ONE MAN, ONE WOMAN FROM ACT I, SCENE 1 OF *CAMELOT* (1960) BY ALAN JAY LERNER AND FREDERICK LOEWE

CHARACTERS: *Arthur*
            Guenevere

SETTING: *A hilltop near the castle at Camelot. There is a large tree onstage in which Arthur is hiding.*

TIME: *Afternoon, a long time ago when King Arthur was a young man.*

SITUATION: *A royal marriage between Arthur and Guenevere has been arranged to bring peace to their people, and Arthur has nervously been waiting in the tree for her to arrive. Guenevere has entered fearfully, running away from the welcoming party, and has just sung "The Simple Joys of Maidenhood."*

COMMENTS: *Guenevere is very young and beautiful; she is wearing a flaming red cloak. Arthur is a boyish young man in his mid-twenties.*

PUBLISHED TEXTS: *Lerner, Alan Jay, and Frederick Loewe.* Camelot. *New York: Random House, 1961.*

Richards, Stanley (ed.). Great Musicals of the American Theatre *Vol. 2. Radnor, PA: Chilton Book Company, 1976.*

(She turns dejectedly towards the foot of the tree. A branch cracks, and ARTHUR *drops to the floor.* GUENEVERE, *startled out of her wits, runs)*

ARTHUR: A thousand pardons, Milady. Wait! Don't run. (*She stops in the corner of the stage and looks at him coweringly*) Please! I won't harm you.

GUENEVERE: You lie! You'll leap at me and throw me to the ground.

ARTHUR: (*Amazed, protesting*) I won't do any such thing. (*He takes a step toward her. She takes a step backwards. He stops*)

GUENEVERE: Then you'll twist my arm and tie me to a tree.

ARTHUR: But I won't.

GUENEVERE: Then you'll sling me over your shoulder and carry me off.

ARTHUR: No, no, no! I swear it! By the Sword Excalibur! I swear I won't touch you.

GUENEVERE: (*Hurt*) Why not? (*Sudden rage*) How dare you insult me in this fashion. Do my looks repel you?

ARTHUR: No. You're beautiful.

GUENEVERE: Well, then? We're alone. I'm completely defenseless. What kind of a cad are you? Apologize at once.

ARTHUR: (*At once*) I apologize. I'm not certain what I've done, but from the depths of my heart, I apologize.

GUENEVERE: (*With sudden wisdom*) Ah! I think I know. You heard me praying.

ARTHUR: I couldn't help it, Milady. You prayed rather loudly.

GUENEVERE: And you know who I am.

ARTHUR: You're Guenevere.

GUENEVERE: Yes, of course. You're afraid because I may be your Queen. That accounts for your respectful, polite, despicable behavior.

Figure 10-1.   Richard Burton as Arthur and Julie Andrews as Guenevere in *Camelot.*
(Courtesy of the Billy Rose Theatre Collection, the New York Public Library at Lincoln Center, Astor, Lenox, and Tilden Foundations.)

ARTHUR: Milady, I would never harm you for any reason. And as for what to do with you, I'm at a loss. I know you are to be Queen and I should escort you back to your carriage. At the same time, you're a maiden in genuine distress. It's chivalry versus country. I can't quite determine which call to obey.

GUENEVERE: (*Looking off toward the foot of the hill*) You'd better decide quickly. They'll soon reach the carriage and discover I'm gone. Then all of Camelot will be searching for me. At least *that* will be exciting. Unless of course everyone in Camelot is like you and they all go home to deliberate.

ARTHUR: (*Thrown off balance, enamored, captivated, and overcome by a great sense of inadequacy*) Oh, why isn't Merlyn here! He usually senses when I need him and appears. Why does he fail me now?

GUENEVERE: Who?

ARTHUR: Merlyn. My teacher. He would know immediately what to do. I'm not accomplished at thinking, so I have Merlyn do it for me. He's the wisest man alive. He lives backwards.

GUENEVERE: I beg your pardon?

ARTHUR: He lives backwards. He doesn't age. He youthens. He can remember the future so he can tell you what you'll be doing in it. Do you understand? (*She comes toward him. He never takes his eyes off her, as the wonder of her comes nearer*)

GUENEVERE: (*Now at ease*) Of course I don't understand. But if you mean he's some sort of fortune-teller, I'd give a year in Paradise to know mine. I can never return to my own castle, and I absolutely refuse to go on to that one.

ARTHUR: (*Sadly*) You refuse to go on—ever?

GUENEVERE: Ever. My only choice is . . . Don't stare. It's rude. Who are you?

ARTHUR: (*After a thought*) Actually, they call me Wart.

GUENEVERE: Wart? What a ridiculous name. Are you sure you heard them properly?

ARTHUR: It's a nickname. It was given to me when I was a boy.

GUENEVERE: You're rather sweet, in spite of your name. And I didn't think I'd like anyone in Camelot. Imagine riding seven hours in a carriage on the verge of hysteria, then seeing that horrible castle rising in the distance, and running away; then having a man plop from a tree like an overripe apple . . . You must admit for my first day away from home it's quite a plateful. If only I were not alone. Wart, why don't you . . . Is it really Wart?

ARTHUR: Yes.

GUENEVERE: Wart, why don't you run away with me? (*She is enchanted by the notion*)

ARTHUR: I? Run away with you?

GUENEVERE: Of course. As my protector. Naturally, I would be brutalized by strangers. I expect that. But it would be dreadful if there were no one to rescue me. Think of it! We can travel the world. France, Scotland, Spain . . .

ARTHUR: What a dream you spin, and how easily I could be caught up in it. But I can't Milady. To serve as your protector would satisfy the prayers of the most fanatic cavalier alive. But I must decline.

GUENEVERE: (*Angrily*) You force me to stay?

ARTHUR: Not at all.

GUENEVERE: But you know you're the only one I know in Camelot. Whom else can I turn to?

ARTHUR: Milady, if you persist in escaping, I'll find someone trustworthy and brave to accompany you.

GUENEVERE: Then do so immediately. There's not much time.

ARTHUR: Oh, do look around you, Milady. Reconsider. Camelot is unique. We have an enchanted forest where the Fairy Queen, Morgan Le Fey, lives in an invisible castle. Most unusual. We have a talking owl named Archimedes. Highly original. We have unicorns with silver feet. The rarest kind. And we have far and away the most equitable climate in all the world. Ordained by decree! Extremely uncommon.

GUENEVERE: Oh, come now.

ARTHUR: (*Sings*)

It's true! It's true! The crown has made it clear:
The climate must be perfect all the year.

A law was made a distant moon ago here,
July and August cannot be too hot;
And there's a legal limit to the snow here
In Camelot.

The winter is forbidden till December,
And exits March the second on the dot.
By order summer lingers through September
In Camelot.

Camelot! Camelot!
I know it sounds a bit bizarre;
But in Camelot, Camelot
That's how conditions are.
The rain may never fall till after sundown.
By eight the morning fog must disappear.
In short, there's simply not
A more congenial spot
For happ'ly-ever-aftering than here
In Camelot.

GUENEVERE: (*Sarcastically*) And I suppose the autumn leaves fall in neat little piles.

ARTHUR: Oh, no, Milady. They blow away completely. At night, of course.

GUENEVERE: Of course.

(*She moves away from him, as if to leave. He leaps after her and blocks her way*)

ARTHUR: (*Sings*)

Camelot! Camelot!
I know it gives a person pause
But in Camelot, Camelot
Those are the legal laws.
The snow may never slush upon the hillside.
By nine p.m. the moonlight must appear.
In short, there's simply not
A more congenial spot
For happ'ly-ever-aftering than here
In Camelot.

CAMELOT

Words by Alan Jay Lerner

(From *Camelot*)

Music by Frederick Loewe

Cue: ARTHUR: Ordained by decree!

...Extremely uncommon.

GUENEVERE: Oh, come now.

SCENE FOR ONE MAN, ONE WOMAN FROM ACT II, SCENE 2 OF *HOW TO SUCCEED IN BUSINESS WITHOUT REALLY TRYING* (1961) BY FRANK LOESSER, ABE BURROWS, JACK WEINSTOCK, WILLIE GILBERT

CHARACTERS: *Finch*
                 Rosemary

SETTING: *Finch's office in the Park Avenue, New York, office building of World Wide Wicket Company, Inc.*

TIME: *Shortly after Finch has become vice president in charge of advertising.*

SITUATION: *Finch has risen rapidly in the company through the advice found in a book that is titled the same as this musical. Now he needs a brilliant advertising idea. A rival, Bud, has deliberately planted with Finch the idea of the firm's sponsoring a TV give-away program called the World Wide Wicket Treasure Hunt, although Bud knows that the boss does not like the concept. Bud has just left, and Finch is thinking about it and looking at a script for the show when his secretary, Rosemary, enters. Because Finch was not paying any attention to her, she has earlier written a letter of resignation, but she has now changed her mind.*

COMMENTS: *Finch is a young man who is consumed with ambition to rise in the company. He started as a window washer and is now a vice president. Rosemary, a sweet, tolerant girl, is in love with him.*

PUBLISHED TEXT: *None. In manuscript only.*

FINCH: (*Left alone, looks at manuscript carefully,* X *above desk*) Treasure hunt. Could be. A thousand dollar bond. This thing needs some kind of a new twist. (ROSEMARY *enters* L)

ROSEMARY: Ponty, I'm back. I changed my mind.

FINCH: (*Still lost in thought*) Oh, Miss Pilkington.

ROSEMARY: (XR *to desk*) I don't blame you for being cold to me. But I did change my mind.

FINCH: (X *back above desk, still preoccupied with manuscript*) About what?

ROSEMARY: About what I said in the letter.

FINCH: What letter?

ROSEMARY: My letter of resignation.

FINCH: Your resignation from what?

ROSEMARY: The Girl Scouts of America.

FINCH: Oh.

ROSEMARY: Don't you understand? (SHE *picks up the letter of resignation from desk, shows it to him, slams it down, then* XL *by settee*) I've quit, resigned, left you forever!

FINCH: Why are you doing that?

ROSEMARY: (*Yelling*) Because I was hurt, humiliated, ignored, upset!

FINCH: (*Startled*) Who did that to you?

ROSEMARY: You.

FINCH: Me. It couldn't have been me. I haven't said ten words to you all week. (ROSEMARY *stares at him*) True?

ROSEMARY: True. (SHE *sits on settee*)

FINCH: Good. Now listen, Miss Pilkington . . .

ROSEMARY: Must you call me that? Can't you call me Rosemary?

FINCH: No. And I want you to call me Mr. Finch, until you're Mrs. Finch.

ROSEMARY: (*Dreamy smile*) Am I really going to be Mrs. Finch?

FINCH: (XL *below desk to her*) Oh come on. I thought that was all settled.

ROSEMARY: I keep thinking maybe you forgot.

FINCH: Well I haven't. You're going to be Mrs. Finch because we're going to be married. Now, may we discuss some serious matters?

ROSEMARY: Oh, sure.

FINCH: Miss Pilkington, I have something I want you to hear. (XR *above desk*) I have finally come up with a new idea for a television program. I'm thinking of calling it the World Wide Wicket Treasure Hunt. (X *to* C) The prize would be a thousand-dollar bond. Do you think that's enough? (ROSEMARY *looks at him raptly, doesn't answer.* FINCH XL *to her*) Maybe we ought to make that twenty-five thousand dollars. Listen carefully, Rosemary. (X *to* C) What would you say if we gave away a hundred thousand dollars? (SHE *doesn't answer.* HE X *to her*) Two hundred thousand?

ROSEMARY: I don't care if you give away the whole company. I love you.

FINCH: (*Stares at her, then looks front with a happy smile on his face*) Say that again.

ROSEMARY: I love you.

FINCH: No, before that.

ROSEMARY: (*Puzzled*) I said I don't care if you give away the whole company.

FINCH: (XR) That's it! We'll give away the company. What a prize! Oh, I don't mean the whole company. (XR *below desk*) I mean stock in the company. Nobody could resist that these days. I've got to have time to work this out. I've got to speak to Mr. Biggley. (HE *picks up phone.* ROSEMARY *rises,* X *to him*) He's got to give me a postponement. (*Hangs up*) No, I'll go see him.

ROSEMARY: Good luck, Mr. Finch.

FINCH: Thank you, Miss Pilkington. (HE *starts off* L)

ROSEMARY: Say . . . (HE *stops and looks at her*) What about taking me to lunch? Nobody has to see us.

FINCH: (*Reprovingly*) Miss Pilkington.

ROSEMARY: (*With a smile*) I'm sorry, Mr. Finch.

(HE *exits* L)

SCENE FOR ONE MAN, ONE WOMAN FROM ACT I, SCENE 13 OF *FUNNY GIRL* (1964) BY JULE STYNE, BOB MERRILL, AND ISOBEL LENNART

CHARACTERS: *Fanny Brice*
Nick Arnstein

SETTING: *A private dining room in Baltimore with a small table, set for two, in front of a fireplace. There is also a red velvet chaise lounge.*

TIME: *Evening: around World War I.*

SITUATION: *Ten months earlier Fanny and Nick were together at an opening night party, but he has not tried to see her since then. She is now on the road starring in Baltimore in the* Ziegfeld Follies, *and she is angry because of his negligence. Nick has checked the table, put a blue marble egg on it, and poured sherry before Fanny enters.*

COMMENTS: *Fanny, who is a star comic and singer with the* Ziegfeld Follies, *is very attracted to Nick. He is a suave, handsome gambler and investor who is equally interested in her. She should use a slight Yiddish accent.*

PUBLISHED TEXT: *Styne, Jule, Bob Merrill, and Isobel Lennart. Funny Girl. New York: Random House, 1964.*

(FANNY *enters—stops for a beat, then, snaps open her fan*)

NICK: May I take your wrap? (SHE X's D *in front of him, turns her back to him and* HE *helps her off with her cape. As* SHE *turns toward him,* HE *looks at her, beautifully attired in a blue dress*) That color is wonderful with your eyes—

FANNY: Just my right eye. I hate what it does to the left. (X's R *above chaise, noticing it for the first time. Feels the material far* R) Tell me are you planning to make advances?

NICK: (X*ing* D C) I wasn't planning but it does seem possible.

FANNY: Before dinner or after dinner?

NICK: (*Smiling*) You look beautiful. (X's U L *and places her cape on chair* L *of table*)

FANNY: (*Sitting on chaise*) You don't have to make leading lady dialogue for me—I'm a comic.

NICK: Onstage.

FANNY: That's where I live—onstage.

NICK: (X*ing* R *to her and sits to her* L) Then you're missing too much.

FANNY: You can't have everything. (*Snaps open fan, rises and* X's U L *to table*)

NICK: (*Turning toward her*) Of course you can—if you insist on it.

FANNY: (*Picking up blue marble egg from table*) Hey—somebody laid a blue marble egg on the table.

NICK: I did. (*Rises,* X's U *to* FANNY) I got that in Europe—ages ago. (*Taking egg from her*) It's one of my favorite things—so I thought you might like it. (*Hands it back to her*)

FANNY: (*Looks at him—then back at table*) A blue marble egg—(*Places it back on table*) white roses—You went to a lot of trouble even though I told you I might not show up.

NICK: I *hoped* you would! Just as I hope you like very dry sherry—(X's R *to table*)

FANNY: I wouldn't know dry from wet. I never got past 3B—remember? (*As* NICK *pours sherry,* SHE *sits* L, X*ing legs quickly, first one way, then the other—trying to find a suitable pose. As* NICK *returns with two glasses of sherry,* SHE *snaps to a position of dignity, sniffing the white roses. Sensing this activity,* HE *stops for a beat,* X's L *to table, handing her a glass.* HE *sits across from her;* THEY *clink glasses in a silent toast and* THEY *drink.* SHE *gulps entire drink in one shot and places glass on table as* NICK *sips his. After a second sip,* HE *places his glass gently on table*)

NICK: Too bad you never made 4B—that's where they teach wine-tasting. (FANNY *getting sick from gulping sherry, quickly fans herself, trying to recover her composure as* NICK *rises,* X's *to above table*) I remember you very well, Fanny. Inquisitive—interested in everything—so full of life you made everyone else look like a sleepwalker. All the things you're trying *not* to be right now—

FANNY: I used to impress very easily—you were my first top hat. But I've met lots of you since then. I'm a little older, you know—

NICK: Funny—you seem so much younger. About eight, I'd say. A bad-tempered eight—determined not to enjoy anything! Why? What are you angry about?

FANNY: (*Rising,* X's R *above chaise. Innocently*) Who's angry? I'm sorry if I'm— disappointing you in some way, but what did you expect? That you could come waltzing into my life after ten months, say, "I have a week before I go to Europe"—
(*Sits*)
and have me fall into your arms?

NICK: (X*ing* D) Why don't you answer the question? Why are you so angry?

FANNY: (*With mounting anger*) I'm NOT ANGRY! And why don't *you* answer the question?! You think I should be flattered because this time your train isn't leaving tomorrow morning. This time, you have a week to kill? Well, I'm not a kid at Keeney's any more! You're not slumming any more!

NICK: (X*ing* D C) I never was—and you *know* it!

FANNY: Don't holler at me!

NICK: I'm not hollering—you are.

FANNY: That's different—I'm a *natural* hollerer! Anyway, I answered your silly question.

NICK: (X*ing* L *and sitting next to her*) No you didn't, my love. Because you got angry the minute you saw me—before I said a word. And that surprised me—because *I* lit up like a Christmas tree when I heard you were here.

FANNY: (*With self-derision*) Just at the thought of great big wonderful me, huh?

NICK: Don't make fun of yourself, Fanny—you don't have to. (FANNY *pulls herself up*) Yes—it *was* at the thought of you. And I didn't think of it as a week to kill. I thought of it as a week to share.

CHAVA:

> Matchmaker, Matchmaker,
> I'll bring the veil,
> You bring the groom,
> Slender and pale.
> Bring me a ring for I'm longing to be
> The envy of all I see.

HODEL:

> For Papa,
> Make him a scholar.

CHAVA:

> For Mama,
> Make him rich as a king.

CHAVA and HODEL:

> For me, well,
> I wouldn't holler
> If he were as handsome as anything.
> Matchmaker, Matchmaker,
> Make me a match,
> Find me a find,
> Catch me a catch.
> Night after night in the dark I'm alone,
> So find me a match
> Of my own.

TZEITEL: Since when are you interested in a match, Chava? I thought you just had your eye on your books. (HODEL *chuckles*) And you have your eye on the rabbi's son.

HODEL: Why not? We only have one rabbi and he only has one son. Why shouldn't I want the best?

TZEITEL: Because you're a girl from a poor family. So whatever Yente brings, you'll take. Right? Of course right. (*Sings*)

> Hodel, oh Hodel,
> Have I made a match for you!
> He's handsome, he's young!
> All right, he's sixty-two,
> But he's a nice man, a good catch—true? True.

> I promise you'll be happy.
> And even if you're not,
> There's more to life than that—
> Don't ask me what.

> Chava, I found him.
> Will you be a lucky bride!
> He's handsome, he's tall—
> That is, from side to side.
> But he's a nice man, a good catch—right? Right.

> You heard he has a temper.
> He'll beat you every night,
> But only when he's sober,
> So you're all right.

Did you think you'd get a prince?
Well, I do the best I can.
With no dowry, no money, no family background
Be glad you got a man.

CHAVA:

Matchmaker, Matchmaker,
You know that I'm
Still very young.
Please, take your time.

HODEL:

Up to this minute
I misunderstood
That I could get stuck for good.

CHAVA and HODEL:

Dear Yente,
See that he's gentle.
Remember,
You were also a bride.
It's not that
I'm sentimental.

CHAVA, HODEL, and TZEITEL:

It's just that I'm terrified!
Matchmaker, Matchmaker,
Plan me no plans,
I'm in no rush.
Maybe I've learned
Playing with matches
A girl can get burned.
So,
Bring me no ring,
Groom me no groom,
Find me no find,
Catch me no catch,
Unless he's a matchless match.

MATCHMAKER, MATCHMAKER

Words by Sheldon Harnick   (From *Fiddler on the Roof*)   **Music by Jerry Bock**

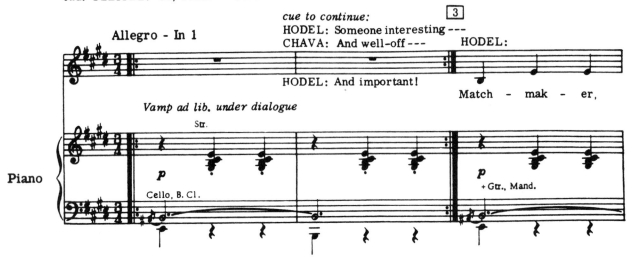

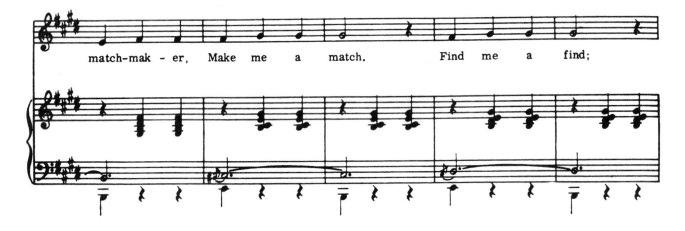

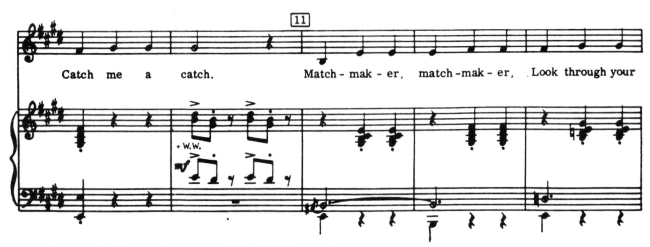

SCENE FOR THREE WOMEN FROM ACT II, SCENE 2 OF *MAME* (1966) BY JERRY HERMAN, JEROME LAWRENCE, AND ROBERT E. LEE

CHARACTERS: *Mame Dennis Burnside*
Vera Charles
Agnes Gooch
Ito, Mame's servant (no lines)

SETTING: *The living room of Mame's elegant Beekman Place apartment in New York City. Because Mame has been away, the furniture is covered, and packing boxes are in the room.*

TIME: *Late 1930s; six months after Mame's husband was killed by falling off an Alp during their honeymoon trip.*

SITUATION: *On arriving home, Mame finds that her friends have brought a dictaphone, typewriter, and Agnes Gooch, a former nanny who is now a secretary, so that Mame can write her memoirs. Vera and Mame have celebrated their reconciliation by singing "Bosom Buddies" and getting slightly drunk. At the end of the song, they have fallen onto the sofa as Agnes enters from the kitchen with a bottle of Dr. Pepper.*

COMMENTS: *Mame, an optimistic, energetic, vital lady of middle years, is fashionably dressed in white. About the same age is Vera, a sophisticated stage star, who is in mourning black. Agnes, who wears oxfords, glasses, and a formless, frumpy dress and slip, is a dowdy, naive, unmarried woman who is awed and fascinated by the two older ladies.*

PUBLISHED TEXT: *Lawrence, Jerome, Robert E. Lee, and Jerry Herman. Mame. New York: Random House, 1967.*

MAME: Vera, it's amazing. When I think of all the same men we dated, and still remained so inseparable.

VERA: Mame! I *never* dated the same man you did.

MAME: How about Carlo, that sexy Argentinian with all those shoulders?

VERA: (*Indignant*)   Carlo! I never dated Carlo. I *married* him, I never dated him.

(AGNES, *fascinated by the conversation, giggles. They both turn and look at her*)

AGNES: Oh, excuse me. But listening to you ladies makes me all goose-pimply. Y'see, I never had one.

VERA: Never had one *what?*

AGNES: A date. With a member of the opposite–you-know-what. (MAME *and* VERA *look at each other; then each takes another long drink, simultaneously. Then they get an inspiration and get up.* AGNES *is baffled as the two women circle her*) Mrs. Burnside, is anything wrong?

MAME: Agnes, you're coming out!

AGNES: (*Clutching the side of her dress*) Where?

VERA: (*Taking off* AGNES' *glasses*) Why, Gooch, you have lovely eyes. Take those glasses off and leave them off forever.

AGNES: But, Miss Charles, I can't see anything out of my right eye.

VERA: Who can? Look out of your left one!

MAME: (*Pointing to* AGNES' *shoes*) What do you call *those* things?

AGNES: Orthopedic oxfords.

MAME: Kick 'em off. (*Baffled*, AGNES *complies*. MAME *pulls her dress tight*) My goodness, Agnes—you *do* have a bust. Where have you been hiding it all these years? (AGNES *breaks away, cowering behind the couch*) All your clothes off, Agnes.

AGNES: Mrs. Burnside! There's a man in the house.

MAME: Don't be a goose, Agnes. Get these clothes off and keep them off. (MAME *and* VERA *peel off* AGNES' *clothes; she stands trembling in a shapeless slip.* MAME *calls*) Ito! Come in here. We've got some work to do.

(ITO *scurries in from the kitchen*)

AGNES: I don't have a very clear picture of what's going on.

VERA: When we're through with you, honey, men will be breaking down your door.

AGNES: What about my virtue?

MAME: Virtue! There's nothing wrong with a harmless smooch.

AGNES: Oh, just the idea of it makes me so nervous, I could die.

MAME: Have a date first—then die. (MAME *hands her a drink*) This'll calm you down.

AGNES: But spirits do the most terrible things to me. I'm not the same girl.

MAME: What's wrong with that?

AGNES: (*Turning to* VERA, *the bibing expert*) Will it mix with Dr. Pepper?

VERA: (*Emphatically*) He'll love it.

(AGNES *drinks it down in one gulp.* MAME *pummels her face*)

MAME: We really should do something about her complexion. For God's sake, Agnes, close your pores. Ito, go upstairs. Drag out that sexy gown I sent from Paris. And get all my cosmetics: face creams, eyebrow pencils, lipstick.

VERA: And a chisel.

(ITO, *giggling, races up the stairs*)

MAME: (*Striking a pose*) Tonight, Agnes, you can be the Queen of Rumania!

(AGNES *tries to imitate the regal pose but immediately gives up, a coward to the core*)

AGNES: Mrs. Burnside, I think I know what you're suggesting I do—and I just don't think I can do anything so—suggestive.

MAME: Agnes, where's your *spine?* Here you've been living in the same house with me all these years, and you don't understand what I believe in. LIVE! That's what I believe.

AGNES: Live?

MAME: Yes! Life is a banquet, and most poor sons-of-bitches are *starving* to death! Live!

(ITO, *at the head of the stairs, giggles, waving a pair of silk stockings like two banners*)

AGNES: Live?

VERA: Live!

MAME, AGNES and VERA: LIVE!

(AGNES *races up the stairs, intoxicated by the idea*)

MAME: We're the greatest team since Romulus and Remus.

SCENE FOR ONE MAN, ONE WOMAN FROM ACT I, SCENE 5 OF *CABARET* (1966) BY JOE MASTEROFF, FRED EBB, AND JOHN KANDER

CHARACTERS: *Clifford Bradshaw*

Sally Bowles

Taxi man (no lines)

SETTING: *Cliff's room in an apartment in Berlin, Germany. It has a single bed, a table, two chairs, washstand, and armoire.*

TIME: *Daytime; January 1, 1930.*

SITUATION: *Cliff, an American, and Ernst, a German, have met on the train to Berlin where Ernst, by putting his briefcase with Cliff's bags, has succeeded in getting it past a Customs officer without being inspected. Ernst has explained to Cliff that he did this because his case contained more gifts from Paris than were permitted. Later, Cliff meets Sally, an English entertainer at the Kit Kat Klub. Although involved with a man named Max, she is attracted to Cliff, and the next day she arrives at his lodgings with the intent of moving in. His landlady, who agrees to this, for more rent, and Ernst have just left the room.*

COMMENTS: *Cliff, who is in his late twenties, is an intelligent, nice-looking writer from Pennsylvania who gives English lessons to earn a living. Sally, a rather pretty and sophisticated English nightclub singer in her early twenties, is wearing a fur coat and green fingernails.*

PUBLISHED TEXTS: *Masteroff, Joe, Fred Ebb, and John Kander.* Cabaret. *New York: Random House, 1967.*

Richards, Stanley (ed.) Great Musicals of the American Theatre. *Vol. 2. Radnor, PA: Chilton Book Company, 1976.*

(SALLY, *still in her fur coat, collapses onto the bed*)

CLIFF: Sally, now what's this all about?

SALLY: Did you guess I was terrified?

CLIFF: Were you?

SALLY: What if you'd—thrown me out? Can you imagine how *that* would feel—being thrown out twice in one day?

CLIFF: You mean—Max . . . ?

SALLY: Dear Max. And you know whose fault it was? (*She points at* CLIFF) If you hadn't come to the Kit Kat Klub—and been so dreadfully attractive—and recited poetry—(*She suddenly sits up*) You know what I'd love? A spot of gin.

CLIFF: Gin?

SALLY: You've *got* some? I mean—I think one *must.*

CLIFF: No, I don't have any . . .

SALLY: Oh, well, Prairie Oysters, then.

CLIFF: Prairie Oysters?

SALLY: I practically live on them. It's just a raw egg whooshed around in some Worcestershire sauce. It's heaven for a hangover.

CLIFF: I haven't got a hangover. (SALLY *takes eggs, salt, pepper and Worcestershire sauce out of her coat pocket.* CLIFF *watches her*) That's quite a coat.

SALLY: It should be. It cost me all I had. Little did I dream how soon I'd be unemployed.

CLIFF: What about your job at the Klub?

SALLY: Well, that's rather complicated. You see, one of the owners of the Klub . . .

CLIFF: Dear Max?

SALLY: You're divinely intuitive! I do hope I'm not going to fall madly in love with you. Are you in the theatre in any way? (CLIFF *shakes his head*) Then you're safe—more or less. Though I do believe a woman can't be a truly great actress till she's had several passionate affairs—and had her heart broken (*Manufacturing the Prairie Oysters,* SALLY *breaks the eggs on this line*) I should have let Ernst pay my cab fare. He's got all that money from Paris.

CLIFF: From Paris?

SALLY: He smuggles it in for some political party.

CLIFF: Ernst is in politics?

SALLY: You didn't know? He goes to Paris about once a month and brings back pots of money.

CLIFF: He has to smuggle it in?

SALLY: It's terribly dangerous. But Ernst is so resourceful. He's discovered the Customs people almost never open the bags of non-Germans. So, just before the border, he finds some innocent-looking Englishman—or American . . . (*She completes the Prairie Oysters*)

CLIFF: It's hard to imagine an American *that* gullible.
(SALLY *hands him his drink. She toasts*)

SALLY: Hals and beinbruch. It means neck and leg break. It's supposed to stop it happening. Though I doubt it does.

CLIFF: (*Toasting*) Look—it's about time we—

SALLY: Drink!
(SALLY *drinks her Prairie Oyster. Then* CLIFF *sips his*)

CLIFF: It's amazing! You know what this tastes like? Peppermint!

SALLY: Oh—well, it's your toothbrush glass. I should have rinsed it. (SALLY *wanders over to the writing table. She picks up a book*) This is your novel! (*She opens it*) It's in German! (*She looks at the cover*) *Mein Kampf?*

CLIFF: It's not my novel. I thought I should know *something* about German politics.

SALLY: Why? You're an American! You know, I've never *known* a novelist. Will I be allowed to watch you work? I promise to be incredibly quiet . . .

CLIFF: I don't think I can write with someone else—on the premises.

SALLY: But I'm hardly noticeable—really. (*Imploring*) I'll go out when you're writing—take long invigorating walks!

CLIFF: In the middle of the night? And there's another thing: I'm not a prude. At least, I don't think I'm a prude. No—no—I've got work to do. I could never explain this arrangement. It's too peculiar.

SALLY: Peculiar? No, not in the least!
  (*Spoken, but the music is playing*)
  I think people are people. I really do, Cliff, don't you?
  I don't think they should be made to apologize for anything they do.
  For example, if I paint my fingernails green—
  And it happens I do paint them green—
  Well, if someone should ask me why,
  I think it's pretty.
  I think it's pretty, *that's* what I reply.
  So, if anyone should ask about you and me one day,
  You have two alternatives:
  You can either say: "Yes, it's true we're living in
  delicious sin,"
  Or you can simply tell them the truth, and say . .
  (SALLY *sings*)
  I met this perfectly marvelous girl
  In this perfectly wonderful place
  As I lifted a glass to the start of a marvelous year.
  Before you knew it she called on the phone, inviting.
  Next moment I was no longer alone,
  But sat reciting some perfectly beautiful verse
  In my charming American style.
  How I dazzled her senses was truly no less than a crime.
  Now I've this perfectly marvelous girl
  In my perfectly beautiful room,
  And we're living together and having a marvelous time.
CLIFF: Sally, I'm afraid it wouldn't work. You're much too distracting.
SALLY: Distracting? No, inspiring! (*She sings*)
  She tells me perfectly marvelous tales
  Of her thrilling scandalous life
  Which I'll probably use as a chapter or two in my book.
  And since my stay in Berlin was to force
  Creation,
  What luck to fall on a fabulous source
  Of stimulation.
  And perfectly marvelous too
  Is her perfect agreement to be
  Just as still as a mouse when I'm giving my novel a whirl.
  Yes, I've a highly agreeable life
  In my perfectly beautiful room,
  With my nearly invisible,
  Perfectly marvelous girl.

(*There is a noise at the door*) Oh, it's the taxi man! (*The door bursts open, and there is the taxi man with a mountain of luggage*) Hello, taxi man. Just put them anywhere. I'll unpack later. (CLIFF, *a little dazed, points to all the baggage*) Things *do* accumulate. I'll throw most of it away—tomorrow! I promise! (CLIFF *helps the taxi man bring in the bags.* SALLY *starts counting the pieces*) One—two—three—four— five—(*She gives up*) There's really not much point in counting. I never remember how many there're supposed to be. (*To* CLIFF) Can you let me have three marks? That includes the tip. (CLIFF *hands her a bill*) Thank you. (SALLY *hands the bill to the taxi man, who tips his cap and exits. There is a pause*) So quite seriously, Cliff—please may I stay?

CLIFF: Sally, I can't afford—

SALLY: Only for a day or two—please?

CLIFF: (*Singing*)
I met this truly remarkable girl
In this really incredible town,
And she's skillfully managed to talk her way into my room.

SALLY: Oh, Cliff!

CLIFF:
I have a terrible feeling I've said a dumb thing;
Besides, I've only got one narrow bed.

SALLY:
We'll think of something.

CLIFF:
And now this wild, unpredictable girl

SALLY:
And this perfectly beautiful man

BOTH:
Will be living together and having a marvelous time.

(*They are in each other's arms as the lights fade*)

PERFECTLY MARVELOUS

Lyrics by Fred Ebb   (From *Cabaret*)   **Music by John Kander**

cue: SALLY: Peculiar? No, not in the least!

Poco agitato

SALLY: *(spoken)* I think people are people, I really do, Cliff. Don't you? I don't think they should be

made to apologize for anything they do. For example, if I paint my fingernails green and it happens I do

paint them green, well, if someone should ask me why I think it's pretty, "I think it's pretty," that's what

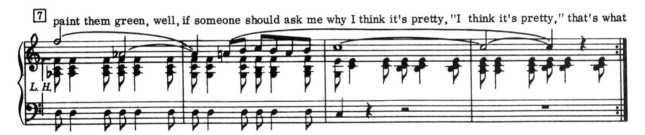

I reply: So, if anyone should ask about you and me one day, you have two alternatives: you can either say

"Yes, it's true. We're living in delicious sin." Or you can simply tell them the truth and say:

SCENE FOR THREE MEN FROM
SCENE 2 OF *1776* (1969) BY
SHERMAN EDWARDS AND PETER STONE

CHARACTERS: *John Adams*
             Benjamin Franklin
             Richard Henry Lee

SETTING: *The Mall in Philadelphia. A bench is onstage.*

TIME: *A day in May, 1776.*

SITUATION: *John Adams is disturbed because the Continental Congress is doing nothing about declaring its independence from Great Britain. He seeks the help of Benjamin Franklin, who is seated on the bench.*

COMMENTS: *Adams, a representative from Massachusetts to Congress, is an energetic egotist of forty-one, short, blunt, and impatient. Franklin, a calm, wise, seventy-year-old diplomat, is one of Pennsylvania's delegates. Lee, a Virginia representative, is a tall, vibrant, aristocratic individual of forty-five.*

PUBLISHED TEXTS: *Stone, Peter, and Sherman Edwards. 1776. New York: The Viking Press, 1970.*

Richards, Stanley (ed.). Ten Great Musicals of the American Theatre. *Radnor, PA: Chilton Book Company, 1973.*

JOHN: Franklin! You heard what I suffered in there?

FRANKLIN: Heard? Of course I heard—along with the rest of Philadelphia. Lord, your voice is piercing, John!

JOHN: I wish to heaven my arguments were. By God, Franklin, when will they make up their minds? With one hand they can raise an army, dispatch one of their own to lead it, and cheer the news from Bunker's Hill—while with the other they wave the olive branch, begging the King for a happy and permanent reconciliation. Why damn it, Fat George has declared us in rebellion—why in bloody hell can't *they?*

FRANKLIN: John, really! You talk as if independence were the rule! *It's never been done before!* No colony has ever broken from the parent stem in the history of the world!

JOHN: Dammit, Franklin, you make us sound treasonous!

FRANKLIN: Do I? (*Thinking*) Treason—"Treason is a charge invented by winners as an excuse for hanging the losers."

JOHN: I have more to do than stand here listening to you quote yourself.

FRANKLIN: No, that was a new one!

JOHN: Dammit, Franklin, we're at war!

FRANKLIN: To defend ourselves, nothing more. *We* expressed our displeasure, the English moved against us, and *we,* in turn, have resisted. Now our fellow Congressmen want to effect a reconciliation *before* it becomes a war.

JOHN: Reconciliation, my ass! The *people* want independence!

FRANKLIN: The people have read Mr. Paine's *Common Sense.* I doubt the Congress has. (*He studies him*) John, why don't you give it up? Nobody listens to you—you're obnoxious and disliked.

JOHN: I'm not promoting John Adams, I'm promoting independence.

FRANKLIN: Evidently they cannot help connecting the two.

JOHN: (*Suspicious*) What are you suggesting?

FRANKLIN: Let someone else in Congress propose.

JOHN: Never! (FRANKLIN *shrugs*) Who did you have in mind?

FRANKLIN: I don't know. I really haven't given it much thought. (RICHARD HENRY LEE, *a tall, loose-jointed Virginia aristocrat of forty-five, enters*)

LEE: You sent for me, Benjamin?

JOHN: (*Looking at* LEE, *then at* FRANKLIN) *Never!!*

LEE: Halloo, Johnny.

JOHN: (*Nodding*) Richard.

FRANKLIN: Richard, John and I need some advice.

LEE: If it's mine t'give, it's yours, y'know that.

FRANKLIN: Thank you, Richard. As you know, the cause that we support has come to a complete standstill. Now, why do you suppose that is?

LEE: Simple! Johnny, here, is obnoxious and disliked.

FRANKLIN: Yes, that's true. What's the solution, I wonder?

LEE: (*It's obvious*) Get someone else in Congress to propose—

FRANKLIN: Richard, that's brilliant! Wasn't that brilliant, John?

JOHN: (*Dully*) Brilliant.

FRANKLIN: Yes. Now the question remains—who can it be? The man we need must belong to a delegation publicly committed to support independence, and at the present time only Massachusetts, New Hampshire, and Delaware have declared our way.

LEE: And Virginia, Benjy—don't forget Virginia.

FRANKLIN: Oh, I haven't, Richard—how could I? But strictly speaking, while Virginia's views on independence are well known, your legislature in Williamsburg has never formally authorized its delegation here in Congress to support the cause. Of course, if we could think of a Virginian with enough influence to go down there and persuade the House of Burgesses—

LEE: Damn me if *I* haven't thought of someone!

FRANKLIN and ADAMS: (*Together*) *Who?*

LEE: *Me!*

FRANKLIN: Why didn't I think of that!

LEE: I'll leave tonight—why, hell, right now, if y'like! I'll stop off at Stratford just long enough to refresh the missus, and then straight to the matter. Virginia, the land that gave us our glorious Commander-in-Chief—(*A short drum roll*)—George Washington, will now give the continent its proposal on independence! And when Virginia proposes, the South is bound to follow, and where the South goes the Middle Colonies go! Gentlemen, a salute! To Virginia, the Mother of American Independence!

JOHN: Incredible! We're free, and he hasn't even left yet! (*To* LEE) What makes you so sure you can do it?
(*Music begins*)

LEE: *Hah!!* (*Singing*)
   My name is Richard Henry Lee!
   Virginia is my home.
   My name is Richard Henry Lee!
   Virginia is my home,
   And may my horses turn to glue
   If I can't deliver up to you
   A resolution—on independency!
   For I am F.F.V.
   The First Family
   In the Sovereign Colony of Virginia.
   The F.F.V.
   The Oldest Family
   In the oldest colony in America!
   And may the British burn my land
   If I can't deliver to your hand
   A resolution—on independency!
   Y'see it's—
   Here a Lee
      There a Lee
      Everywhere a Lee, a Lee!
FRANKLIN and LEE: (*Alternating*)
   Social—
            LEE!
   Political—
            LEE!
   Financial—
            LEE!
   Natural—
            LEE!
   *In*ternal—
            LEE!
   *Ex*ternal—
            LEE!
   *Fra*ternal—
            LEE!
   E-ternal—
            LEE!
   (*Together*)
   The F.F.V.,
   The First Family
   In the Sovereign Colony of Virginia!
LEE:

   And may my wife refuse my bed
   If I can't deliver (as I said)
   A resolution—on independency!
JOHN: (*Speaking*) Spoken modest-*Lee*. God help us!
FRANKLIN: He will, John! He will!

LEE: (*Singing*)
> They say that God in Heaven
> Is everybody's God.

FRANKLIN:
> Amen!

LEE:

> I'll admit that God in Heaven
> Is everybody's God.
> But I tell y', John, with pride,
> God leans a little on the side
> Of the Lees! The Lees of old Virginia!
> Y'see it's
> Here a Lee, there a Lee
> Everywhere a Lee—a Lee!

FRANKLIN and LEE:
> Here a Lee, there a Lee
> Everywhere a Lee—

LEE:

> Look out! There's
> > Arthur Lee!
> > "Bobby" Lee! . . . an'
> > General "Lighthorse" Harry Lee!
> > Jesse Lee!
> > Willie Lee!

FRANKLIN:
> And Richard H.—

LEE:

> *That's me!!*
> And may my blood stop running blue
> If I can't deliver up to you
> A resolution—on independency!
> (*He begins strutting, a military cakewalk*)
> Yes sir, by God, it's
> Here a Lee!
> There a Lee!
> Come on, boys, join in with me!
> (*They do,* JOHN *reluctantly*)
> Here a Lee! There a Lee!

FRANKLIN: (*Speaking*) When do y'leave?

LEE: (*Singing*)
> Immediate-*Lee!*
> Here a Lee! There a Lee!

FRANKLIN: (*Speaking*) When will you return?

LEE: (*Singing*)
> Short-*Lee!*
> Here a Lee! There a Lee!
> And I'll come back
> Triumphant-*Lee!*

FRANKLIN and JOHN:

> Here a Lee! There a Lee!
> Ev'rywhere a Lee! A Lee!

LEE:

> Forrr-warrr . . .
> *Ho-ooo!*

> (LEE *struts off.* FRANKLIN *and* JOHN *follow him almost as far as the wings, then drop out and return, breathless but relieved*)

JOHN: (*Speaking*) That was the most revolting display I ever witnessed.

FRANKLIN: They're a warm-blooded people, Virginians!

JOHN: Not him, Franklin—*you!* You and your infernal obsession for deviousness! If you'd come right out and asked him straight, he'd've been gone a half hour ago!

FRANKLIN: Cheer up, John. At this very moment our cause is again riding high— sitting straight in the saddle and in full gallop for Virginia!

THE LEES OF OLD VIRGINIA

Broadway Production by Stuart Ostrow (From *1776*) Music and Lyrics by Sherman Edwards

SCENE FOR TWO MEN, ONE WOMAN FROM ACT I, SCENE 2 OF *COMPANY* (1970) BY STEPHEN SONDHEIM AND GEORGE FURTH

CHARACTERS: *Robert*
   Sarah
   Harry

SETTING: *Sarah and Harry's chic living room on the ground floor of a garden apartment.*

TIME: *After dinner.*

SITUATION: *The three have just finished dinner and are now having coffee.*

COMMENTS: *Sarah and Harry are a middle-aged married couple. They are very fond of Robert, a good-looking but thin bachelor of thirty-five.*

PUBLISHED TEXTS: *Furth, George, and Stephen Sondheim.* Company. *New York: Random House, 1970.*

   Richards, Stanley (ed.). Ten Great Musicals of the American Theatre. *Radnor, PA: Chilton Book Company, 1973.*

SARAH: (*Pouring coffee*) There's cinnamon in the coffee, Robert . . . The odd taste is cinnamon. Sugar and cream?

ROBERT: Both. May I have lots of both?

SARAH: Of course you may.

HARRY: Do you want some brandy in it, Robert? Or do you just want some brandy?

ROBERT: You having some?

SARAH: We don't drink, but you have some, you darling. Go ahead.

HARRY: Or do you want a real drink? We have anything you want.

ROBERT: Well, Harry, if you don't mind, could I have some bourbon?

HARRY: Right. (*He goes to the bar and begins the elaborate preparation of* ROBERT's *drink*)

SARAH: Sweetheart!

HARRY: Okay, darling.

ROBERT: (*As* HARRY *gets the bourbon*) Are you both on the wagon? Sarah? You're not on the wagon?

SARAH: Goodness, Robert, all the questions! Or do you just collect trivia like some old quiz kid? We spend half of our lives with you and now you notice Harry's on the wagon?

HARRY: A year and a half.

SARAH: No, love. Just a year.

HARRY: It was a year in February. It's a year and a half now.

SARAH: I know for a fact next month it will be a year.

HARRY: And a half.

SARAH: One year. Count it, one! Harry got arrested for being drunk, and quit out of some kind of humiliation.

HARRY: I quit to see if I could is actually what happened. C'mon, I must have told you about all that.

ROBERT: Never. You never mentioned it or I never would have brought you the bourbon. How were you arrested?

SARAH: Another question! Here, why don't you have one of these brownies you brought?

HARRY: I was in California on business and I really got soused one night and these guys drove me back to my hotel, but instead of going in, I walked down to the corner to get something to eat to sober up. (*He has poured the bourbon into* ROBERT's *glass, and sniffs it longingly*)

SARAH: (*Interrupting*) You said it was three blocks away.

HARRY: No, just the corner.

SARAH: (*In a stage whisper to* ROBERT) Three blocks away.

HARRY: Anyway, this patrol car stopped me and said, "You're drunk." I said, "Drunk? I'm clobbered." He said, "I'm taking you in." "Take me to my hotel, for God's sake," I said. "It's just on the corner." (*He cracks the ice and adds the soda*)

SARAH: Three blocks away.

(ROBERT *moves to the bar and reaches for his drink, but is stopped by* HARRY, *who indicates that the lemon peel has not yet been added*)

HARRY: Anyway, they mugged me and booked me for being drunk. Unbelievable. California is a police state, though. And then, Robert, the very next time I was out there, I got arrested all over again—drunk driving. I only had wine—

SARAH: Only five bottles . . .

HARRY: And I *insisted* on taking a drunk test. I flunked it by one point. (*He adds lemon peel to the drink with a flourish*)

SARAH: And that is when you quit, precious. He always thinks it was the first arrest, but it was the second. We never told you that? Curious, I thought Harry had told *everybody.*

HARRY: (*His gaze fixed on* ROBERT's *drink*) Anyway, I quit to see if I really had a drinking problem, and I don't.

SARAH: Just a problem drinking.

(ROBERT *finally takes the drink from* HARRY, *breaking* HARRY's *"trance"*)

ROBERT: Do you miss it?

SARAH: See how you talk in questions! Harry, do you miss it?

HARRY: No. No, I really don't.

SARAH: (*Loud whisper to* ROBERT) Yes. Yes, he really does. (*Full voice, and a wave to* HARRY) Hi, darling.

HARRY: Anyway, I stopped. Haven't had a drink since.

SARAH: Whoops.

HARRY: What's whoops? I haven't had a drink since.

SARAH: (*She sings this*)
        At Evelyn and George's wedding.

HARRY: A toast, for God's sake. Sorry, Robert, you must have noticed how staggering falling-down drunk I got on one swallow of champagne.

SARAH: I *never* said you got drunk, but you did have the champagne.

HARRY: A swallow. One swallow.

SARAH: And it was gone. An elephant's swallow.

ROBERT: I'd like to ask for another bourbon, but I'm terrified.

(HARRY *grabs the glass and runs back to the bar*)

SARAH: Darling Robert, put a nipple on the bottle for all we care. Don't you want a brownie?

ROBERT: God, no. I'll bust.

SARAH: Bust? *You* bust! You skinny thing. Just look at you. Bones. You're skin and bones. I bet when you get on a scale it goes the other way—minus.

ROBERT: Well, thank you, Sarah. I am touched and honored. And I think I was just insulted.

SARAH: (*Takes a brownie from the box*) Oh, Robert, I was praying that you'd eat just one so I could watch.

ROBERT: Sarah! Is it possible you've become a food voyeur?

SARAH: Mexican food. What I crave without cease is Mexican food. With all the Tabasco sauce in the world.

HARRY: (*With his back to* SARAH, *but knowing what she's up to*) Don't eat that brownie!

SARAH: I'm not. I'm just smelling it. Oh, Robert, you eat one!

ROBERT: Not with bourbon. (*Takes his second drink*) Thank you, Harry.

(HARRY *looks upset, as he hasn't the lemon nor his other "extras"*)

SARAH: And chocolate. I'd kill for chocolate. Or a baked potato with sour cream and chives. Doesn't that just make you writhe? Or hot sourdough bread and all the butter there is.

HARRY: Chili.

SARAH: Oh, chili, dear God, yes, chili!

HARRY: Manicotti.

SARAH: Manicotti. One teaspoon of manicotti.

HARRY: Sara Lee cake.

SARAH: Sara Lee cake! Sara Lee is the most phenomenal woman since Mary Baker Eddy.

HARRY: How about sweet and sour shrimp?

SARAH: How about sweet and sour pork?

(*She pretends to pass out by falling behind the sofa, but* ROBERT *has seen her stick a brownie in her mouth on the way down. She eats it, hidden from their sight behind the sofa.* ROBERT *watches this, and turns in time to see* HARRY *stealing one swallow of bourbon*)

ROBERT: (*Crosses to the sofa and calls to the hidden* SARAH) I get the impression you guys are on diets.

HARRY: Not me. Sarah.

SARAH: (*Rises and crosses from behind the sofa, still chewing*) Look at these pants. You can put your fist in there. That's how much weight I've lost.

HARRY: She always does that. Look, I can put my fist in my pants too, you know. She thinks I buy that.

SARAH: Darling, I've lost eight pounds already.

HARRY: It's the magazines, Robert. Did you ever look at any of those women's magazines? Pages and pages of cakes and pies and roasts and potatoes. I bet Sarah subscribes to about forty magazines. It's a sickness. We're up to our ass in magazines.

SARAH: I read them all.

HARRY: Don't.

SARAH: Do.

HARRY: Look at this, Robert. Wrestling. She even subscribes to a magazine on wrestling.

SARAH: Karate, not wrestling. It's karate.

HARRY: Wouldn't you like to see it? All those fat broads in her gym learning karate. What wouldn't you give to see that?

SARAH: Strangely enough, darling, I'm terribly good at it.

ROBERT: How long have you been studying it?

SARAH: (*To* ROBERT, *in a mock-scolding tone*) Who asked that question? Oh, Robert! Seven months.

HARRY: Show us some karate.

SARAH: No. Robert, would you like some more coffee, love? You, Harry?

HARRY: No. I want some karate. I want to see how my money is being wasted.

SARAH: No.

ROBERT: Do one thing.

SARAH: No.

ROBERT: (*Flirtatiously*) Come on, Sarah, I really would give anything to see you do just one. I bet you are *excellent*. Hey, I'll be your partner.

SARAH: (*Responding girlishly*) No. Oh, Harry, this is embarrassing.

HARRY: Aw, come on.

SARAH: My God—all right.

HARRY: Hooray!

SARAH: One throw!

HARRY: Hooray!

SARAH: Harry, do you want to stand there?

HARRY: Where?

SARAH: There.

HARRY: All right. I'm standing here. Now what?

(SARAH, *with intense concentration, goes into her karate preparation ritual, complete with kneebends, deep-breathing, grunts and a variety of chops and holds*)

SARAH: Okay. Now just come at me.

HARRY: Okay.

(*He does, and she lets out a piercing samurai sound, "Hyieeeee," flipping him spread-eagle to the floor.* SARAH *does a Japanese bow to* HARRY, *and does a feminine tiptoe dance to the sofa, where she lies majestically and adorably, looking at her fingernails*)

ROBERT: Fantastic. That's hysterical.

HARRY: (*Gets up and moves away, doing some sort of twist to loosen his back from the impact of the fall*) Actually, I could have prevented that.

SARAH: How?

HARRY: By blocking it.

SARAH: No, that can't be blocked.

HARRY: It certainly can. I just didn't do it.

SARAH: Anyway, Robert, that can't be blocked.

HARRY: Let's do it again.

SARAH: All right, darling. (*She is the sweet killer, arranging herself*)

HARRY: I'll come at you again.

SARAH: Okay. (*He goes at her. She attempts the same thing and he blocks it by lifting her and putting her over his shoulder. Taken by surprise,* SARAH *quickly reworks the movement in her mind and comes up with her mistake*) Oh, I see. Put me down. Okay, do it again.

(*He does it again and she overcomes his block, throwing him again. She then gives a karate scream and jumps on top of him, pinning him down.*)

SCENE FOR ONE MAN, TWO WOMEN
FROM ACT I, SCENE 6 OF *GREASE* (1972)
BY JIM JACOBS AND WARREN CASEY

CHARACTERS: *Sandy Dumbrowski*
        Danny Zuko
        Patty Simcox

SETTING: *Rydell High School*

TIME: *Late 1950s, soon after the beginning of the school year.*

SITUATION: *Sandy, who is new to Rydell High School, is surprised to find that Danny, whom she met and was attracted to last summer, is also a student here. As the scene begins, she is practicing for the cheerleaders' tryouts, to which she has been invited by Patty. The Band-Aid on her ear is the result of a girl's piercing her ear for earrings.*

COMMENTS: *Danny is the leader of his gang, a well-built, nice-looking, confident boy with a cool charm. Sandy is cute, wholesome, and naive. Patty is a cheerleader who is attractive and athletic, but rather catty.*

PUBLISHED TEXTS: *Jacobs, Jim, and Walter Casey.* Grease. *New York: Winter House Ltd., 1972.*
        Richards, Stanley (ed.). Great Rock Musicals. *New York: Stein and Day, 1979.*

(SANDY *runs on with pom-poms, dressed in a green baggy gymsuit.* SHE *does a Rydell cheer.*)

SANDY:

Do a split, give a yell,
Throw a fit for old Rydell.
Way to go, green and brown,
Turn the foe upside down.

(SANDY *does awkward split.* DANNY *enters*)

DANNY: Hiya, Sandy.
(SANDY *gives him a look and turns her head so that* DANNY *sees the Band-Aid on her ear*)
Hey, what happened to your ear?

SANDY: Huh? (SHE *covers her ear with her hand, answers coldly*) Oh, nothing. Just an accident.

DANNY: Hey, look, uh, I hope you're not bugged about that first day at school. I mean, couldn't ya tell I was glad to see ya?

SANDY: Well, you could've been a little nicer to me in front of your friends.

DANNY: Are you kidding? Hey, you don't know those guys. They just see ya talkin' to a chick and right away they think she puts . . . well, you know what I mean.

SANDY: I'm not sure. It looked to me like maybe you had a new girlfriend or something.

DANNY: Are you kiddin'! Listen, if it was up to me, I'd never even look at any other chick but you. (SANDY *blushes*) Hey, tell ya what. We're throwin' a party in the park tonight for Frenchy. She's gonna quit school before she

Figure 10-2. *Grease,* as produced at Marshall University. Scene designer: Bruce Greenwood.

(Photo: Rick Haye.)

flunks again and go to Beauty School. Howdja like to make it on down there with me?

SANDY: I'd really like to, but I'm not so sure those girls want me around anymore.

DANNY: Listen, Sandy. Nobody's gonna start gettin' salty with ya when I'm around. Uh-uhh!

SANDY: All right, Danny, as long as you're with me. Let's not let anyone come between us again, okay?

PATTY: (*Rushing onstage with two batons and wearing cheerleader outfit*) Hiiiii-iiiii, Danny! Oh, don't let me interrupt. (*Gives* SANDY *baton*) Here, why don't you twirl this for a while. (*Taking* DANNY *aside*) I've been dying to tell you something. You know what I found out after you left my house the other night? My mother thinks you're cute. (*To* SANDY) He's such a lady-killer.

SANDY: Isn't he, though! (*Out of corner of mouth, to* DANNY) What were you doing at her house?

DANNY: Ah, I was just copying down some homework.

PATTY: Come on, Sandy, let's practice.

SANDY: Yeah, let's! I'm just dying to make a good impression on all those cute lettermen.

DANNY: Oh, that's why you're wearing that thing—gettin' ready to show off your skivvies to a bunch of horny jocks?

SANDY: Don't tell me you're jealous, Danny.

DANNY: What? Of that buncha meatheads! Don't make me laugh. Ha! Ha!

SANDY: Just because they can do something you can't do?

DANNY: Yeah, sure, right.

SANDY: Okay, what have *you* ever done?

DANNY: (*To* PATTY, *twirling baton*) Stop that! (*Thinking a moment*) I won a Hully Gully contest at the "Teen Talent" record hop.

SANDY: Aaahh, you don't even know what I'm talking about.

DANNY: Whattaya mean, look, I could run circles around those jerks.

SANDY: But you'd rather spend your time copying other people's homework.

DANNY: Listen, the next time they have tryouts for any of those teams I'll show you what I can do.

PATTY: Oh, what a lucky coincidence! The track team's having tryouts tomorrow.

DANNY: (*Panic*) Huh? Okay, I'll be there.

SANDY: Big talk.

DANNY: You think so, huh? Hey, Patty, when'dja say those tryouts were?

PATTY: Tomorrow, tenth period, on the football field.

DANNY: Good, I'll be there. You're gonna come watch me, aren't you?

PATTY: Oooohh, I can't wait!

DANNY: Solid. I'll see ya there, sexy. (*Exits*)

PATTY: Toodles! (*Elated, turns to* SANDY) Ooohh, I'm so excited, aren't you?

SANDY: Come on, let's practice.

SUGGESTED READING

MUSICAL THEATRE

Balk, H. Wesley. *The Complete Singer-Actor.* 2d ed. Minneapolis: University of Minnesota Press, 1985.

——. *Performing Power.* Minneapolis: University of Minnesota Press, 1985.

Bordman, Gerald. *American Musical Revue.* New York: Oxford University Press, 1985.

——. *American Musical Theatre.* Expanded ed. New York: Oxford University Press, 1986.

——. *American Operetta.* New York: Oxford University Press, 1981.

Cohen, Selma Jeanne (ed.). *Dance as a Theatre Art.* New York: Dodd, Mead & Company, 1974.

Craig, David. *On Performing.* New York: McGraw-Hill Book Company, 1987.

——. *On Singing On Stage.* New York: Schirmer Books, 1978.

Engel, Lehman. *American Musical Theatre.* Rev. ed. New York: The Macmillan Company, 1975.

——. *Getting the Show On.* New York: Schirmer Books, 1983.

——. *The Making of a Musical.* New York: Macmillan Publishing Co., Inc., 1977.

——. *Planning and Producing the Musical Show.* Rev. ed. New York: Crown Publishers, Inc., 1966.

Ewen, David. *Complete Book of the American Musical Theater.* New York: Henry Holt and Company, 1958.

——. *The Story of America's Musical Theatre.* Philadelphia: Chilton Book Co., 1968.

Frankel, Aaron. *Writing the Broadway Musical.* New York: Drama Book Specialists (Publishers), 1977.

Green, Stanley. *Encyclopaedia of the American Musical Theatre.* New York: Dodd, Mead & Co., Inc., 1976.

——. *The World of Musical Comedy.* 4th ed. New York: Da Capo Press, Inc., 1984.

Jacob, Ellen. *Dancing: A Guide for the Dancer You Can Be.* Reading, MA: Addison-Wesley Publishing Co., 1981.

Kislan, Richard. *Hoofing on Broadway.* New York: Prentice-Hall Press, 1987.

——. *The Musical.* Englewood Cliffs, NJ: Prentice-Hall, Inc., 1980.

Kosarin, Oscar. *The Singing Actor.* Englewood Cliffs, NJ: Prentice-Hall, Inc., 1983.

Laufe, Abe. *Broadway's Greatest Musicals.* Rev. ed. New York: Funk & Wagnalls, Inc., 1973.

MANNERS AND CUSTOMS

Oxenford, Lyn. *Playing Period Plays*. London: J. Garnet Miller Ltd., 1958.
Russell, Douglas A. *Period Style for the Theatre*. Boston: Allyn and Bacon, Inc., 1980.

STAGE FIGHTING

Gordon, Gilbert. *Stage Fights*. New York: Theatre Arts Books, 1973.
Hobbs, William. *Stage Combat*. New York: St. Martin's Press, 1981.
Katz, Albert M. *Stage Violence*. The Theatre Student Series. New York: Richards Rosen Press, Inc., 1976.
Kezer, Claude D. *Principles of Stage Combat*. Schulenburg, TX: I. E. Clark, Inc., 1983.
Martinez, J. D. *Combat Mime*. Chicago: Nelson-Hall Publishers, 1982.

STAGE MAKEUP

Corson, Richard. *Stage Makeup*. 7th ed. Englewood Cliffs, NJ: Prentice-Hall, Inc., 1986.
Smith, C. Ray (ed.). *The Theatre Crafts Book of Make-up, Masks and Wigs*. Emmaus, PA: Rodale Press, 1974.
Terry, Ellen and Lynne Anderson. *Make-up and Masks*. The Theatre Student Series. New York: Richards Rosen Press, Inc., 1971.
Westmore, Michael. *The Art of Theatrical Makeup for Stage and Screen*. New York: McGraw-Hill Book Co., 1973.

GLOSSARY OF THEATRICAL TERMS

Above Upstage or away from the audience; to move above someone or a property is to move upstage of that person or prop.

Ad-lib To improvise words and actions.

Air The places in a song where singers do not sing but music is played.

Apron The part of the stage that is downstage of the front curtain.

Aria An operatic solo.

Aside A short remark made by a character to the audience that other people onstage are not supposed to hear.

Backdrop (or **drop**) A large sheet of painted canvas or muslin that hangs at the back of a set.

Backstage The areas behind the stage set, including the dressing rooms.

Balance (1) An aesthetically pleasing integration of performers, set, properties, and lighting on a stage. (2) A person's steadiness that results when all parts of the body are properly adjusted to each other.

Bar (1) In music, one bar is one measure. (2) (often spelled *barre*) A handrail used by dancers in exercising.

Below Downstage or toward the audience; to move below someone or a property is to move downstage of that person or prop.

Belt To sing in a forceful manner using the chest voice.

Bit part A small role.

Blackout A sudden darkening of the stage; used in many musicals at the ends of scenes.

Block To plan the movements of performers.

Border A drapery or short drop hanging across the stage above the acting area to mask the fly loft and overhead lights.

Box office The place where tickets are sold for admission to performances.

Box set A realistic representation of a room with three walls and often a ceiling.

Breakaway A costume or prop that is especially constructed to come apart easily onstage and to be assembled quickly for the next performance.

Bridge (1) See **release.** (2) See **segue.**

Build To increase the loudness, rate of speed, and energy of a line, speech, scene, or song in order to reach a climax.

Burn (or **slow burn**)   A slow, comic realization that something bad has happened; the disgust and anger builds within the comedian until he or she explodes in rage.

Business   See **stage business**.

Call   (1) Announcement to performers or crews that they are needed for a rehearsal or performance. (2) Warning to performers to get ready for an entrance.

Callboard   The place backstage in a theatre where company rules, announcements, notes, and messages are posted.

Cheat   To move slightly to improve the stage picture or to turn more toward the audience for better audibility.

Chorus   (1) A group of people who sing and/or dance. (2) (also called the **refrain**) The main part of a song, often having thirty-two measures.

Closed turn   A turn made away from the audience, so that the spectators see the back of the actor.

Combo   A small combination of instrumentalists who usually play piano, bass, percussion, and, perhaps, another instrument or two.

Counter (or **dress stage**)   A small movement made by an actor to better the stage picture after a cross by another performer.

Cover   (1) To stand accidentally in front of someone so that the audience cannot see that person. (2) To deceive an audience by concealing an action, such as a stabbing.

Cross   (sometimes abbr. X) To move from one place to another on a stage.

Cue   The signal for performers and technicians to speak, enter, turn on lights, play a tape, and so forth.

Curtain call   Bowing and receiving the audience's applause at the end of the show or, sometimes in opera, at the end of an act.

Cyclorama (abbr. **cyc,** pronounced "sike")   A curved curtain, drop, or wall often painted to look like the sky and used at the rear and sides of the stage.

Deadpan   An impassive, matter-of-fact manner with no facial expressions.

Double   (1) To play more than one role in a production. (2) One who resembles a member of the cast and takes his or her place in scenes needing special skills.

Double take   A delayed reaction to a line or situation after an initial failure to see anything unusual.

Dress rehearsal   A final rehearsal in which costumes, makeup, and hairstyles are worn to make the rehearsal as close to a performance as possible.

Dress stage   See **counter**.

Drop   See **backdrop**.

Elevator stage   Stage in which sections of the floor may be raised or lowered to change scenery.

Ensemble   A group of singers, dancers, actors, or musicians.

Entr'acte   (1) The orchestral opening to the second act of a musical. (2) A dance, musical number, or interlude performed between the acts of a play.

Entrance   (1) Entering the stage. (2) An opening in the set that is used for entering.

Exit   (1) Leaving the stage. (2) An opening in the set that is used for leaving.

Extra (or **walk-on**)   A person who is onstage to provide atmosphere and background and who may speak only with a group.

Feed line   See **straight line**.

Flat   A wooden frame covered with canvas or muslin that is painted and used as part of a set.

Floor plan (or **ground plan**)   A line drawing of a stage set as seen from above; it shows the placement on the stage floor of the scenic elements, such as walls, doors, windows, fireplaces, platforms, steps, furniture, and other set props.

Fly loft (or **flies**)   The space above the stage from which scenery and lights may hang.

Focal point   The place onstage of greatest interest to the audience at that moment.

Focus   (1) To look at someone or something. (2) To adjust the beam size of a spotlight.

Follow spotlight   A lighting instrument operated in the back of the house by an electrician who moves it to follow the movements of one or more performers.

Freeze   To stop all movement.

Give stage   To permit another actor to have the dominant position.

Greenroom   A traditional backstage waiting lounge and reception room for performers.

Ground plan   See **floor plan**.

Heads up!   A warning to those onstage that something is falling or being lowered from the flies and that everyone should look up to determine if he or she is in danger of being hit.

Heavy   The role of a villain.

House   (1) The places where the audience is seated, the lobby, and other areas in front of the stage curtain. (2) The audience.

Ingenue   The role of a young girl.

In one   In a wing and drop setting, it is the area that is downstage of the first set of wings and drop.

Jackknife stage   Large wagon that, when it is facing the audience, is permanently pivoted at one corner (usually a downstage corner in the right or left wing area) and is swung on and offstage in a motion resembling the opening and closing of a jackknife.

Juvenile   The role of a young man.

Kill   (1) To lose the effectiveness of a line, action, or stage effect. (2) To eliminate something, such as a light.

Laugh line   See **punch line**.

Libretto (Italian word meaning "little book")   The text of an opera or musical.

Malapropism   The use of an incorrect word that sounds similar to the intended word.

Measure   A group of notes indicated on a musical staff between vertical bar lines.

Monologue   A long speech by one character.

Move in (or **on**)   To move toward the center of the stage.

Move out (or **off**)   To move away from the center of the stage.

Mug   To use exaggerated facial expressions.

Open turn   A turn made toward the audience so that the spectators see the front of the actor.

Open up   To turn toward the audience.

Orchestra   (1) A group of musicians who perform together. (2) The main floor of a theatre.

Orchestra pit   See **pit**.

Out front   The auditorium, lobby, and other public areas.

Overplay   To exaggerate or use more force than is needed.

Overture   The orchestral beginning of a musical, opera, or play.

Pantomime   To perform an action in character without speaking words, although sounds may be uttered.

Pas de deux   A dance for two people.

Phrase   (1) A thought-group of words. (2) A small part, typically two to four measures, of a melody. (3) A small series of dance movements.

Pick up   To speed up or shorten the time between a cue and the next line.

Pit (or **orchestra pit**)   The area between the stage and the front row of seats where the orchestra usually plays.

Plant   To emphasize a line or a prop because of its later importance to the plot.

Pointe (or **point**)   A position in ballet in which dancers wearing toeshoes dance on the tips of their toes.

Point up (or **play up**)   To make a line or action more emphatic.

Practical   Any onstage prop, light, or piece of scenery that can be used by performers and is not just decorative; for example, a table lamp that can be turned on or a window that can be opened.

Pratfall   A fall on the buttocks.

Promptbook   A copy of the script in which all information is recorded that is essential for the production of the show.

Prompter   Person who holds the promptbook offstage during rehearsals and performances and provides lines to forgetful performers.

Property (or **prop**)   An article or object that is carried by performers (such as a cane, sword, or fan) or is used on the set (such as a piece of furniture, pillow, picture, or drapery).

Proscenium   The permanent architectural arch that separates the stage from the audience.

Punch line (or **laugh line**)   A line that should get a laugh from the audience.

Ramp   A sloping walkway that rises gradually from one level to another.

Recitative   Operatic dialogue that is sung in a way that suggests the inflections of speech.

Refrain (or **chorus**)   The main part of a song, often having thirty-two measures.

Release (or **bridge**)   In an AABA format for a song, the release is the B section; it has a different melody than the A section.

Reprise   The repetition of a song or part of a song.

Revolve   A circular platform that can be turned to change sets; it may be permanently built into the stage or mounted temporarily on the floor.

Revolving stage   A stage that has a revolve.

Rideout   The end of a song, including the singer's last syllable and the following music.

Ring down   Close the front curtain.

Ring up   Open the front curtain.

Running gag   Comic business that is repeated throughout a show.

Run-through   A rehearsal in which a scene, act, or entire show is played without interruption.

Scrim A curtain, drop, or set made of net or gauze that is opaque when lighted from the front but becomes transparent when lighted from behind.

Script The dialogue, lyrics, and stage directions of a musical or play.

Segue (pronounced "seg-way") (also termed **bridge**) Transition from one musical number to another.

Share To have two or more performers equally dominant onstage.

Shtick (also spelled **shtik** or **schtick**) A repeated bit of comic business, routine, or gimmick used by a star performer.

Sides Half sheets of paper that have one character's speaking lines and lyrics with cues and stage directions.

Sight gag Visual humor from a funny prop, costume, makeup, hairstyle, or movement.

Sight lines Imaginary lines from the seats at the sides of the house and the top of the balcony to the stage to determine what parts of the acting area will be visible to audience members sitting in those seats.

Slapstick (from a device made of two slats that makes a loud noise when used by a performer to strike someone) Comedy that stresses horseplay and wild physical buffoonery.

Soliloquy The revelation of thoughts and feelings by a character when alone onstage.

Spectacle The visual elements of a stage production (the scenery, properties, lighting, costumes, makeup, movements, and dancing) and, by extension, those productions in which the visual elements are predominant.

Spike To mark the stage floor with chalk or tape to indicate the position of furniture, properties, or scenery so that they will be placed correctly during scene shifts.

S.R.O. A sign meaning "Standing Room Only" that is displayed at the box office when all seats have been sold for a performance.

Stage business Not a major movement, but a smaller activity, such as smoking a cigarette, playing with eyeglasses, or sewing, that helps to establish characterization or mood.

Stage convention A departure from reality that audiences accept, such as a character breaking into song accompanied by an orchestra.

Stage picture The arrangement on a stage of performers and the visual production elements (scenery, properties, lighting, and costumes).

Standby A well-known performer who is prepared to substitute for a star in case of an emergency; unlike an understudy, the standby does not appear in the musical at other times.

Steal (1) To "steal a scene" is to take attention away from the performer(s) who should receive it. (2) To move without attracting the audience's attention.

Straight line (or **feed line**) A line that sets up a punch line so it will get a laugh.

Straight man (or **woman**) One who delivers straight lines to a comic.

Strike To remove a prop or a light or to dismantle a set.

Style A distinctive manner of expression in the writing, designing, or performing; the characteristics of a show that make it different from others.

Subtext (literally, *under the text*) The underlying meaning of a scene.

Swing A singer and/or dancer who is prepared to substitute for chorus members who are unable to perform.